FOOD LABELING - NUTRITION LABELING OF STANDARD MENU ITEMS IN RESTAURANTS AND SIMILAR RETAIL FOOD ESTABLISHMENTS (US FOOD AND DRUG ADMINISTRATION REGULATION) (FDA) (2018 EDITION)

Updated as of May 29, 2018

THE LAW LIBRARY

TABLE OF CONTENTS

AGENCY	5
ACTION	5
SUMMARY	5
DATES	5
ADDRESSES	5
FOR FURTHER INFORMATION CONTACT	6
SUPPLEMENTARY INFORMATION	6
Table of Contents	6
Executive Summary	6
Purpose and Coverage of the Final Rule	6
Summary of the Major Provisions of the Final Rule	6
Costs and Benefits	6
Executive Summary	10
I. Background	13
II. Legal Authority	15
III. General Comments on the Proposed Rule	16
IV. Comments and FDA Response on Proposed Conforming Amendments	18
V. Key Terms That FDA Proposed To Define (Proposed § 101.11(a))	20
VI. Comments and FDA Response on the Proposed Definitions of Terms Related to the Scope of Establishments Covered by the Rule (Proposed § 101.11(a))	20
VII. Comments and FDA Response on the Proposed Definition of Menu or Menu Board (Proposed § 101.11(a))	45
VIII. Comments and FDA Response on the Proposed Definition of Terms Related to Foods Covered by the Rule (Proposed § 101.11(a))	56
IX. Comments and FDA Response on Proposed § 101.11(b)(1)(i)—Food Subject to the Labeling Requirements	63
X. Comments and FDA Response on Proposed § 101.11(b)(1)(ii)—Food Not Subject to the Labeling Requirements	63
XI. Comments and FDA Response on Proposed § 101.11(b)(2)(i)(A)(	74
XII. Additional Format Requirements That Apply When Declaring Calories on Menus and Menu Boards for Variable Menu Items, Combination Meals, and Toppings (Final § 101.11(b)(2)(i)(A)(	84
XIII. Additional Requirements That Apply to Beverages That Are Not Self-Service or on Display (Final § 101.11(b)(2)(i)(A)(	99
XIV. Comments and FDA Response on Proposed § 101.11(b)(2)(i)(B)—Succinct	

Statement That Must Be on Menus and Menu Boards To Provide Context About Calories in a Daily Diet	100
XV. Comments and FDA Response on Proposed § 101.11(b)(2)(i)(C)—Statement That Must Be on Menus and Menu Boards About Availability of Written Nutrition Information	110
XVI. Comments and FDA Response on Proposed § 101.11(b)(2)(ii)—Nutrition Information That Must Be Made Available in Written Form	113
XVII. Comments and FDA Response on Proposed § 101.11(b)(2)(iii)—Requirements for Food That Is Self-Service or on Display	125
XVIII. Comments and FDA Response on Proposed § 101.11(c)(1) to (c)(5)—Determination of Nutrient Content (Final § 101.11(c)(1) to (c)(2))	144
XIX. Comments and FDA Response on Proposed § 101.11(c)(6)—Substantiation Documentation (Final § 101.11(c)(3))	152
XX. Comments and FDA Response on Proposed Section 101.11(d)—Voluntary Registration To Elect To Be Subject to the Rule	160
XXI. Comments and FDA Response on Proposed § 101.11(e)—Signatures	162
XXII. Comments and FDA Response on Proposed § 101.11(f)—Misbranding	163
XXIII. Comments and FDA Response on Effective Date	163
XXIV. Comments and FDA Response on Compliance	168
XXV. Final Regulatory Impact Analysis	173
XXVI. Paperwork Reduction Act of 1995	174
XXVII. Federalism	182
XXVIII. Environmental Impact	187
XXIX. References	187
LIST OF SUBJECTS	190
REGULATORY TEXT	190
PART 11 ELECTRONIC RECORDS ELECTRONIC SIGNATURES	190
Authority:	190
§ 11.1 Scope.	190
PART 101 FOOD LABELING	191
Authority:	191
§ 101.9 Nutrition labeling of food.	191
§ 101.10 Nutrition labeling of restaurant foods whose labels or labeling bear nutrient content claims or health claims.	192
§ 101.11 Nutrition labeling of standard menu items in covered establishments.	192

AGENCY

Food and Drug Administration, HHS.

ACTION

Final rule.

SUMMARY

To implement the nutrition labeling provisions of the Patient Protection and Affordable Care Act of 2010 (Affordable Care Act or ACA), the Food and Drug Administration (FDA or we) is requiring disclosure of certain nutrition information for standard menu items in certain restaurants and retail food establishments. The ACA, in part, amended the Federal Food, Drug, and Cosmetic Act (the FD&C Act), among other things, to require restaurants and similar retail food establishments that are part of a chain with 20 or more locations doing business under the same name and offering for sale substantially the same menu items to provide calorie and other nutrition information for standard menu items, including food on display and self-service food. Under provisions of the ACA, restaurants and similar retail food establishments not otherwise covered by the law may elect to become subject to these Federal requirements by registering every other year with FDA. Providing accurate, clear, and consistent nutrition information, including the calorie content of foods, in restaurants and similar retail food establishments will make such nutrition information available to consumers in a direct and accessible manner to enable consumers to make informed and healthful dietary choices.

DATES

Effective date: December 1, 2015.

Compliance date: Covered establishments must comply with the rule by December 1, 2015. See section XXIII for more information on the effective and compliance dates.

Comment Date: Submit comments on information collection issues under the Paperwork Reduction Act of 1995 by December 31, 2014 (see section XXVI, the "Paperwork Reduction Act of 1995" section of this document).

ADDRESSES

To ensure that comments on the information collection are received, the Office of Management and Budget (OMB) recommends that written comments be faxed to the Office of Information and Regulatory Affairs, OMB, Attn: FDA Desk Officer, FAX: 202-395-7285, or emailed to oira_submission@omb.eop.gov. All comments should be identified with the OMB control number 0910-New and title "Food Labeling: Nutrition Labeling of Standard Menu Items in Restaurants and Similar Retail Food Establishments." Also include the FDA docket number found in brackets in the heading of this document.

FOR FURTHER INFORMATION CONTACT

Daniel Y. Reese, Center for Food Safety and Applied Nutrition (HFS-820), Food and Drug Administration, 5100 Paint Branch Pkwy., College Park, MD 20740, 240-402-2371, email: Daniel.Reese@fda.hhs.gov.

SUPPLEMENTARY INFORMATION

Table of Contents

Executive Summary

Purpose and Coverage of the Final Rule

Summary of the Major Provisions of the Final Rule

Costs and Benefits

I. Background

II. Legal Authority

III. General Comments on the Proposed Rule

A. Introduction

B. Description of General Comments and FDA Response

IV. Comments and FDA Response on Proposed Conforming Amendments

A. Section 11.1(g)—Electronic Signatures

B. Sections 101.9(j)(1)(i), (j)(2), and (j)(3)—Nutrition Labeling of Food

C. Section 101.10—Nutrition Labeling of Restaurant Foods Whose Labels or Labeling Bear Nutrient Content Claims or Health Claims

V. Key Terms That FDA Proposed to Define (Proposed § 101.11(a))

VI. Comments and FDA Response on the Proposed Definitions of Terms Related to the Scope of Establishments Covered by the Rule (Proposed § 101.11(a))

A. Introduction

B. Restaurant or Similar Retail Food Establishment

C. Restaurant Food and Restaurant-Type Food

D. Part of a Chain With 20 or More Locations

E. Doing Business Under the Same Name

F. Offering for Sale Substantially the Same Menu Items

G. Authorized Official of a Restaurant or Similar Retail Food Establishment

H. Covered Establishment

I. Revisions to Several Provisions to Clarify the Applicability of the Rule to Those Restaurants and Similar Retail Food Establishments That Are Covered Establishments

VII. Comments and FDA Response on the Proposed Definition of Menu or Menu Board (Proposed § 101.11(a))

VIII. Comments and FDA Response on the Proposed Definition of Terms Related to Foods Covered by the Rule (Proposed § 101.11(a))

A. Restaurant Food and Restaurant-Type Food

B. Standard Menu Item

C. Combination Meal

D. Variable Menu Item

E. Food on Display

F. Self-Service Food

G. Custom Order

H. Daily Special

I. Food That Is Part of a Customary Market Test

J. Temporary Menu Item

IX. Comments and FDA Response on Proposed § 101.11(b)(1)(i)—Food Subject to the Labeling Requirements

X. Comments and FDA Response on Proposed § 101.11(b)(1)(ii)—Food Not Subject to the Labeling Requirements

A. The Proposed Requirements

B. Alcohol

C. Condiments

D. Daily Specials, Temporary Menu Items, Custom Orders, and Food That Is Part of a Customary Market Test

E. Additional Comments on Food That Is Part of a Customary Market Test

XI. Comments and FDA Response on Proposed § 101.11(b)(2)(i)(A)(1) to (b)(2)(i)(A)(3)—General Requirements for Calorie Declaration on Menus and Menu Boards

XII. Additional Format Requirements That Apply When Declaring Calories on Menus and Menu Boards for Variable Menu Items, Combination Meals, and Toppings (Final § 101.11(b)(2)(i)(A)(4) Through (b)(2)(i)(A)(8))

A. Proposed Format for Declaring Calories for Variable Menu Items

B. Decision To Require Option 4

C. Requirements That Apply to Individual Variable Menu Items (Final § 101.11(b)(2)(i)(A)(4))

D. Requirements That Apply to a Variable Menu Item That Is Offered for Sale With the Option of Adding Toppings Listed on the Menu or Menu Board (Final § 101.11(b)(2)(i)(A)(5))

E. Requirements That Apply to a Combination Meal (Final § 101.11(b)(2)(i)(A)(6))

F. Format Requirements for Declaring Calories for an Individual Variable Menu Item, a Combination Meal, and Toppings as a Range, if Applicable (Final § 101.11(b)(2)(i)(A)(7))

G. Exception for a Variable Menu Item When There Is No Clearly Identifiable Upper Bound to the Range of Calories (Final § 101.11(b)(2)(i)(A)(8))

H. Declaring Calories Using Interactive Menus or New Technology

XIII. Additional Requirements That Apply to Beverages That Are Not Self-Service or on Display (Final § 101.11(b)(2)(i)(A)(9))

XIV. Comments and FDA Response on Proposed § 101.11(b)(2)(i)(B)—Succinct Statement That Must Be on Menus and Menu Boards To Provide Context About Calories in a Daily Diet

A. The Proposed Requirements

B. Principles for Establishing the Succinct Statement

C. Wording of the Succinct Statement

D. Succinct Statement on Menus Targeted to Children

E. Requirements for the Succinct Statement To Be Prominent, Clear, and Conspicuous

F. Placement of the Succinct Statement on Menus and Menu Boards

XV. Comments and FDA Response on Proposed § 101.11(b)(2)(i)(C)—Statement That Must Be on Menus and Menu Boards About Availability of Written Nutrition Information

A. Proposed Wording of the Statement of Availability

B. Requirements for the Statement of Availability To Be Prominent and Conspicuous

C. Placement of the Statement of Availability

XVI. Comments and FDA Response on Proposed § 101.11(b)(2)(ii)—Nutrition Information That Must Be Made Available in Written Form

A. Required Nutrients

B. Manner of Presentation of the Written Nutrition Information

C. Nutrients in Insignificant Amounts

D. Variable Menu Items

E. Form of the Written Nutrition Information

XVII. Comments and FDA Response on Proposed § 101.11(b)(2)(iii)—Requirements for Food That Is Self-Service or on Display

A. Applicability of § 101.11(b)(2)(i) to Food That Is Self-Service or on Display

B. Placement of Calories for Self-Service Foods and Foods on Display

C. Declaring Calories "Per Item" or "Per Serving"

D. Declaring Calories "Per Serving" for Self-Service Beverages

E. Manner of Declaring Calories for Self-Service Foods and Foods on Display

F. Applicability of Requirements for Written Nutrition Information, Succinct Statement, and Statement of Availability to Self-Service Foods and Foods on Display

G. Succinct Statement and Statement of Availability for Self-Service Foods and Foods on Display

H. The Written Nutrition Information That Must Be Provided for Food That Is Self-Service or on Display

XVIII. Comments and FDA Response on Proposed § 101.11(c)(1) to (c)(5)—Determination of Nutrient Content (Final § 101.11(c)(1) to (c)(2))

XIX. Comments and FDA Response on Proposed § 101.11(c)(6)—Substantiation Documentation (Final 101.11(c)(3))

XX. Comments and FDA Response on Proposed § 101.11(d)—Voluntary Registration to Elect To Be Subject to the Rule

XXI. Comments and FDA Response on Proposed § 101.11(e)—Signatures

XXII. Comments and FDA Response on Proposed § 101.11(f)—Misbranding

XXIII. Comments and FDA Response on Effective Date

A. Proposed Effective Date and Request for Comment

B. Comments on Proposed Effective Date

C. Effective Date and Compliance Date for This Rule

XXIV. Comments and FDA Response on Compliance

XXV. Final Regulatory Impact Analysis

XXVI. Paperwork Reduction Act of 1995

XXVII. Federalism

XXVIII. Environmental Impact

XXIX. References

Executive Summary

Purpose and Coverage of the Final Rule

More than two thirds of adults and about a third of children in the United States are overweight or obese. Overconsumption of calories is one of the primary risk factors for overweight and obesity. About half of consumers' annual food dollars are spent on, and a third of total calories come from, foods prepared outside the home, including foods from restaurants and similar retail food establishments. Many people do not know, or underestimate, the calorie and nutrient content of these foods. To help make nutrition information for these foods available to consumers in a direct, accessible, and consistent manner to enable consumers to make informed and healthful dietary choices, section 4205 of the ACA requires that calorie and other nutrition information be provided to consumers in restaurants and similar retail food establishments that are part of a chain with 20 or more locations doing business under the same name and offering for sale substantially the same menu items (chain retail food establishment). Section 4205 of the ACA also provides that a restaurant or similar retail food establishment that is not a chain retail food establishment may elect to be subject to section 4205's nutrition labeling requirements by registering every other year with FDA.

To be covered by this rule, an establishment must satisfy several criteria. First, the establishment must be a restaurant or similar retail food establishment. Under this rule, that means a retail establishment that offers for sale restaurant-type food, except if it is a school as defined in 7 CFR 210.2 or 220.2. Restaurants and similar retail food establishments include bakeries, cafeterias, coffee shops, convenience stores, delicatessens, food service facilities located within entertainment venues (such as amusement parks, bowling alleys, and movie theatres), food service vendors (e.g., ice cream shops and mall cookie counters), food take-out and/or delivery establishments (such as pizza take-out and delivery establishments), grocery stores, retail confectionary stores, superstores, quick service restaurants, and table service restaurants.

The rule defines "restaurant-type food" in a way that both focuses on the food most like the food offered for sale in restaurants and reflects the statutory context of section 4205 of the ACA. The table that follows provides examples of foods that generally would be considered restaurant-type food (e.g., foods that are usually eaten on the premises, while walking away, or soon after arriving at another location), as well as examples of foods that generally would be not be considered restaurant-type food (e.g., foods that are grocery-type items that consumers often store for use at a later time or customarily further prepare), for the purposes of this rule.

Examples of Foods That Generally Would or Would Not Be Considered Restaurant-Type Food

Examples of foods that generally would be considered restaurant-type food	Examples of foods that generally would not be considered restaurant-type food
• Food for immediate consumption at a sit-down or quick service restaurant• Food purchased at a drive-through establishment• Food purchased at a drive-through establishment• Take-out and delivery pizza; hot pizza at grocery and convenience stores that is ready to eat; pizza slice from a movie theater• Hot buffet food, hot soup at a soup bar, and food from a salad bar• Foods ordered from a menu/menu board at a grocery store intended for individual consumption (e.g., soups, sandwiches, and salads)• Self-service foods and foods on display that are intended for individual consumption (e.g., sandwiches, wraps, and paninis at a deli counter; salads plated by the consumer at a salad bar; cookies from a mall cookie counter; bagels, donuts, rolls offered for individual sale)	• Certain foods bought from bulk bins or cases (e.g., dried fruit, nuts) in grocery stores• Foods to be eaten over several eating occasions or stored for later use (e.g., loaves of bread, bags or boxes of dinner rolls, whole cakes, and bags or boxes of candy or cookies)• Foods that are usually further prepared before consuming (e.g., deli meats and cheeses)• Foods sold by weight that are not self-serve and are not intended solely for individual consumption (e.g., deli salads sold by unit of weight such as potato salad, chicken salad), either prepacked or packed upon consumer request

Consistent with the statute, to be covered by the rule, a restaurant or similar retail establishment must be "part of a chain with 20 or more locations doing business under the same name (regardless of the type of ownership of the locations) and offering for sale substantially the same menu items." A restaurant or similar retail food establishment that does not satisfy these criteria may choose to be covered by the rule by registering with FDA using a process established in the rule.

Under the rule, "location" means a fixed position or site. Transportation venues such as trains and airplanes are not covered by the rule because they do not have a fixed position or site. "Doing business under the same name" means a restaurant or similar retail food establishment must share the same name as other establishments in the chain (regardless of the type of ownership of the locations, e.g., individual franchises). The term "name" refers to either the name of the establishment presented to the public or, if there is no name of the establishment presented to the public (e.g., an establishment with the generic descriptor "concession stand"), the name of the parent entity of the establishment. "Offering for sale substantially the same menu items" means offering for sale a significant proportion of menu items that use the same general recipe and are prepared in substantially the same way with substantially the same food components, even if the name of the menu item varies.

The nutrition labeling requirements of the rule apply to standard menu items offered for sale in covered establishments. "Standard menu item" means a restaurant-type food that is routinely included on a menu or menu board or routinely offered as a self-service food or food on display. The nutrition labeling requirements are not applicable to certain foods, including foods that are not standard menu items, such as condiments, daily specials, temporary menu items, custom orders, and food that is part of a customary market test; and self-service food and food on display that is offered for sale for less than a total of 60 days per calendar year or fewer than 90 consecutive days in order to test consumer acceptance. In addition, the rule exempts alcohol beverages that are food on display and are not self-service food (e.g., bottles of liquor behind the bar used to prepare mixed drinks) from the labeling requirements that apply to food on display.

Summary of the Major Provisions of the Final Rule

The rule includes provisions that:

- Define terms, including terms that describe criteria for determining whether an establishment is subject to the rule;

- Establish which foods are subject to the nutrition labeling requirements and which foods are not subject to these requirements;

- Require that calories for standard menu items be declared on menus and menu boards that list such foods for sale;

- Require that calories for standard menu items that are self-service or on display be declared on signs adjacent to such foods;

- Require that written nutrition information for standard menu items be available to consumers who ask to see it;

- Require, on menus and menu boards, a succinct statement concerning suggested daily caloric intake (succinct statement), designed to help the public understand the significance of the calorie declarations;

- Require, on menus and menu boards, a statement regarding the availability of the written nutrition information (statement of availability);

- Establish requirements for determination of nutrient content of standard menu items;

- Establish requirements for substantiation of nutrient content determined for standard menu items, including requirements for records that a covered establishment must make available to FDA within a reasonable period of time upon request; and

- Establish terms and conditions under which restaurants and similar retail food establishments not otherwise subject to the rule could elect to be subject to the requirements by registering with FDA.

Costs and Benefits

The statute requires nutrition labeling for standard menu items on menus and menu boards for certain restaurants and similar retail food establishments and calorie labeling for food sold from certain vending machines. FDA is issuing two separate final rules (one for menu labeling and one for vending machine labeling) to implement those labeling requirements. Taken together the labeling requirements (of the menu labeling and vending machine labeling rules combined) are estimated to have benefits exceeding costs by $477.9 million on an annualized basis (over 20 years discounted at 7 percent).

Summary of Costs and Benefits of Menu Labeling and Vending Machine Rules

	Rate	Potential benefits	Estimated costs	Net benefits
Total for Labeling (menu and vending rules) over 20 years*	3	$9,221.3	$1,697.9	$7,523.4
	7	6,752.8	1,333.9	5,418.9
Annualized for Labeling (menu and vending rules) over 20 years*	3	601.9	110.8	491.1
	7	595.5	117.6	477.9
Total for Menu Labeling over 20 years	3	9,221.3	1,166.8	8,054.5
	7	6,752.8	932.8	5,820.0
Annualized for Menu Labeling over 20 years	3	601.9	76.9	525.01
	7	595.5	84.5	510.99

I. Background

More than two thirds of adults and about a third of children in the United States are overweight or obese (Refs. 1 and 2). Overconsumption of calories is one of the primary risk factors for overweight and obesity (Ref. 3). About half of consumers' annual food dollars are spent on, and a third of total calories come from, foods prepared outside the home, including foods from restaurants and similar retail food establishments (Refs. 4 to 6). Research indicates that many people do not know, or underestimate, the calorie and nutrient content of these foods (Ref. 7).

Since the early 1990s, the Nutrition Labeling and Education Act of 1990 (NLEA) and our regulations in § 101.9 (21 CFR 101.9) implementing the NLEA have required that the labeling for many foods bear nutrition information, including calorie information. However, as we noted in the proposed rule (76 FR 19192 at 19193; April 6, 2011), the NLEA left a gap in the Federal requirements for nutrition labeling through certain exemptions. The NLEA included an exemption for nutrition labeling for food that is "served in restaurants or other establishments in which food is served for immediate human consumption" or "sold for sale or use in such establishments" (section 403(q)(5)(A)(i) of the FD&C Act) (21 U.S.C. 343(q)(5)(A)(i)). The NLEA also included an exemption for food of the type described in section 403(q)(5)(A)(i) that is primarily processed and prepared in a retail establishment, ready for human consumption, "offered for sale to consumers but not for immediate human consumption in such establishment and which is not offered for sale outside such establishment" (section 403(q)(5)(A)(ii) of the FD&C Act). However, these exemptions were contingent on there being no nutrient content claims or health claims made on the label or labeling, or in the advertising, for the food. Current provisions in § 101.10 (21 CFR 101.10) require restaurants and other establishments in which food is offered for human consumption that make either a nutrient content claim (defined in § 101.13 (21 CFR 101.13)) or health claim (defined in 21 CFR 101.14) to provide certain nutrition information upon request. For example, if a menu lists an entree as being low in fat, information about the amount of fat in the entree must be available upon request (§ 101.10).

Section 101.9(j)(2) of our regulations implementing the NLEA includes examples of restaurants or other establishments in which food sold for immediate human consumption generally was exempted from nutrition labeling requirements under the NLEA. Section 101.9(j)(3) of these regulations includes examples of food sold in establishments in which food is processed and prepared, ready for human consumption, offered for sale to consumers but not for immediate consumption, and not offered for sale outside of the establishments.

Several State and local governments enacted their own laws requiring nutrition labeling on menus and menu boards to fill the gap in the Federal requirements. However, these State and local requirements vary significantly in their substantive requirements and the set of establishments to which they apply.

On March 23, 2010, the ACA (Pub. L. 111-148) was signed into law. Section 4205 of the ACA amends section 403(q) of the FD&C Act, which governs nutrition labeling requirements, and section 403A of the FD&C Act (21 U.S.C. 343-1), which governs Federal preemption of State and local food labeling requirements. As amended, section 403(q)(5)(H) of the FD&C Act requires chain retail food establishments with 20 or more locations to provide calorie information for standard menu items, including food on display and self-service food, and to provide, upon consumer request, additional written nutrition information for standard menu items (21 U.S.C. 343(q)(5)(H)(i) to (iii)). Section 403(q)(5)(H) of the FD&C Act also provides that a restaurant or similar retail food establishment not otherwise subject to the requirements of section 403(q)(5)(H) (e.g., a restaurant that is not part of a chain with 20 or more locations) may elect to be subject to the requirements of section 403(q)(5)(H) by registering every other year with FDA (21 U.S.C. 343(q)(5)(H)(ix)). Thus, "covered establishments" include both chain retail food establishments and other restaurants or similar retail food establishments that voluntarily register to be subject to the rule. A standard menu item offered for sale in a covered establishment is deemed to be misbranded if the requirements of section 403(q)(5)(H) are not met.

Section 4205 of the ACA became effective on the date the law was signed, March 23, 2010; however, FDA must issue rules before some provisions can be required. On July 7, 2010, we published a notice in the Federal Register to solicit comments and suggestions on the new law (2010 docket notice) (75 FR 39026). On August 25, 2010, we published for public comment a draft guidance entitled "Draft Guidance for Industry: Questions and Answers Regarding Implementation of the Menu Labeling Provisions of Section 4205 of the Patient Protection and Affordable Care Act of 2010" (draft implementation guidance) (Ref. 8) (75 FR 52426), describing which provisions became requirements upon enactment of the law, which provisions we would implement through rulemaking, and draft interpretations of certain provisions, including a broad interpretation of the scope of establishments covered. On January 25, 2011, we published in the Federal Register a notice withdrawing the draft implementation guidance (76 FR 4360) and announcing our intent to exercise our enforcement discretion until we complete the notice and comment rulemaking process.

In the Federal Register of April 6, 2011 (76 FR 19192), we issued a proposed rule (proposed rule) to implement the requirements of section 4205 of the ACA for the nutrition labeling of standard menu items in certain restaurants and similar retail food establishments. We requested public comments on the proposed requirements and some alternatives by June 6, 2011. In the Federal Register of May 24, 2011 (76 FR 30050), we issued a document (correction document) correcting errors in the proposed rule, including errors in cross-references, an incomplete address, and a typographical error in the codified section of the document. In the Federal Register of May 24, 2011 (76 FR 30051), we extended the comment period until July 5, 2011.

In the proposed rule, we described both the provisions that became requirements upon enactment (i.e., they are self-executing) and the provisions that depend on FDA to issue rules before they can become effective (76 FR 19192 at 19194). We also noted that we had published the draft implementation guidance and described the issues addressed by the draft implementation guidance. In the proposed rule, we reiterated that we intended to exercise enforcement discretion for the self-executing provisions of section 4205 of the ACA and described our reasons for doing so (76 FR 19192 at 19194).

After considering comments to the proposed rule, we are issuing this final rule to implement the requirements of section 4205 of the ACA for the nutrition labeling of standard menu items in certain chain restaurants and similar retail food establishments.

In addition to the nutrition labeling requirements for standard menu items, other amendments made by section 4205 of the ACA to the FD&C Act (specifically, section 403(q)(5)(H)(viii)(I)) establish calorie disclosure requirements for certain articles of food sold from vending machines. We published a proposed rule to implement the vending machine provisions of section 403(q) of the FD&C Act on April 6, 2011 (76 FR 19238; the proposed vending machine rule). Elsewhere in this issue of the Federal Register, we are issuing a final rule to implement the vending machine provisions of section 403(q)(5)(H)(viii)(I) of the FD&C Act.

II. Legal Authority

On March 23, 2010, the ACA was signed into law. Section 4205 of the ACA amended section 403(q)(5) of the FD&C Act by amending section 403(q)(5)(A) and by creating new clause (H), which requires, in relevant part, covered establishments to provide certain nutrient declarations for standard menu items in the labeling for such foods. Under section 403(f) of the FD&C Act, any word, statement, or other information required by or under authority of the FD&C Act to appear on the label or labeling of a food is required to be prominently placed thereon with such conspicuousness (as compared with other words, statements, designs, or devices, in the labeling) and in such terms as to render it likely to be read and understood by the ordinary individual under customary conditions of purchase and use. Under section 403(a)(1) of the FD&C Act, food labeling must be truthful and non-misleading. Because food that is not in compliance with section 403 is deemed misbranded, food to which these requirements apply is deemed misbranded if these requirements are not met. In addition, under section 201(n) of the FD&C Act (21 U.S.C. 321(n)), the labeling of a food is misleading if it fails to reveal facts that are material in light of representations made in the labeling or with respect to consequences that may result from use. Section 403(q)(5)(H)(x) of the FD&C Act requires that the Secretary of Health and Human Services (Secretary) issue regulations to carry out requirements in section 403(q)(5)(H). Section 701(a) of the FD&C Act (21 U.S.C. 371(a)) vests the Secretary with the authority to issue regulations for the efficient enforcement of the FD&C Act. Thus, we have the authority to issue this final rule under sections 201(n), 403(a)(1), 403(f), 403(q)(5)(H), and 701(a) of the FD&C Act.

We have revised our labeling regulations by adding new § 101.11 to require that covered establishments provide calorie and other nutrition information for standard menu items, including food on display and self-service food. Also, we are establishing the terms and conditions for voluntary registration by establishments that are not otherwise subject to the requirements of section 4205 of the ACA but elect to become subject to such requirements.

III. General Comments on the Proposed Rule

A. Introduction

We received approximately 900 submissions on the proposed rule by the close of the comment period, each containing one or more comments. We received submissions from consumers; consumer groups; trade organizations; industry (including restaurants, entertainment venues, food service operations, and grocery stores); public health organizations; public advocacy groups; contractors; Congress; Federal, State, and local Government Agencies; and other organizations.

We describe and respond to the comments in sections III, IV, VI through XXIV, and XXVII of this document. To make it easier to identify comments and our responses, the word "Comment," in parentheses, appears before the comment's description, and the word "Response," in parentheses, appears before our response. We have also numbered each comment and response to help distinguish between different comments and responses. The number assigned to each comment is purely for organizational purposes and does not signify the comment's value or importance or the order in which it was received.

B. Description of General Comments and FDA Response

Many comments made general remarks supporting or opposing the rule and did not focus on a particular section of the rule. The majority of these comments expressed general support for nutrition labeling of standard menu items in covered establishments, and we do not discuss them in detail. In the following paragraphs, we discuss general comments that did not support the rule as proposed.

(Comment 1) Some comments stated that people do not need to be told what to eat. Some comments asserted that calorie disclosure on menus will either cause eating disorders or affect those with eating disorders. Other comments asserted that the menu labeling requirements will not affect consumer behavior, there will be information overload, and people will ignore the information. Some comments considered that the menu labeling requirements will promote healthier choices, whereas other comments considered that the menu labeling requirements will not promote healthier choices. Some comments supported the menu labeling requirements but considered that education is needed to fight obesity.

(Response 1) The rule does not tell consumers what they should or should not eat. The nutrition labeling required by section 4205 of the ACA will provide nutrition information to consumers in covered establishments in a direct, accessible, and consistent manner to enable consumers to make informed choices about the foods they purchase in such establishments.

About half of consumers' annual food dollars are spent on, and a third of total calories come from, foods prepared outside of the home, including foods from restaurants or similar retail food establishments (Refs. 4 to 6). Further, research indicates that many people do not know, or underestimate, the calorie and nutrient content of these foods (Ref. 7). Accordingly, providing direct access to nutrition information for these foods will enable consumers to make informed decisions within the context of nutrition regarding the foods they purchase in restaurants or similar retail food establishments. Providing nutrition information to consumers for standard menu items offered for sale in covered establishments will give consumers much needed access to essential nutrition information for a large and growing number of the foods they purchase and consume. In addition, it will allow consumers to make informed nutritional comparisons between different foods and informed purchase decisions. Further, section 4205 of the ACA and this rule require covered establishments to post, on menus and menu boards, a succinct statement concerning suggested daily caloric intake designed to enable consumers to understand, in the context of a total daily diet, the significance of the calorie information provided on menus and menu boards. This statement, along with the required calorie information, will enable consumers to better understand the significance of the calorie information provided on menus and menu boards and the potential impacts of overconsumption of calories. As a result, the information will enable consumers to assess their calorie intake during short- or long-term settings and better understand how the foods that they purchase at covered establishments fit within their daily caloric and other nutritional needs.

The comments provided no evidence that the provision of nutrition labeling at the point of purchase causes or adversely affects those with eating disorders. For nearly two decades, consumers have had access to this type of information on the labels of packaged foods that bear the Nutrition Facts label in accordance with § 101.9. We are not aware of data or other information demonstrating that the availability of nutrition information through the Nutrition Facts Panel has either caused eating disorders or negatively impacted persons with eating disorders. In addition, Congress, through section 4205 of the ACA, requires covered establishments to provide calorie and other nutrition information for standard menu items. This rulemaking implements that Congressional mandate.

(Comment 2) Some comments considered that the requirements are unnecessary because most "fast food" restaurants have the information already. One comment considered that the proposed requirements constitute a tax increase designed to relieve the individual of personal responsibility.

(Response 2) Section 4205 of the ACA requires covered establishments to provide calorie and other information for standard menu items on menus, menu boards, signs adjacent to self-service foods and foods on display and additional nutrition information for standard menu items in written form, available on the premises, to consumers on request. Therefore, section 4205 of the ACA requires covered establishments to provide nutrition information to consumers in a direct, accessible, and consistent manner, typically at points of purchase, where consumers make order selections. While some "fast food" establishments may already have some nutrition information available to consumers in some fashion, these establishments are a subset of the establishments required to comply with the requirements of this rule, and these establishments may not be providing nutrition information to consumers in the manner required by section 4205 of the ACA.

Regarding the comment asserting that the proposed requirements somehow negate personal responsibility, we reiterate that the requirements do not tell consumers what they should or should not eat or otherwise interfere with a consumer's ability to purchase foods. In fact, as we noted previously, this rule requires covered establishments to provide accurate nutrition information to consumers in a direct and accessible manner to enable consumers to make informed and healthful dietary choices.

(Comment 3) Some comments addressed concerns related to enforcement. One comment expressed concern that the proposed rule did not set forth a clear "chain of liability" for food that is misbranded under the rule and related provisions of the FD&C Act, specifically sections 201(n), 403(a), or 403(q) of the FD&C Act. The comment stated that it is unclear whether FDA might impose vicarious liability on the franchisor or licensor of a restaurant for such misbranded food, particularly where the franchisor or licensor retains power over the menus and menu boards used by the restaurants. The comment also expressed concern that restaurants that "unwittingly 'misbrand' their menu offerings" will be held liable for their food that is misbranded under this rule and related provisions of the FD&C Act.

(Response 3) Persons exercising authority and supervisory responsibility over a restaurant or similar retail food establishment can be held responsible for violations under the FD&C Act. See United States v. Park, 421 U.S. 658, 659 (1978). ("The Act imposes upon persons exercising authority and supervisory responsibility reposed in them by a business organization not only a positive duty to seek out and remedy violations but also, and primarily, a duty to implement measures that will insure that violations will not occur . . . .") (citing United States v. Dotterweich, 320 U.S. 277 (1943)). Agency decisions regarding enforcement actions will be determined on a case by case basis.

(Comment 4) Some comments addressed issues unrelated to the specific nutrition labeling requirements of section 4205 of the ACA, such as labeling of genetically engineered foods, allergens, gluten, food additives (including preservatives), artificial sweeteners, ingredients, pesticides, and organic foods; labeling to indicate whether a food has been irradiated; labeling of alcohol as a toxin; labeling the country of origin; and labeling the "gender of meat products."

(Response 4) Section 4205 of the ACA requires covered establishments to provide certain nutrition information for standard menu items. It does not address the labeling issues raised in these comments. Therefore, we do not address these issues in this document.

(Comment 5) Some comments directed to what establishments would be covered by the rule pointed to a report submitted by a U.S. House of Representatives Appropriations Committee explaining an appropriations bill for Agriculture, Rural Development, Food and Drug Administration, and Related Agencies for fiscal year 2012 (Ref. 9). The comments quoted an excerpt from the report (". . . and the Committee believes that the FDA should define the term restaurant to mean only restaurants doing business marketed under the same name or retail establishments where the primary business is the selling of food for immediate consumption . . .") to signify Congressional intent on the scope of establishments subject to section 4205 of the ACA or as evidence supporting their own recommendations regarding the establishments that should be covered by the rule. (We note that some comments reported the date of the report as June 3, 2011, and one comment reported the date of the report as May 27, 2011. We identified a report dated June 3, 2011 (Ref. 9), but did not identify a report dated May 27, 2011. For the purpose of this document, we assume that the comments are referring to the report dated June 3, 2011.)

(Response 5) We disagree that an Appropriations Committee report from a Congress subsequent to the Congress that passed section 4205 of the ACA can be used as evidence of the intent of the previous Congress that passed section 4205. The Appropriations Committee report cited by the comments is dated after the ACA was passed, so it is not part of the relevant legislative history and carries no interpretive weight on this issue (see, e.g., Bruesewitz v. Wyeth, 131 U.S. 1068, 1081 (2011)).

IV. Comments and FDA Response on Proposed Conforming Amendments

A. Section 11.1(g)—Electronic Signatures

Proposed § 11.1(g) (21 CFR 11.1(g)) would provide that 21 CFR part 11 regarding electronic signatures does not apply to electronic signatures obtained under the voluntary registration provision for covered restaurants and similar retail food establishments at proposed § 101.11(d).

We received no comments on this proposed provision and are finalizing it without change.

B. Sections 101.9(j)(1)(i), (j)(2) and (j)(3)—Nutrition Labeling of Food

Our proposed amendment to § 101.9(j)(1)(i) would specify that claims or other nutrition information subject the food to the nutrition labeling provisions of § 101.11 as well as § 101.9 or § 101.10 (nutrition labeling of restaurant foods), as applicable.

Our proposed amendments to § 101.9(j)(2) and (j)(3) would change the introductory text of paragraphs (j)(2) and (j)(3) to add the phrase "Except as provided in § 101.11, food products that are:".

We received no comments on these proposed provisions and are finalizing them without change. However, we also are adding a conforming amendment to add the phrase "Except as provided in § 101.11" to the beginning of the first sentence in § 101.9(j)(4). As with § 101.9(j)(2) and (j)(3), § 101.9(j)(4) needs to be revised to exclude standard menu items sold in covered establishments and reference the special labeling requirements for those foods in § 101.11 (see § 101.11(b)(2)(ii)(B)).

C. Section 101.10—Nutrition Labeling of Restaurant Foods Whose Labels or Labeling Bear Nutrient Content Claims or Health Claims

Our proposed amendment to § 101.10 would provide that the information in the written nutrition information required by § 101.11(b)(2)(ii)(A) for standard menu items that are offered for sale in covered establishments (as defined in § 101.11(a)) will serve to meet the requirements of § 101.10.

We received no comments on this proposed provision. Given our removal of the term "restaurant food" and our revision of the term "restaurant-type food" in § 101.11, we are adding a conforming amendment to ensure that the use of the term "restaurant foods" in § 101.10, which predates the ACA, is not confusing. We are inserting three sentences between the current first and second sentences of § 101.10, to clarify that the scope of § 101.10 includes those foods described in section 403(q)(5)(A)(i) and (ii) of the FD&C Act. These sentences describe that, for the purposes of § 101.10, restaurant food includes two categories of food. The first category of food is that which is served in restaurants or other establishments in which food is served for immediate human consumption or which is sold for sale or use in such establishments. The second category of food is that which is processed and prepared primarily in a retail establishment, which is ready for human consumption, which is of the type described in the first category, and which is offered for sale to consumers but not for immediate consumption in such establishment and which is not offered for sale outside such establishment. This scope is reflected in numerous prior Agency statements, including in the preamble to our final rule entitled "Food Labeling: Nutrient Content Claims, General Principles, Petitions, Definition of Terms; Definitions of Nutrient Content Claims for the Fat, Fatty Acid, and Cholesterol Content of Food" (58 FR 2302, 2386, January 6, 1993), and in our 2008 "Guidance for Industry: A Labeling Guide for Restaurants and Other Retail Establishments Selling Away-From-Home Foods" (Ref. 10). This change does not alter the meaning or applicability of § 101.10.

V. Key Terms That FDA Proposed To Define (Proposed § 101.11(a))

To establish the scope of establishments, labeling, and food covered by section 4205 of the ACA, we proposed to define key terms (proposed § 101.11(a)). We also proposed to establish that the definitions in section 201 of the FD&C Act apply when used in § 101.11 (proposed § 101.11(a)). We received no comments regarding the use of statutory definitions in section 201 of the FD&C Act, and we are finalizing that provision without change.

In the next section of this document, we discuss the final definitions and related comments, organized into three categories: (1) Terms related to the scope of establishments covered by the rule, (2) the terms menu and menu board, and (3) terms related to foods covered. This organization is consistent with our discussion of our proposed terms in the preamble to the proposed rule.

VI. Comments and FDA Response on the Proposed Definitions of Terms Related to the Scope of Establishments Covered by the Rule (Proposed § 101.11(a))

A. Introduction

To specify establishments that would be subject to the nutrition labeling requirements of section 4205 of the ACA, we proposed to define "covered establishment" to mean a restaurant or similar retail food establishment that is a part of a chain with 20 or more locations doing business under the same name (regardless of the type of ownership, e.g., individual franchises) and offering for sale substantially the same menu items, as well as a restaurant or similar retail food establishment that is registered to be covered under section 403(q)(5)(H)(ix) of the FD&C Act. (Emphasis added).

Importantly, the definition of "covered establishment" includes several terms, identified in italics, that are defined in the rule. In addition, the proposed definition of one of these terms—i.e., "restaurant or similar retail food establishment"—includes other terms we proposed to define—i.e., "restaurant food" and "restaurant-type food." Thus, any revisions we make to the proposed definitions of any of these terms may affect whether a particular establishment is a "covered establishment" for the purposes of this rule. As discussed more fully in sections VI.B, VI.C, VI.D, VI.E, and VI.F:

- We have revised the definition of "restaurant or similar retail food establishment" to mean a retail establishment that offers for sale restaurant-type food, except if it is a school as defined in 7 CFR 210.1 or 220.2;

- We have revised the definition of the term "restaurant-type food" to focus on the food most like the food offered for sale in restaurants;

- We are adding a definition of "locations" to clarify our interpretation of "part of a chain with 20 or more locations";

- We have revised the definition of "doing business under the same name" so that the term "name" refers to either (1) the name of the establishment presented to the public or (2), if there is no name of the establishment presented to the public (e.g., an establishment with the generic descriptor "concession stand"), the name of the parent entity of the establishment; and

- We have revised the definition of "offering for sale substantially the same menu items" to add a qualitative description of the number of menu items that must be shared in order for the criterion of "offering for sale substantially the same menu items" to be met.

We proposed to define the term "gross floor area" because we proposed that it be used in the definition of restaurant or similar retail food establishment. While we received comments on this proposed definition, as discussed in section VI.B.2 the definition of restaurant or similar retail food establishment in this rule no longer considers gross floor area. Therefore, we are deleting the proposed definition of "gross floor area" because it is no longer relevant to the scope of establishments covered by this rule.

B. Restaurant or Similar Retail Food Establishment

1. The Proposed Definition

Proposed § 101.11(a) would define "restaurant or similar retail food establishment" as a retail establishment that offers for sale restaurant or restaurant-type food, where the sale of food is the primary business activity of that establishment. Proposed § 101.11(a) would provide that the sale of food is the retail establishment's primary business activity if the establishment presents itself, or has presented itself publicly as a restaurant (primary purpose 1), or a total of more than 50 percent of that retail establishment's gross floor area is used for the preparation, purchase, service, consumption, or storage of food (primary purpose 2). (See Figure 1 in the proposed rule (76 FR 19192 at 19201), in which we coined the terms "primary purpose 1" and "primary purpose 2." We did not include these coined terms in the regulatory text of the definition. In this document, we are using these coined terms to simplify the discussion. We also are coining the term "primary business test" to simplify the discussion of the criterion for the primary business activity of the establishment.) Under an alternative approach we discussed in the proposed rule (76 FR 19192 at 19197) (the alternative revenue approach), "primary purpose 2" would be that more than 50 percent of the retail establishment's gross revenues are generated by the sale of food rather than that more than 50 percent of the retail establishment's gross floor area is used for the preparation, purchase, service, consumption, or storage of food.

In the proposed rule (76 FR 19192 at 19198), we also discussed an alternative (the restaurant-type food alternative) in which the sale of restaurant or restaurant-type food (rather than the sale of food in general) would be the primary business activity of the establishment. Under the restaurant-type food alternative, "primary purpose 2" would be that a total of more than 50 percent of a retail establishment's gross floor area is used for the preparation, purchase, service, consumption, or storage of restaurant or restaurant-type food or its ingredients.

In the proposed rule (76 FR 19192 at 19198), we acknowledged that many facilities that sell restaurant or restaurant-type food are located within larger retail establishments, such as coffee shops in bookstores or concession stands in movie theaters. We considered that some of these facilities would be separate retail establishments, while others would be part of their larger retail establishments. We explained that if a facility that is inside a larger establishment is part of a chain with locations outside of the chain of the larger establishment, the facility would be considered a separate establishment. For example, if a coffee shop in a bookstore is part of a chain of coffee shops with locations outside of the chain of bookstores, the coffee shop would be considered a separate retail establishment. By contrast, if a facility is not part of a chain with locations outside of the chain of the larger establishment, the facility would be considered part of the larger establishment. Thus, a movie theater concession stand that appears only in other movie theaters in that particular chain of movie theaters would not be considered a separate establishment for the purposes of this proposed rule.

As an example of how all of the elements of the proposed definition of restaurant or similar retail food establishment fit together, movie theaters would not have met the proposed definition of restaurant or similar retail food establishment. Movie theaters usually do not present themselves as restaurants. In addition, movie theaters usually neither dedicate more than 50 percent of their gross floor area to the sale of food, nor generate more than 50 percent of their gross revenues from the sale of food. Thus, under the proposed definition of "restaurant or similar retail food establishment," movie theater concession stands generally would not have been covered regardless of whether "primary purpose 2" is based on the percent of gross floor area dedicated to the sale of food or on the alternative revenue approach based on the percent of gross revenues from the sale of food.

In the proposed rule (76 FR 19192 at 19197 to 19199), we acknowledged that the statutory language is ambiguous with respect to the scope of establishments covered by section 4205 of the ACA, and asked for comments on:

- Whether we should use "primary business activity," or a different test, as a basis for determining whether an establishment is a restaurant or similar retail food establishment;

- Whether we should use the sale of food in general, or the sale of restaurant-type food, as the criterion for "primary business activity";

- Whether we should use the alternative revenue approach, rather than a floor space approach, in "primary purpose 2";

- Whether we should choose a different number for the cutoff for the percent of gross floor area for determining the primary business activity of the retail establishment;

- Whether we should choose a different criteria for determining primary business activity, such as whether the consumer pays for admission to the establishment; and

- Whether a facility selling restaurant or restaurant-type food that is not part of a chain with locations outside of the chain of a larger retail establishment should be included within the definition of restaurant or similar retail food establishment. We particularly requested comment on this approach with respect to larger retail establishments such as movie theaters, other entertainment-type venues, and superstores that offer restaurant or restaurant-type food.

In the following paragraphs, we discuss comments on the proposed definition of "restaurant or similar retail food establishment." After considering these comments, we have revised the proposed definition to eliminate the primary business test.

Importantly, the proposed definition of "restaurant or similar retail food establishment" included the terms "restaurant and restaurant-type food" and, thus, revisions to those terms also may affect whether a particular establishment is a "restaurant or similar retail food establishment" for the purposes of this rule. As discussed more fully in section VI.C, we are deleting the term "restaurant food" throughout the rule and establishing a revised definition of "restaurant-type food" that better reflects the food most like the food offered for sale in restaurants.

With these changes, in this rule "restaurant or similar retail food establishment" means a retail establishment that offers for sale restaurant-type food, except if it is a school as defined in 7 CFR 210.2 or 220.2. Establishments such as bakeries, cafeterias, coffee shops, convenience stores, delicatessens, food service facilities located within entertainment venues (such as amusement parks, bowling alleys, and movie theatres), food service vendors (e.g., ice cream shops and mall cookie counters), food take-out and/or delivery establishments (such as pizza take-out and delivery establishments), grocery stores, retail confectionary stores, superstores, quick service restaurants, and table service restaurants would be restaurants or similar retail food establishments if they sell restaurant-type food.

2. Primary Business Test

(Comment 6) A few comments generally opposed having any primary business test within the definition of "restaurant or similar retail food establishment." One of these comments recommended that the primary purpose of the definition be related to "whether the establishment optimizes the nation's health through their food distribution channels, rather than a profit/commerce approach." This comment acknowledged that a "profit/commerce approach" may be more tangibly measured but believed that the definition of restaurant or similar retail food establishment should reflect what the comment considered to be the purpose of the ACA: To inform consumers on healthy food choices. Another comment considered that the floor space test we proposed as "primary purpose 2" is not a rational basis for defining a restaurant or similar retail food establishment. Another comment asserted that both the proposed definition of "restaurant or similar retail food establishment" and the "alternative revenue approach" would have covered grocery stores but not superstores, putting grocery stores at a competitive disadvantage.

One comment recommended that we define a restaurant or similar retail food establishment as any chain establishment selling restaurant or restaurant-type food. The comment asserted that this broader interpretation is consistent with the language in the statute. The comment pointed out that the statute does not include text to suggest that in order to qualify as a retail food establishment, an entity must have the sale of food as its primary business activity.

One comment recommended that the definition cover all of the establishments exempted from nutrition labeling by the NLEA. Some comments referred to examples of covered establishments that we had included in our draft implementation guidance (which we withdrew on January 25, 2011) and agreed that these types of establishments should be covered by the rule. The examples in the draft implementation guidance included table service restaurants, quick service restaurants, coffee shops, delicatessens, food take-out and/or delivery establishments (e.g., pizza take-out and delivery establishments), grocery stores, convenience stores, movie theaters, cafeterias, bakeries/retail confectionary stores, food service vendors (e.g., lunch wagons, ice cream shops, mall cookie counters, and sidewalk carts), and transportation carriers (e.g., airlines and trains). These examples reflected the establishments that sell certain food previously exempted from nutrition labeling by the NLEA under sections 403(q)(5)(A)(i) and (ii) of the FD&C Act, including those mentioned in § 101.9(j)(2) and (j)(3) as well as some additional examples (i.e., similar food served in coffee shops, grocery stores, and movie theaters). Some of the establishments that would have been covered under the draft implementation guidance (such as transportation carriers and facilities located within movie theaters) would be excluded under a definition that includes any primary business test presented in the proposed rule (i.e., regardless of whether the criterion is the proposed criterion based on the sale of food in general or the restaurant-type food alternative based on the sale of restaurant-type food, and regardless of whether "primary purpose 2" relates to gross floor area or gross revenue). Other examples (such as grocery stores and convenience stores) would be excluded from coverage under the restaurant-type food alternative but not under the proposed criterion based on the sale of food in general.

Several comments recommended that we define a restaurant or similar retail food establishment using the restaurant-type food alternative. Some comments that opposed coverage of grocery and convenience stores asserted that selling prepared foods does not make grocery stores similar to restaurants or food court facilities that have on-premises consumption. According to some of these comments, the primary purpose of grocery stores is to sell packaged food, which is already labeled with nutrition information. One comment that opposed covering convenience stores considered that the proposed criterion for a primary business activity based on the sale of food in general, including prepackaged food, is an activity in which restaurants do not engage. The comment recommended that we view the phrase "similar retail food establishment" as a single cohesive term and define those that are in fact similar to restaurants.

Some comments opposed "primary purpose 1" of the proposed primary business test because it would be difficult to enforce. One comment asserted that some bowling alleys list themselves as restaurants in the phone book or have signs indicating that they serve as a restaurant, whereas others do not. The comments maintained that FDA and State and local inspectors would have to determine how many establishments in the chain present themselves as restaurants, which would make enforcement difficult.

One comment agreed with the proposed criterion for "primary purpose 2"—i.e., that greater than 50 percent of a retail establishment's gross floor area is used for the preparation, purchase, service, consumption, or storage of food. One comment asserted that the amount of floor space used for the preparation, purchase, service, consumption, or storage of food would be difficult to determine. Another comment considered that "primary purpose 1" is sufficient for determining whether an establishment is covered, but considered that the floor space criterion would be a more accurate approach than the alternative revenue approach if a second approach for "primary business activity" is needed. One comment asked us to clarify that "gross floor area" includes outdoor space for parks as part of the calculation of the percentage of gross floor area used for the preparation, purchase, service, consumption, or storage of food. A few comments recommended that seating areas, including outside seating, be included in the floor space.

A few comments preferred the alternative revenue approach for "primary purpose 2." One comment reported that the Internal Revenue Service uses revenue to determine a business's primary activity. One comment suggested that we add to the proposed definition "or a total of more than 50 percent of that retail establishment's revenues are generated by the sale of food."

A few comments opposed the alternative revenue approach for "primary purpose 2." These comments considered that it would be difficult for FDA and the States to ascertain the revenue of a restaurant or similar retail food establishment and the revenue may change from day to day. One comment noted that the proposed rule did not include a defined time period for revenue. Another comment asserted that basing "primary purpose 2" on revenue would be complicated when a primary non-food related service or good is paired with an ancillary service such as the sale of food in one price. The comment asserted that it would be difficult to distinguish or separate the percentage of the fee for the non-food related service or good from the percentage of the fee for the food.

A few comments suggested a lower cutoff (20 to 25 percent) for the alternative revenue approach but provided no rationale for the lower cutoff. One comment, which also supported the coverage of movie theaters, stated that movie theaters derive much of their revenue from food in concession stands.

Some comments agreed with our discussion in the proposed rule that a facility within a larger facility should not be considered to be a separate establishment if it is not part of a chain outside that establishment. Some comments specifically agreed that facilities located within movie theaters and other entertainment venues should not be covered by the provisions of section 4205 of the ACA. However, many comments opposed a definition of "restaurant or similar retail food establishment" that would exclude facilities located within a larger facility, specifically facilities in movie theaters and other entertainment venues. Some of these comments provided the following reasons for including such facilities:

- Excluding facilities located within movie theaters removes information from consumers, which defeats the very purpose of the law.

- Food in entertainment venues is high in calories and some of these venues cater to children and have many less healthy options (e.g., fries, ice cream, cotton candy).

- Covering facilities located within movie theaters would not be burdensome for them because they have limited menu options and many packaged foods that have Nutrition Facts.

- Movie theaters derive large revenue from the sale of food; some much more than chain restaurants. It is irresponsible to send the message that consumption of calories in popcorn offered for sale at movie theaters is not as important as consumption of calories in menu items offered for sale at drive-through restaurants.

- Movies attract sedentary people.

- Congress intended that the law apply to movie theaters, bowling alleys, bookstore cafes, and other establishments; the phrase "and similar retail establishments" was used to reach beyond restaurants.

- Excluding facilities located within movies theatres and other entertainment venues is unfair to competing venues.

- Providing other services or entertainment does not affect the need for nutrition information.

- Menu labeling is feasible in venues not covered by the proposed rule. Movie theaters in California, New York City, and counties in New York are providing this information with no problem. To capriciously exempt movie theaters defeats the purpose of the law. One comment asserted that there is 98 percent compliance for menu labeling by movie theaters in New York City.

- Excluding such venues raises equal protection concerns (U.S. Const. 14 Amend. section 1 for similarly situated entities).

One comment considered that we would have to broaden the scope of covered establishments to include other places (such as bowling alleys, airlines, trains, and hotels), regardless of whether they fit the proposed definition of a restaurant or similar retail food establishment, if the rule covered establishments such as facilities located within movie theaters. This comment argued that there is no mention in the legislative history, committee reports, or Congressional floor debates of facilities located within movie theaters being covered. The comment considered that no one would associate "chain retail food establishment" with movie theaters because the primary purpose of going to movies or other entertainment venues is not to eat food and noted that many States and localities do not include these establishments in their laws. Another comment suggested that we add the following statement to our proposed definition: "This definition does not include businesses or establishments that sell food incidental to their primary purpose of providing or hosting entertainment at venues such as movie and live theaters, arenas, amusement parks, sports facilities, concert venues, and other similar establishments."

(Response 6) We have revised the definition of "restaurant or similar retail food establishment" to eliminate the primary business test. Most of the comments opposed one or more aspects associated with our proposal to include a primary business test, and we are persuaded by them. The comments we received were diverse and raised important considerations, including issues related to fairness; public health impact; accessibility of nutrition information; enabling informed decision-making; statutory purpose and Congressional intent; enforcement challenges; and feasibility of complying with the rule. We are convinced that any primary purpose test presented in the proposed rule will be problematic.

Congress did not define the term "restaurant or similar retail food establishment" in section 4205 of the ACA or elsewhere in the FD&C Act. As we stated in the proposed rule, we look to statutory context as a starting point for the regulatory definition of "restaurant or similar retail food establishment." As we noted, the 1990 NLEA amendments exempted two categories of food relevant for this discussion: (1) Food "which is served in restaurants or other establishments in which food is served for immediate human consumption or which is sold for sale or use in such establishments," (termed "restaurant food" in the proposed rule); and (2) food "which is processed and prepared primarily in a retail establishment, which is ready for human consumption, which is of the type described in [(1)] and which is offered for sale to consumers but not for immediate human consumption in such establishment and which is not offered for sale outside such establishment" (termed "restaurant-type food" in the proposed rule). Section 4205 of the ACA amended both of these statutory exemptions. In determining the scope of section 4205 of the ACA, we must determine which of these foods should remain wholly exempt from Federal nutrition labeling requirements and which should be covered by the new nutrition labeling requirements in this rule.

Instead of using a primary purpose test within the definition of restaurant or similar retail food establishment to set the scope of the new law, we are finalizing a broader definition of restaurant or similar retail food establishment, consistent with many of the comments. In response to concerns about overreaching in establishments that sell a significant amount of food that is not typical of food sold in restaurants, such as grocery and convenience stores (see also discussion in section VI.B.3), we are narrowing the set of food covered by removing the term "restaurant food" from this rule and redefining "restaurant-type food" to include only the set of food described in sections 403(q)(5)(A)(i) and (ii) of the FD&C Act that is most like the food served in restaurants (see discussion in section VI.C). Retail food establishments that offer for sale this type of food are either restaurants or are relevantly similar to restaurants in that they offer for sale the kind of food that restaurants do. Therefore, the final definition focuses on those establishments that offer for sale food that is most like food served in restaurants; overall, it is generally broader than the definition provided in the proposed rule, but narrower than what we put forward in the draft implementation guidance.

Most of the comments that addressed the floor space approach or the alternative revenue approach to "primary purpose 2" expressed a preference for one or the other without providing strong and convincing arguments as to why their preferred alternative is superior to the alternative that they opposed. Several comments identified challenges to enforcing the rule if the definition of "restaurant or similar retail food establishment" included either the floor space approach or the alternative revenue approach.

We agree with several points made by the comments about facilities within entertainment venues such as movie theaters and amusement parks—e.g., that providing nutrition information to consumers at such venues will make such nutrition information available to consumers in a direct and accessible manner to enable consumers to make informed and healthful dietary choices; food in entertainment venues is similar to food offered for sale in other restaurants or similar retail food establishments; and covering entertainment venues would create a level playing field. Under the revised definition of "restaurant or similar retail food establishment," such facilities in entertainment venues will be covered by the rule if they offer for sale restaurant-type food and satisfy the other criteria in the definition of "covered establishment"—i.e., part of a chain with 20 or more locations, doing business under the same name, and offering for sale substantially the same menu items. Similarly, some superstores that may not have been covered under the proposed definition likewise may be considered a "restaurant or similar retail food establishment" under the final definition established in the rule. Under the definition of "restaurant or similar retail food establishment" in this rule, a superstore, like a grocery store, would be covered if it sells restaurant-type food and is part of a chain with 20 or more locations, doing business under the same name, and offering for sale substantially the same menu items. Hotel restaurants are another type of establishment that we stated generally would not have been covered under the proposed rule (76 FR 19192 at 19198), but would be covered under the final rule if they sell restaurant-type food and are part of a chain of hotel restaurants with 20 or more fixed locations, doing business under the same name, and offering for sale substantially the same menu items.

We disagree that the legislative history of section 4205 of the ACA demonstrates any express intent of Congress to exclude facilities located within entertainment venues such as movie theaters and bowling alleys from the rule. The legislative history of section 4205 of the ACA is very sparse; the section was discussed on few occasions, and when it was discussed, few specifics were mentioned, including specifics about the scope of the law.

We discuss transportation venues later in this document (see Response 27).

(Comment 7) One comment considered the proposed requirement that the sale of food be the retail establishment's primary business to be at odds with the approach taken in the proposed vending machine rule. The comment pointed out that we concluded that only 5,000 of 10,000 vending machine operators operate vending machines as their primary business, yet the proposed vending machine rule would apply to those with 20 or more machines, which includes all 10,000 of the vending machine operators.

(Response 7) The provisions of the proposed vending machine rule, including criteria for determining coverage of that rule, are not relevant to the criteria for determining coverage of this rule. Regardless, this comment is moot because the definition of "restaurant or similar retail food establishment" established in this rule no longer includes a primary business test.

(Comment 8) A few comments recommended that we separately define "restaurant" and "similar retail food establishment." One of these comments recommended that we define "restaurant" separately from "similar retail food establishment" because Congress uses the word "or" in the phrase "restaurant or similar retail food establishment," and thus "restaurants" and "similar retail food establishments" are clearly two separate things. Another comment recommended that we define a restaurant as one that uses greater than 50 percent gross floor space for preparation, purchase, service, consumption of restaurant food and a similar retail food establishment as an establishment that meets the same standard but does not present itself as a restaurant.

(Response 8) We disagree that we should separately define "restaurant" and "similar retail food establishment." As an initial matter, while Congress does use the word "or" between "restaurant" and "similar retail food establishment" in some places, it also uses the word "and" between them in others. For example, section 403(q)(5)(H)(i) of the FD&C Act contains both constructions ("General requirements for restaurants and similar retail food establishments" and "the restaurant or similar retail food establishment shall disclose"). We interpret the choice of the words "and" and "or" in section 403(q)(5)(H) of the FD&C Act to be a function of appropriate grammar, not to indicate Congressional intent to conceptualize "restaurants" separately from "similar retail food establishments." Moreover, given that the requirements in section 403(q)(5)(H) of the FD&C Act are the same for restaurants and similar retail food establishments, we see no practical reason to create separate regulatory definitions.

(Comment 9) One comment recommended that we include as part of the regulation table 1 from the proposed rule to help the public interpret the regulation.

(Response 9) In the proposed rule (77 FR 19192 at 19198 and 19199), tables 1 and 2 identify establishments that generally would, or would not, be a "restaurant or similar retail food establishment" for the purposes of this rule. We included these tables to demonstrate the likely impact for many establishments of the proposed and alternative criteria for a "primary business test" within the definition of "restaurant or similar retail food establishment." The definition of "restaurant or similar retail food establishment" established in this rule no longer has a primary business test. Any establishment that sells restaurant-type food is a "restaurant or similar retail food establishment" for the purposes of this rule. Therefore, we see no value added in including such tables in this final rule.

3. Coverage of Grocery Stores and Convenience Stores

(Comment 10) Several comments recommended that grocery stores be covered. Some of these comments considered that grocery stores should be covered because they sell a great deal of food for immediate consumption. One of these comments referred to the "Food Marketing Institute's 2010 U.S. Grocery Shopper Trends" (Ref. 11) as evidence that the number of consumers who express interest in supermarket ready-to-eat food is at its highest point in 4 years. One comment asserted that the law does not exempt grocery stores or take-out food.

(Response 10) We agree with these comments. Grocery stores that sell restaurant-type food and are part of a chain with 20 or more locations doing business under the same name and offering for sale substantially the same menu items are covered by the rule.

(Comment 11) One comment argued that the plain meaning of section 4205 of the ACA precludes including grocery stores as "restaurants and similar retail food establishments." The comment stated that Congress used other words elsewhere in the FD&C Act to refer to the set of establishments that include grocery stores, such as "food retailer" and "retail establishment" in section 403(q) of the FD&C Act. In addition, our regulation at 21 CFR 1.227 defines "retail food establishment" to include grocery stores for the purposes of food facility registration. Given that Congress chose a different term here, the comment argued that we must assume "similar retail food establishments" has a different meaning.

(Response 11) We disagree with this comment. We do interpret the phrase "similar retail food establishment" to have a different meaning than the terms "food retailer" and "retail establishment" that appear elsewhere in section 403(q) of the FD&C Act or "retail food establishment" in 21 CFR 1.227. Both our proposed and final definitions are different from the definitions of these other terms. If a retail food establishment does not offer for sale restaurant-type food, it would not be a "restaurant or similar retail food establishment" for the purposes of section 403(q)(5)(H) of the FD&C Act, even though it could be a "food retailer" or a "retail establishment" or "retail food establishment."

(Comment 12) One comment argues that the heading of section 4205 of the ACA, "Nutrition Labeling of Standard Menu Items at Chain Restaurants," indicates that "restaurants or similar retail food establishments" is an ambiguous term, and should be interpreted narrowly to exclude grocery stores.

(Response 12) We disagree with this comment. First, while we recognize that the heading of a statute may be considered part of a section's legislative history, the heading is not part of the law itself (Ref. 12). Second, it is clear that the heading is not meant to describe the scope of the requirements in section 4205 of the ACA, given that section 4205 includes requirements for "restaurants and similar retail food establishments" and requirements for vending machine operators.

(Comment 13) One comment argued that the legislative history of section 4205 of the ACA demonstrates that grocery stores should not be included in the menu labeling requirements. The comment cited a floor speech by Senator Harkin where he favorably compares the nutrition information available in grocery stores to the lack of nutrition information available at restaurants. For example, "It makes no sense that American consumers can go to a grocery store and find nutrition information on just about anything, but then they are totally in the dark when they go to a restaurant for dinner." (Ref. 13) The comment also argued that the legislative history does not include any hearing or debate indicating that we were being given authority to regulate chain grocery stores through section 4205 of the ACA.

Some comments stated that some State and local jurisdictions did not cover grocery stores. One comment remarked that State and local laws related to menu labeling referred to in the legislative history of section 4205 of the ACA did not cover grocery stores. Specifically, the comment mentions that the New York City Health Code provisions on menu labeling, which the comment characterizes as the first and most extensively discussed law cited by Senator Harkin, does not regulate supermarkets.

(Response 13) We disagree that the legislative history demonstrates that grocery stores should not be included in the nutrition labeling requirements of this rule. First, the most straightforward interpretation of Senator Harkin's statements is that the food in grocery stores he had in mind was packaged food already required to bear nutrition information under Federal law.

Second, the fact that none of the State or local jurisdictions with menu labeling requirements explicitly covered grocery stores does not mean that Congress did not intend to cover grocery stores under the Federal law. Many State and local jurisdictions with menu labeling requirements predating the ACA did not cover self-service food or food on display, which is most likely to be the type of food in grocery stores covered by this rule. However, it is clear that Congress intended for self-service food and food on display to be covered, because section 403(q)(5)(H)(iii) explicitly establishes statutory requirements specific to self-service food and food on display. In addition, for at least some local governments, including New York City, the regulation of grocery stores fell outside of their jurisdiction (Ref. 14). So, the fact that grocery stores were not covered by New York City cannot be assumed to be a choice by local authorities.

Finally, we recognize that the legislative history of section 4205 of the ACA does not include any hearing or debate indicating specifically mentioning chain grocery stores. However, this does not imply that Congress intended for grocery stores to be excluded. As already noted, the legislative history of section 4205 of the ACA is very sparse; the section was discussed on few occasions, and when it was discussed, few specifics were raised, including specifics about the scope of the law. The comment does not provide evidence to the contrary. Our final rule represents a reasonable interpretation of the statute, given the language of section 4205 of the ACA and the scant legislative history.

(Comment 14) Some comments asserted that if Congress had intended broad application, it would have overhauled 21 U.S.C. 343(q)(5)(A)(i) and (ii) of the FD&C Act rather than letting those stand and adding 21 U.S.C. 343(q)(5)(H). Further, these comments stated that if Congress had wanted to include all establishments exempted by the NLEA, it would have cross-referenced to the NLEA exemption or just removed the exemption.

(Response 14) We agree with some of these comments and disagree with others. We agree that Congress did not intend for all establishments exempted by the NLEA to be covered by section 4205 of the ACA. Under the rule, there are many establishments, including establishments that meet the regulatory definition of restaurant or similar retail food establishment, that will not be covered. For example, food described in section 403(q)(5)(A)(i) of the FD&C Act served in certain sit-down restaurants that are not part of a chain of 20 or more locations will continue to be exempt from the Federal nutrition labeling requirements in sections 403(q)(1) to (4). In addition, section 403(q)(5)(A)(i) and (ii) of the FD&C Act continue to exempt all food that is described in sections 403(q)(5)(A)(i) and (ii), including food offered for sale in restaurants and similar retail food establishments, from the nutrition labeling requirements in sections 403(q)(3) and (4). Therefore, irrespective of the breadth of section 403(q)(5)(H) of the FD&C Act, Congress's amendment to sections 403(q)(5)(A)(i) and (ii) leaves a large portion of the exemption intact. Congress could not have removed the exemption in sections 403(q)(5)(A)(i) and (ii) of the FD&C Act and achieved the same result.

Instead, Congress amended sections 403(q)(5)(A)(i) and (ii) of the FD&C Act to cross-reference section 403(q)(5)(H). The cross-references to section 403(q)(5)(H) of the FD&C Act in sections 403(q)(5)(A)(i) and (ii) indicate that the requirements in 403(q)(5)(H) must apply to at least a subset of those foods described in both sections 403(q)(5)(A)(i) and (ii). Congress did not provide a statutory definition of "restaurant or similar retail food establishment" in section 403(q)(5)(H) of the FD&C Act, leaving ambiguity in the statute as to the breadth of the set of establishments covered. Our definition of restaurant or similar retail food establishment is a reasonable interpretation of this ambiguous term, and is consistent with section 4205's amendments to section 403(q)(5)(A)(i) and (ii) of the FD&C Act.

(Comment 15) One comment argued that the restaurant industry supported section 4205 of the ACA, because the law would provide them with a nationally uniform regulatory scheme. The comment asserted that grocery stores "did not ask for this law," and should therefore not be covered.

(Response 15) In general, whether an industry asks to be regulated is not determinative of whether that industry should be regulated. In addition, grocery stores are increasingly offering for sale restaurant-type food, including food for immediate consumption that is prepared and processed on the premises.

(Comment 16) A few comments maintained that there is too much variability in grocery store food because food is seasonal and grocery stores make prepared food from food in the store. Some comments also noted that some grocery stores offer unique menu items, such as a unique chicken salad based on the personal recipe of a chef at a particular grocery store's location, that are not available at all grocery stores in the chain. These comments asserted that it would be difficult to calculate the nutrient information if grocery stores were covered under the final rule.

(Response 16) A grocery store is required to make calorie declarations for its standard menu items if it meets the definition of "covered establishment" in this rule; including, in relevant part, that the grocery store is "offering for sale substantially the same menu items" as other grocery stores in the chain (see section VI.F for discussion on "offering for sale substantially the same menu items"). However, if a food is not routinely included on a menu or menu board or routinely offered as a self-service food or food on display at a covered establishment, it is not a standard menu item at that establishment and therefore not covered by this rule (see section VIII.B for discussion on the definition of standard menu item). For example, if a food's ingredients and recipe changes daily based on food available in the store, it is likely that such food would not be a standard menu item. However, for food offerings that are standard menu items, even if unique to only one location in the chain, a covered establishment has many options for determining nutrient content, including, for example, calculating the required nutrient information from the recipe for the food offering using nutrient databases (see § 101.11(c)). Per the statute, in those cases where seasonal availability is limited to less than 60 days, the food offering may be exempt from the nutrition labeling requirements of this rule as a temporary menu item or a self-service food and food on display that is offered for sale for less than a total of 60 days per calendar year.

(Comment 17) One comment maintained that menu labeling is needed in small grocery stores and convenience stores because of the disparity in low-income neighborhoods that do not have many large grocery stores or superstores but do have small grocery stores and convenience stores. According to the comment, grocery stores, convenience stores, and drug store chains have expanded their businesses to include ready-to-eat food offerings. The comment maintained that these establishments are in direct competition with restaurants and have grown so rapidly over the past decade that some are being called "grocerants."

(Response 17) Small grocery stores and convenience stores are covered by the rule if they sell restaurant-type food and are part of a chain with 20 or more locations, doing business under the same name, and offering for sale substantially the same menu items.

(Comment 18) One comment considered that grocery stores should not be covered by the menu labeling requirements because they do not have menus and menu boards.

(Response 18) We disagree with this comment. First, the comment suggests that no grocery stores have menus or menu boards. However, some grocery stores do have menus and menu boards, including for example, menus and menu boards for sandwiches that are prepared upon the consumer's request. Second, the comment implies that a restaurant or similar retail food establishment must have a menu or menu board in order to be covered by this rule. This is not the case. Consistent with section 403(q)(5)(H) of the FD&C Act, this rule requires that covered establishments provide certain nutrition information for standard menu items, even the standard menu items that do not appear on menus or menu boards. For example, section 403(q)(5)(H)(iii) of the FD&C Act requires nutrition labeling for standard menu items that are self-service foods and foods on display, irrespective of whether they are listed on a menu or menu board.

4. Confectionery Stores

(Comment 19) A few comments recommended that confectionery stores not be covered because they do not sell restaurant food. According to one of these comments, most candy sold in retail confectionery stores is not generally consumed immediately where purchased or while walking away. Instead, the comment stated, most candy sold in retail confectionery stores is either prepackaged (e.g., boxed chocolates) or selected by the consumer and placed in a box or other packaging for consumption at a later time. Thus, according to this comment, food served in retail confectionery stores without facilities for consumption on the premises would continue to be covered by the nutrition labeling requirements in § 101.9. Another comment acknowledged that some confectionary stores do sell some restaurant-type foods, such as chocolate from display cases, shakes, and specialty items dipped in chocolate, but that the primary focus of the business was the sale of packaged food such as "gift box" packaged chocolates.

(Response 19) We disagree that confectionery stores, as a class of retail food establishments, should not be covered. Based on these comments, some foods sold in some confectionery stores are restaurant-type foods. As discussed in section VI.C, we are establishing a revised definition of "restaurant-type food" that would cover food that is usually eaten on the premises, while walking away, or soon after arriving at another location (see Response 24). A prepackaged box of candy sold in a confectionery store is not likely to be a restaurant-type food, because a box of candy is not usually eaten on the premises, while walking away, or soon after arriving at another location. However, individual pieces of candy sold to a consumer from a display case, shakes, and specialty items dipped in chocolate likely would be restaurant-type foods, because they are generally consumed on the premises, while walking away, or soon after arriving at another location. Under this rule, a confectionery store that sells restaurant-type food would be covered if it is part of a chain with 20 or more locations doing business under the same name and offering for sale substantially the same menu items. We note that the only foods covered by this rule in a covered establishment are restaurant-type foods that are standard menu items.

5. Facilities Within Facilities

(Comment 20) One comment asked us to clarify that the independent franchise restaurant that operates within an amusement park is liable for adherence to the final regulation, not the park. The comment maintained that the park would have no way of knowing if the franchisee is compliant.

(Response 20) The covered establishment bears the responsibility to comply with the rule. In addition, see Response 3.

6. Schools

(Comment 21) One comment asked us to clarify whether a school food service contractor that uses a central kitchen or cooks the same food for 20 schools would be covered. One comment stated that these establishments should provide calories on menu boards, online menus, and menus sent home to parents.

(Response 21) We have decided not to include schools in the definition of "restaurant or similar retail food establishment" for the purposes of this rule. As previously discussed (see Response 6) Congress did not define the term "restaurant or similar retail food establishment" in section 4205 of the ACA or elsewhere in the FD&C Act. The term is ambiguous, and we look to statutory context as a starting point for our regulatory definition. As discussed in section I of this document, while the NLEA required that the labeling of many foods bear nutrition information, it exempted certain food from such nutrition labeling requirements, including food that is "served in restaurants or other establishments in which food is served for immediate human consumption" (section 403(q)(5)(A)(i) of the FD&C Act). In FDA's regulations implementing the NLEA, we included schools among the list of examples of "other establishments in which food is served for immediate human consumption" (§ 101.9(j)(2)) Section 4205 of the ACA amended this statutory exemption, among others, to account for new nutrition labeling requirements for standard menu items in restaurants and similar retail food establishments. Therefore, we must determine whether standard menu items in schools should remain wholly exempt from FDA nutrition labeling requirements or whether they should be eligible to be covered by the new nutrition labeling requirements in this rule.

Traditionally, the U.S. Department of Agriculture (USDA) has exercised a primary role in setting the standards for foods served in schools through school lunch and breakfast programs. USDA regulates such foods, under various Federal statutes, including the Child Nutrition Act of 1996 and the Richard B. Russell National School Lunch Act. Given the traditional and long-standing role of USDA in setting standards, including nutrition requirements, for foods served in schools through school lunch and breakfast programs, as established by Federal legislation and implemented by Federal Agencies, we conclude that it is reasonable to interpret the term "restaurant or similar retail food establishment" to not include schools. Therefore, we have revised the definition "restaurant or similar retail food establishment" to mean a retail establishment that offers for sale restaurant-type food, except if it is a school as defined in 7 CFR 210.2 or 220.2.

C. Restaurant Food and Restaurant-Type Food

A key term in the final definition of "restaurant or similar retail food establishment" is the term "restaurant-type food." The terms "restaurant food" and "restaurant-type food" also were important to the proposed definition of "restaurant or similar retail food establishment." Proposed § 101.11(a) would define "restaurant food" as food that is served in restaurants or other establishments in which food is served for immediate human consumption, i.e., to be consumed either on the premises where that food is purchased or while walking away; or which is sold for sale or use in such establishments. (As a typographical error, the proposed rule incorrectly stated "where that the food is purchased" rather than "where that food is purchased.") Proposed § 101.11(a) would define "restaurant-type food" as food of the type described in the definition of "restaurant food" that is ready for human consumption, offered for sale to consumers but not for immediate consumption, processed and prepared primarily in a retail establishment, and not offered for sale outside of that establishment.

In the following paragraphs, we discuss comments on these proposed definitions. After considering comments, we are deleting the proposed definition of "restaurant food" and establishing a revised definition of "restaurant-type food" that better reflects the food most like the food offered for sale in restaurants. As conforming amendments, we are deleting the term "restaurant food" from other proposed definitions that had included this term—i.e., the proposed definitions for "food on display," "restaurant or similar retail food establishment," "self-service food," and "standard menu item."

(Comment 22) One comment recommended that food be covered if prepared for immediate human consumption regardless of whether consumers choose to consume on or off the premises. The comment recommended that we remove the term "walking away" from the definition of restaurant food because it would be clearer to state simply that foods that are served in restaurants or similar retail food establishments and are prepared for immediate human consumption are covered, whether customers choose to consume them on or off the premises. The comment considered that whether foods are actually consumed on or off the premises should not be a determining factor as to whether a food or facility is covered by the rule. The comment asked us to clarify that food from facilities serving take-away food that meet the other criteria are covered.

(Response 22) We decline the specific suggestion that we replace our proposed criterion that food may be "consumed either on the premises where the food is purchased or while walking away" with a criterion mentioning that consumers may consume the food "on or off the premises." The comment did not disagree that restaurant food should include food that is consumed while walking away but rather suggested communicating this differently.

While restaurants do offer for sale food that is consumed off the premises, in general that food is consumed while walking away or upon arriving at another location. Other foods, like groceries, are also consumed "off the premises" of the store that sells them (e.g., a grocery or convenience store), but they are often consumed at a later time or over a period of days. Our aim is to cover the food most like the food offered for sale in restaurants, and not food that is more similar to food traditionally thought of as groceries. Therefore, the phrase "on or off the premises" is too broad for our final definition of restaurant-type food.

In general, take-away food is consumed while walking away or upon arriving at another location. Therefore, take-away food is likely to be "restaurant-type food," and retail establishments that offer for sale take-away food are likely to meet the definition of restaurant or similar retail food establishment. Take-away food that satisfies the definition of "restaurant-type food" established in this rule would be subject to the nutrition labeling requirements of this rule if it is a standard menu item that is offered for sale in a covered establishment.

(Comment 23) One comment recommended that the phrase "not offered for sale outside that establishment" be deleted from the definition of restaurant food because some restaurants market frozen meals from their restaurants.

(Response 23) We are retaining the phrase "not offered for sale outside such establishment" in the definition of restaurant-type food. This phrase comes from section 403(q)(5)(A)(ii) of the FD&C Act. FDA previously has interpreted this phrase (see 58 FR 2079 at 2146 (January 6, 1993)). The frozen meals described by the comment appear to be packaged foods. Most packaged foods are subject to the labeling requirements of § 101.9. The sale of such packaged, frozen food outside of a restaurant, e.g., in a grocery store, will not affect whether the food in a restaurant is covered by this rule.

(Comment 24) One comment urged us to remove the term "restaurant-type food" from the rule and recognize that the sale of food to consumers for immediate consumption is a primary distinguishing factor of a restaurant. The comment contended that our definition of restaurant or similar retail food establishment is overly broad because it includes an establishment that sells not only restaurant food but also restaurant-type food. The comment maintained that we did not explain our rationale for including restaurant-type food in the proposed rule, especially when our existing regulation on restaurants refers only to restaurant food.

A few comments were concerned that because of the definition of restaurant-type food grocery stores would have to label prepared foods for immediate consumption as well as every loaf of bread, roll, cookie and deli item except cold cuts; these comments estimated that approximately 6,400 service deli, prepared foods, and bakery items would be included, which would be very costly. One comment contended that the increase in cost may limit the items that grocery stores would carry, which would limit sales growth. According to a few comments 95 percent of items in grocery stores have Nutrition Facts and the costs to cover the remaining 5 percent vastly outweighs benefits.

(Response 24) We agree that sale of food to consumers for immediate consumption is a common characteristic of restaurants but disagree that it follows that only "restaurant food" is relevant to this rulemaking. In the proposed rule, we explained that section 4205 of the ACA amended both sections 403(q)(5)(A)(i) and (ii) of the FDA&C Act. Under section 403(q)(5)(A)(ii) of the FD&C Act, except as provided in section 403(q)(5)(H)(ii)(III) of the FD&C Act (i.e., the requirement for written nutrition information for food covered by this rule) the nutrition labeling requirements of section 403(q)(1), (2), (3), and (4) of the FD&C Act shall not apply to food which is processed and prepared primarily in a retail establishment, which is ready for human consumption, which is of the type described in section 403(q)(5)(A)(i), and which is offered for sale to consumers but not for immediate human consumption in such establishment and which is not offered for sale outside such establishment (emphasis added). To implement the phrase "except as provided in section 403(q)(5)(H)(ii)(III)" of the FD&C Act, some set of food described in section 403(q)(5)(A)(ii)—that is not for immediate consumption—is covered by this rule.

We acknowledge that the proposed definition of restaurant-type food includes some foods that are sold in grocery or convenience stores that are not generally offered for sale in restaurants, foods that are more like groceries, and we have amended that definition in the final rule. After considering all of the comments directed to the proposed definitions of "restaurant food" or "restaurant-type food," in addition to the comments related to the scope of the rule more generally, given the relationship between these terms and the definition of restaurant or similar retail food establishment, we are convinced that this rule should cover only those foods described in sections 403(q)(5)(A)(i) and (ii) of the FD&C Act that are most like the food sold in restaurants and should not cover foods that are more commonly considered to be groceries. Therefore, we are deleting the proposed definition of "restaurant food" and establishing a revised definition of "restaurant-type food" that reflects the food most like the food offered for sale in restaurants. Under that new definition, restaurant-type food means food that is (1) usually eaten on the premises, while walking away, or soon after arriving at another location; and (2) either (i) served in restaurants or other establishments in which food is served for immediate human consumption or which is sold for sale or use in such establishments; or (ii) processed and prepared primarily in a retail establishment, ready for human consumption, of the type described in (i), and offered for sale to consumers but not for immediate human consumption in such establishment and which is not offered for sale outside such establishment. The first part of this definition focuses on the food most like the food offered for sale in restaurants, while the second part of this definition reflects the statutory context of sections 403(q)(5)(A)(i) and (ii) of the FD&C Act. The new definition includes food for immediate consumption at a sit-down or quick service restaurant; food purchased at a drive-through establishment; take-out and delivery pizza; hot pizza at grocery and convenience stores that is ready to eat; pizza slice from a movie theater; hot buffet food, hot soup at a soup bar, and food from a salad bar; foods ordered from a menu/menu board at a grocery store intended for individual consumption (e.g., soups, sandwiches, and salads); and self-service foods and foods on display that are intended for individual consumption (e.g., sandwiches, wraps, and paninis at a deli counter; salads plated by the consumer at a salad bar; cookies from a mall cookie counter; bagels, donuts, rolls offered for individual sale). Foods that are similar to grocery items that may be ready for immediate consumption but that consumers usually store for use at a later time or customarily further prepare would not be included within the meaning of "restaurant-type food." Foods that we therefore would not consider to be within the meaning of "restaurant-type food" include foods to be eaten over several eating occasions or stored for later use (e.g., loaves of bread, bags or boxes of dinner rolls, whole cakes, and bags or boxes of candy or cookies); foods sold by weight that are not self-serve and are not intended solely for individual consumption (e.g., deli salads sold by unit of weight such as potato salad, chicken salad), either prepacked or packed upon consumer request; and foods that are usually further prepared before consuming (e.g., deli meats and cheeses).

(Comment 25) One comment asked us to clarify that only food offered "for sale" in a restaurant or similar retail food establishment should be considered in determining whether an establishment is a covered establishment. The comment noted that the statute expressly limits the application of food labeling to items that are "offered for sale," and considered that the menu labeling regulations should adopt a similar limitation.

(Response 25) The rule only applies to food offered for sale.

D. Part of a Chain With 20 or More Locations

In the proposed rule (76 FR 19192 at 19195), we noted that we did not propose a definition of the statutory criterion "part of a chain with 20 or more locations" and that we were assuming the common meaning of the words in the phrase. However, we requested comment on whether the phrase should be defined in the final rule, and particularly on whether the terms "chain" and "location" should be defined in context of the various types of corporate or other business arrangements that may be relevant, including contracting arrangements.

In the following paragraphs, we discuss comments on the terms "chain" and "location." After considering these comments, we are adding a definition of "locations" to clarify our interpretation of "part of a chain with 20 or more locations."

(Comment 26) A few comments responded to our request for comment on the term "chain." One comment recommended that we define "chain" as a covered establishment doing business under the same name as those that share the same name under the ownership, control, and operation of a single corporate entity. This comment considered that this is consistent with the commonly accepted dictionary definition of a chain as "a group of enterprises or institutions of the same kind or function under a single ownership, management, or control." Another comment cited the following dictionary definition for "chain": "A range of retail outlets which share a brand and central management, usually with standardized business methods". This comment also cited the following dictionary definition for "restaurant chain": "A set of restaurants, usually with the same name in many different locations either under shared corporate ownership or franchising agreements. Typically, the restaurants within a chain are built to a standard format and offer a standard menu."

(Response 26) Section 4205 of the ACA covers restaurants or similar retail food establishments that are part of a chain with 20 or more locations doing business under the same name "regardless of the type of ownership of the locations." Both definitions suggested by comments refer to management structure, corporate control, and/or ownership. Because the statute directs us to disregard the type of ownership of the locations when determining whether an establishment is "part of a chain with 20 or more locations doing business under the same name," neither of these definitions for the word "chain" is appropriate.

According to the dictionary definitions, the word "chain" means, among other things, "a group of enterprises, establishments, institution, or constructions of the same kind or function linked together into a single system" (Ref. 15), a "series or group of things or people that are connected to each other in some way" (Ref. 15), and "a series of closely linked or connected things" (Ref. 16). In section 403(q)(5)(H)(i) of the FD&C Act, Congress provides the ways in which restaurants or similar retail food establishments must be connected to or linked to each other in order to be covered by the new law: They must be doing business under the same name and offering for sale substantially the same menu items, and there must be 20 or more locations of them. Therefore, we continue to use the common meaning of the word "chain" and do not consider an additional regulatory definition necessary for this broad term. The statute specifies the particular criteria for the set of chains that are relevant for this rulemaking, and we provide regulatory definitions for those criteria specifically.

(Comment 27) One comment recommended that we not rely solely on the terms "chain" and "location" because some restaurants and food establishments have locations at the same address, such as a mall. The comment asked us to either use the term "selling post" or to clarify that the location includes chains with restaurants in the same physical building. Another comment asked us to clarify that mobile facilities (such as food trucks) are covered. Some comments noted that transportation venues have menus that look like those in sandwich shops. Other comments noted that it is feasible for transportation venues to comply with the rule.

(Response 27) We disagree that we should add the term "selling post" to the definition to specify restaurants and similar retail food establishments that are part of the same chain and are located in the same shopping mall or otherwise in the same physical building. However, this comment demonstrates that there is a need to define the term "locations," even assuming its common meaning. Unlike "chain," where a definition is unnecessary given that we are establishing definitions for more specific, relevant criteria, we are convinced that establishing a regulatory definition of "locations" would provide clarity and facilitate a better understanding of regulatory expectations.

The dictionaries define "location" to mean, among other things, "a position or site occupied . . . a tract of land designated for a purpose" (Ref. 17); "an area or tract of land" (Ref. 18); "a place where something is or could be located; a site . . . a tract of land that has been surveyed and marked off" (Ref. 19). This evidences that the common meaning of the word "location" involves a specific or fixed position on land or portion of land. For clarity, we are defining "location" to mean "a fixed position or site." Therefore, for the purposes of determining whether an establishment is part of a chain with "20 or more locations," we would consider each of the establishments occupying separate fixed positions or sites within the same shopping mall or physical building as separate establishments. One result of this definition of "location" is to exclude food facilities that do not have a fixed position or site, such as trains and airplanes. Additionally, mobile food operations such as food trucks without a fixed position or site are not covered by the rule.

E. Doing Business Under the Same Name

Proposed § 101.11(a) would define "doing business under the same name" as sharing the same name, where "same name" would include names that are either exactly the same, or are slight variations of each other, for example, due to the region, location, or size (e.g., "New York Ave. Burgers" and "Pennsylvania Ave. Burgers" or "ABC" and "ABC Express"). In the proposed rule (76 FR 19192 at 19199), we requested comment on whether the term should be understood to refer to the underlying name of ownership such as the name of the parent company, or the name of the entity conducting corporate business on behalf of the establishment, e.g., the name of a contractor operating the establishment, regardless of the public name used by the individual establishment.

In the following paragraphs, we discuss comments on this proposed definition. After considering comments, we have revised the definition to clarify that the term "name" refers to either (a) the name of the establishment presented to the public or (b), if there is no name of the establishment presented to the public (e.g., an establishment with the generic descriptor "concession stand"), the name of the parent entity of the establishment.

(Comment 28) Several comments supported the proposed definition. One comment recommended that the definition be broadened to include those with the same underlying name of ownership (parent company or contractor). A few comments recommended that the definition not be based on the underlying name of ownership. Based on the language of the statute, the comments considered that "regardless of . . . ownership" means that the ownership is not determinative and, therefore, the term should refer to the name used when doing business with the public and not the parent company, franchise owner, or other ownership entity. One comment argued that the phrase "regardless of . . . ownership" means that the corporate structure should not be considered when determining coverage; instead, the determining factor should be whether the name of the restaurant is the same. Another comment maintained that to include the underlying name of ownership in the definition would stifle investment in smaller locally based restaurants, i.e., it would place a cap on the number of restaurants an investor or entity could have before subjecting them to menu labeling.

One comment recommended that the definition not be based on the name of the parent company because the name of the parent company has no bearing on the similarity of menu offerings. The comment argued that to do so would ignore the plain language of the statute, which clearly meant the public name of the location. One comment asserted that our proposed definition would expand the definition beyond the statutory language and Congress' express intent by covering smaller restaurant chains that offer creative menus and, thus, thwart the purpose and intent behind thoughtfully designed restaurants.

(Response 28) We agree with comments that considered that the statutory phrase "regardless of the type of ownership of the locations" means that the type of ownership is not determinative. We also agree that "doing business under the same name" should, in general, refer to the name used when doing business with the public (e.g., the branded name that appears on the establishment's signage) rather than the name of the person or legal entity that owns the establishment. However, we are aware that some establishments have no specific name presented to the public. For example, concession stands in entertainment venues or cafeterias in office buildings may simply have a sign with a general descriptor, such as "Hot Dogs" or "Concession Stand" or "Building 1 Café," or they may have no sign at all. In instances where there is no specific name presented to the public, we find it reasonable to conclude that the name under which they are doing business is the name of the parent entity of the facility. Consequently, we have revised the definition of the term "doing business under the same name" in § 101.11(a) to add that the term "name" refers to the name of the facility presented to the public or, if there is no name of the facility presented to the public (e.g., a facility with the generic descriptor "concession stand"), the name of the parent entity of the facility.

(Comment 29) One comment addressed the examples we included in the proposed definition of establishments doing business under the same name. As discussed in the proposed rule (76 FR 19192 at 19199), these examples include names that are slight variations on each other due, for example, to the region, location, or size. The comment asserted that it is inappropriate to imply that same name means slight variation. Another comment recommended that the rule apply to facilities in grocery stores with 20 or more locations even if the facilities' names vary from store to store.

(Response 29) We disagree that the examples we included in the proposed definition of establishments doing business under the same name are inappropriate. Establishments that are part of large chains have slight variations in the name, e.g., to reflect a limited menu based on the space that the establishment occupies. For example, "XYZ" chain may have "XYZ" restaurant in a free-standing store and "XYZ Express" in an airline terminal, food court in a shopping mall, or grocery store. Even though the names are slight variations of each other, they are sufficiently similar that it is clear that the establishments are affiliated with one another. Generally, these establishments also have the same trade dress (e.g., trade name, logo, graphics and other distinctive elements of a brand) as the other establishments in the chain.

(Comment 30) One comment recommended that we require that a chain remain covered if it initially is subject to the rule but the parent company changes the name of some locations to get below 20.

(Response 30) Individual restaurants and similar retail food establishments would be subject to the rule if they satisfy the criteria for a "covered establishment." If a restaurant or similar retail food establishment satisfies all the criteria for a covered establishment, and subsequently changes its name, it must reconsider whether it continues to satisfy all the criteria for a covered establishment, including whether it "is part of a chain with 20 or more locations doing business under the same name." We anticipate that the benefits to an establishment to continue to do business under the same name as other establishments in the chain will keep establishments from changing their names in order to avoid being covered by this rule.

F. Offering for Sale Substantially the Same Menu Items

Proposed § 101.11(a) would define "offering for sale substantially the same menu items" as offering for sale menu items that use the same general recipe and are prepared in substantially the same way with substantially the same food components, even if the name of the menu item varies (e.g. "Bay View Crab Cake" and "Ocean View Crab Cake"). Under the proposed definition, "menu items" would refer to food items that are listed on a menu or menu board or that are offered as self-service food or food on display. The proposed definition would also provide that restaurants and similar retail food establishments that are part of a chain can still be offering for sale substantially the same menu items if the availability of some menu items varies within the chain.

In the following paragraphs, we discuss comments on this proposed definition. After considering comments, we have revised the definition to:

- Add a qualitative description of the number of menu items that must be shared in order for the criterion of "offering for sale substantially the same menu items" to be met; and

- Add a statement that having the same name may indicate, but does not necessarily guarantee, that menu items are substantially the same.

(Comment 31) Several comments supported the definition. One comment asserted that the proposed rule was not clear on what "substantially" the same menu items means quantitatively and suggested that it could mean anywhere between 51 and 99 percent. Another comment asked us to clarify what constitutes "offering for sale menu items that use the same general recipe and are prepared with substantially the same food components even if the name varies." This comment pointed out that some restaurants in a chain may have some unique items or may vary the recipes and therefore, it is not clear if the restaurant is "offering for sale substantially the same menu items." The comment gave as an example a kosher restaurant that uses the same name as non-kosher restaurants that are part of the same chain. The comment noted that due to the kosher restaurant's following of the kosher laws, the kosher restaurant may offer for sale some menu items that vary from the menu items offered for sale in a non-kosher restaurant in the chain. In addition, the comment noted that the kosher restaurant may offer for sale unique menu items, such as schwarma, that are not offered for sale in the non-kosher restaurants in the chain. This comment requested an exemption for franchise restaurants that offer specialty menu items or items altered to accommodate a specific dietary practice (e.g., kosher).

One comment pointed out that menu items in chain restaurants and similar retail food establishments vary between States and within States to accommodate local tastes, even if the menu items have the same name. The comment cited chili as an example, stating that in Cincinnati it is common for chili to be made with cocoa and cinnamon thinned out with finely ground meat over spaghetti, whereas in Texas, chili is made with large chunks of meat, often with beans, served alone in a bowl.

One comment stated that some food service contractors provide clients with menus that may change daily, weekly, or monthly and with rotating cycle menus that can use up to several hundred recipes with cycle menus that vary from 3, 4, or 5 week cycles and from 5, 6, or 7 day service weeks. Due to the variability in menus in locations that rely on contract food services, the comment recommended that the definition of "offering for sale substantially the same menu item" be changed to "establishments in a chain that offer standard menus comprised of menu items that use the same general recipes and are prepared in substantially the same ways with substantially the same food components, even if the name of the menu item varies."

(Response 31) We decline to name a proportion or percentage of menu items that must be shared between establishments. Restaurants and similar retail food establishments regularly offer new and reformulated menu items in their establishments. It would be burdensome and impractical for establishments and inspectors to continually evaluate all of the establishments in the chain to count the numbers of standard menu items in common in order to determine whether a given establishment is covered. In addition, some establishments that are part of a large chain may not offer for sale all of the standard menu items offered in other locations of that chain. For example, some chains have a handful of locations in airports or other venues notated by the term "Express" added to the name, that sell a subset of the foods that are carried by the larger establishments in the chain. Finally, as the comments point out, some restaurants that are part of large chains have some unique or regional items or may vary recipes in a unique way. These types of minor variations should not exclude establishments from the requirements of this rule.

Based on the comments and on the considerations discussed previously in this document, we are not finalizing a specific proportion or percentage of menu items that covered establishments within a chain must share. However, we understand from the comments that our definition should speak to the number of menu items that must be shared more clearly. Therefore, we are adding a qualitative, not quantitative, description of the number of menu items that must be shared in order for the criterion of "offering for sale substantially the same menu items" to be met. Given the statutory language, along with the practicalities of and variations within the industry, we are adding "offering for sale a significant proportion of menu items" to the definition of "offering for sale substantially the same menu items." For example, if establishments only share one or two menu items, those establishments would not meet the criterion of "offering for sale substantially the same menu items."

We recognize that some establishments in a chain may have some menu items with ingredients that vary based on regional taste or source. Some menu items may be designed or prepared to meet certain dietary practices (e.g., Kosher or Halal) or contain a "secret ingredient." This is why our definition of "offering for sale substantially the same menu items" includes the criteria "us[ing] the same general recipe, prepared in substantially the same way, with substantially the same food components." By "the same general recipe," we mean that the establishments share a recipe, even if one establishment subsequently tweaks that recipe due to regional tastes or dietary practices. By "prepared in substantially the same way," we mean to include slight deviations from the recipe, because of, for example, food service worker variability. By "with substantially the same food components," we mean to include situations where ingredients may vary based on local availability or sourcing, including those used to conform to certain dietary practices (e.g., Kosher meat).

We also agree with comments that having the same name may indicate that the menu items are substantially the same, but it does not always do so. As comments pointed out, menu items that reflect regional differences may be so different that the name of the menu item sheds little light on whether the menu items use the same general recipe and are prepared in substantially the same way with substantially the same food components. For example, in some regions of the United States a menu item named "barbecue" may refer to a food prepared from pulled pork, whereas in other regions a menu item named "barbecue" may refer to a food prepared from beef ribs. Therefore, we have revised the definition to add a new sentence stating that having the same name may indicate, but does not necessarily guarantee, that menu items are substantially the same.

The definition for "substantially the same menu items" would also apply to establishments relying on food contractors. If such an arrangement caused menu rotations, the relevant question would still be whether those establishments are offering for sale substantially the same menu items, including whether they are selling a significant proportion of menu items that use the same general recipe and are prepared in substantially the same way with substantially the same food components, even if not necessarily at the same time. In other words, the focus is on whether the menu items are substantially the same, not on whether the menus or menu boards are substantially the same. We decline to accept the suggestion from the comment to revise the definition to include "establishments in a chain that offer standard menus comprised of menu items that . . . ." because it reflects a misunderstanding that an establishment needs to have a menu, or a "standard menu" more specifically, to be covered by the new law.

(Comment 32) One comment maintained that convenience stores in a chain do not have identical business plans and the same food; the food varies per establishment and is not prepared to corporate policy as it is in restaurants.

(Response 32) As explained previously in this document, establishments can be "offering for sale substantially the same menu items" even if not all of their menu items are exactly the same. Depending on the extent to which the menu items vary, a convenience store may or may not meet the criterion of offering for sale substantially the same menu items as defined in the rule.

(Comment 33) One comment described itself as a family-owned restaurant operator with 25 restaurants located entirely within a single State. Two of its restaurants also contain sushi operations, each under a different name and with entirely different menus than the larger establishment. The comment asked us to confirm that the rule would not apply to these sushi operations.

(Response 33) Based on the information in the comment, the two sushi operations do not appear to be covered by the rule because they are neither doing business under the same name (see section VI.E) nor offering for sale substantially the same menu items as 18 other establishments.

G. Authorized Official of a Restaurant or Similar Retail Food Establishment

Proposed § 101.11(a) would define "Authorized official of a restaurant or similar retail food establishment" as the owner, operator, agent in charge, or other person authorized by the owner, operator, or agent in charge to register the restaurant or similar retail food establishment, which is not otherwise subject to section 403(q)(5)(H) of the FD&C Act, with FDA for the purposes of § 101.11(d). (Section 101.11(d) pertains to voluntary registration to become subject to the requirements of section 403(q)(5)(H) of the FD&C Act.)

We received no comments on the proposed definition and are finalizing it without change.

H. Covered Establishment

As already noted in section VI.A, proposed § 101.11(a) would define "covered establishment" as a restaurant or similar retail food establishment that is a part of a chain with 20 or more locations doing business under the same name (regardless of the type of ownership, e.g., individual franchises) and offering for sale substantially the same menu items, as well as a restaurant or similar retail food establishment that is registered to be covered under section 403(q)(5)(H)(ix) of the FD&C Act. (Emphasis added).

In the following paragraphs, we discuss general comments on this proposed definition. We are finalizing the definition of "covered establishment" without change, except to refer to § 101.11(d) instead of section 403(q)(5)(H)(ix) of the FD&C Act. However, as already discussed (see sections VI.B, VI.C, VI.D, VI.E, and VI.F), changes we are making to other terms (i.e., adding a definition of "location," revising the definition of "restaurant or similar retail food establishment," revising the definition of "restaurant-type food," revising the definition of "doing business under the same name," and revising the definition of "offering for sale substantially the same menu items") affect the overall set of covered establishments.

1. General Comments on the Definition of Covered Establishment

(Comment 34) One comment considered that our proposed definition would make it conceivable for the requirements to apply to a single, completely unique "restaurant concept" that is owned by a chain with 20 or more other restaurants. The comment described a "restaurant concept" as separate and distinct operations by virtue of the individual restaurant's menu offerings or recipes, name, decor, and other distinguishing characteristics such as different dining experiences with higher quality food and different menu items that may be unrecognizable to the average diner as being operated by the larger chain. This comment also considered that applying the menu labeling requirements to these individual "restaurant concepts" would not be consistent with the statute or intent of Congress. Another comment expressed concern that a person who operates more than 20 chain retail food establishments and wants to start a "new concept" would be required to provide nutrition information if this "new concept" is only in one location.

(Response 34) We disagree that we need to revise the definition of a covered establishment to prevent a misinterpretation that a single, completely unique "restaurant concept" that is owned by a chain with 20 or more other restaurants generally would be covered by the rule. An establishment that is "single" and a "completely unique restaurant concept" is unlikely to have "20 or more locations" and be "offering for sale substantially the same menu items" as 20 or more other restaurants. Thus, such an establishment is unlikely to satisfy the criteria in the proposed definition to be a "covered establishment" as it is currently written. Likewise, if a person operates more than 20 chain retail food establishments and starts a "new concept," that "new concept" establishment would not be a covered establishment unless it is part of a chain with 20 or more locations doing business under the same name and offering for sale substantially the same menu items. We are retaining our definition, which, as we described in the proposed rule, is derived from sections 403(q)(5)(H)(i) and (xi)(I) of the FD&C Act (76 FR 19192 at 19195).

(Comment 35) One comment recommended that we revise the definition of covered establishment to use the following language from its State's regulation: "A food establishment that: (1) Is engaged in the business of preparing and selling food items for immediate human consumption on the premises or off the premises, . . . and (2) offers for sale substantially the same menu items, utilizing menus, menu boards or food item tags, in servings that are standardized for portion size and content, and (3) is one of a group of . . . food establishments . . . that (a) operates under common ownership or control, or (b) operates as franchised outlets of a parent business, or (c) does business under the same name." The comment cited only those portions of its regulation relevant to the questions raised by the definition of covered establishment in our proposed rule, and used ellipses to indicate text that was in the State regulation but not being offered as part of the definition of "covered establishment" in this rule.

(Response 35) We disagree with this comment and are not revising the definition of "covered establishment" to incorporate its suggestions. Our definition of covered establishment is derived from the Federal statutory language. The only basis offered by the comment was that the suggestions are used in a State law; the comment did not state why these changes were necessary from a policy perspective or legally justified under the Federal law.

(Comment 36) One comment recommended that the rule apply to most restaurants, and not just those with more than 20 locations, possibly excluding only establishments with a very small seating capacity. The comment contended that consumers already know that fast food is "bad for you" and they need to know the nutrition information about the food in other restaurants.

(Response 36) This rule implements section 4205 of the ACA, which, in general, covers only restaurants and similar retail food establishments that are part of a chain with 20 or more locations. Section 4205 of the ACA allows other restaurants and similar retail food establishments to register with FDA to become subject to the Federal requirements, but it does not require them to do so.

(Comment 37) One comment asked us to clarify whether the rule would apply to foreign establishments of a particular chain that has 20 or more establishments in the United States, and also has an establishment located in a foreign location, such as Italy.

(Response 37) The rule applies to locations in the United States, including any State or Territory of the United States, the District of Columbia, and the Commonwealth of Puerto Rico. This geographic scope is consistent with the definitions of "State" and "Territory" in section 201(a) of the FD&C Act.

(Comment 38) A few comments asked us to clarify that contractors and managed food service operations would be covered if they offer for sale substantially the same menu items.

(Response 38) Whether any other specific contractor or managed food service would be subject to the rule would depend on whether it satisfied all criteria established within the definition of "covered establishment." Thus, to be a covered establishment, an establishment operated by a contractor or managed food service must be a restaurant or similar retail food establishment that is a part of a chain with 20 or more locations doing business under the same name and offering for sale substantially the same menu items. We expect that some establishments operated by contractors and managed food services will satisfy all of these criteria.

2. Cooperatives

(Comment 39) Some comments addressed cooperatives and discussed multiple aspects related to the definition of "covered establishment," including "part of a chain," "doing business under the same name," and "offering for sale substantially the same menu items." One comment considered that cooperatives should not be exempt because the law expressly states "regardless of . . . ownership." One comment considered that the type of ownership of grocery stores, such as a cooperative, is irrelevant to whether a store is part of a chain. This comment maintained that the law clearly requires chains operating under the same name to disclose calories, regardless of the type of ownership. This comment also maintained that grocery store cooperatives face a similar situation as that faced by independent franchise owners of chain restaurants.

Other comments generally expressed the view that cooperatives should not be covered by the rule. One comment asserted that establishments associated with the same wholesaler or cooperative should not be considered "part of a chain" regardless of whether they operate under the same "banner" or under a different "banner." The comment considered that cooperatives are the opposite of chains because they are owned by individual members, operate independently, and are not bound by franchise agreements, whereas chains are centrally controlled with little say or choice by participants. The comment asked us to recognize that independent grocers are not part of a chain of 20, doing business under same name and selling the same items, even if we believe cooperatives are similar retail food establishments.

A few comments maintained that the definition for "doing business under the same name" does not apply to cooperatives because they are independent and exercise their independence more than franchised restaurants. According to one comment, independent retailers own, control, and operate their stores independently as customers of voluntary wholesalers and members of cooperatives. The comment explained that the food distribution system allows independent retailers to take advantage of economies of scale when procuring goods and services, as well as marketing and advertising, thus helping independent operators effectively compete with large national chain stores. The comment also explained that these entities are independently owned and operated businesses that often compete with other stores under the same banner name, and that menu items can have different general recipes and be prepared in substantially different ways with substantially different food components.

One comment asked us to recognize that members of cooperatives are not "doing business under the same name." For example, the comment considered that "Fred's Thriftway" is not the same as "Bob's Thriftway." The comment considered that "Thriftway" signals that these establishments are part of a cooperative but maintained that they are two different stores.

One comment contended that the term "offering for sale substantially the same menu items" may not apply to some foods, such as brownies or potato salad, made in grocery store cooperatives, although those foods may be offered for sale under the same name in those stores. According to the comment, "Bob's Thriftway" and "Mike's Thriftway" may both sell brownies made from the same general recipe, (e.g., flour, sugar, eggs, chocolate and butter); however, because independent grocers compete with each other, each is likely to include a secret ingredient, and as a result, the brownies are not the same.

(Response 39) We agree with some comments that the type of ownership of an establishment is not relevant to whether it is covered. To be subject to the rule, a cooperative must satisfy all the criteria in the definition of "covered establishment." In other words, to be subject to the rule a cooperative must be a restaurant or similar retail food establishment that sells restaurant-type food and is a part of a chain with 20 or more locations doing business under the same name (regardless of the type of ownership, e.g., individual franchises) and offering for sale substantially the same menu items. As we explain in section VI.D., we are not defining the term "chain" in this rulemaking. In addition, for the reasons we provide in section VI.E., we continue to define doing business under the same name to include names that are slight variations of each other. Independent businesses that are cooperatives, even those that are similarly named, are not covered establishments if, for example, they are only connected insofar as they take advantage of economies of scale when procuring goods and services, or for marketing and advertising purposes, but are not "offering for sale substantially the same menu items."

However, given the way cooperatives generally are structured, we do not expect that two cooperatives would be offering for sale substantially the same menu items. Unless a food such as a brownie offered for sale in Bob's Thriftway has the same general recipe, prepared in substantially the same way, with substantially the same food components as a brownie offered for sale in Mike's Thriftway, the two cooperatives' brownies would not be "substantially the same." However, if Bob's Thriftway and Mike's Thriftway share a recipe such as a brownie recipe, and the only difference between the two brownie recipes is that Mike's Thriftway has added a "secret ingredient," the brownies could be considered substantially the same menu item, depending on the importance of that ingredient. Note that even in this circumstance, Bob's Thriftway and Mike's Thriftway would not be "offering for sale substantially the same menu items" if the brownie is the only menu item that the two cooperatives share.

In addition, we note that a cooperative that is a restaurant or similar retail food establishment and does not satisfy all of the criteria to be a covered establishment, but voluntarily registers to be covered in accordance with § 101.11(d), would be subject to the rule.

I. Revisions to Several Provisions To Clarify the Applicability of the Rule to Those Restaurants and Similar Retail Food Establishments That Are Covered Establishments

This rule applies to restaurants and similar retail food establishments that satisfy the definition of "covered establishment" in this rule. Several provisions of the proposed rule that would apply to "covered establishments" used the term "restaurant or similar retail food establishment" rather than "covered establishment." To make clear that those provisions only apply to those restaurants and similar retail food establishments that satisfy the definition of "covered establishment," we are replacing the term "restaurant or similar retail food establishment" with "covered establishment" in those provisions. The affected provisions are:

- The definition of "custom order" (§ 101.11(a));

- The definition of "menu or menu board" (§ 101.11(a));

- The introductory text of § 101.11(b)(2)(ii) regarding nutrition information for a standard menu item that must be available in written form;

- The introductory paragraph of proposed § 101.11(c)(6) (which we are establishing in § 101.11(c)(3)) regarding information that must be provided to FDA substantiating nutrient information; and

- A subparagraph of proposed § 101.11(c)(6) regarding specific substantiation documentation (i.e., proposed paragraph (c)(6)(ii)(D), which we are establishing as paragraph (c)(3)(ii)(D)).

We note these changes in our discussion of each of these specific provisions.

VII. Comments and FDA Response on the Proposed Definition of Menu or Menu Board (Proposed § 101.11(a))

Proposed § 101.11(a) would define "menu or menu board" as the primary writing of the restaurant or similar retail food establishment from which a customer makes an order selection, including, but not limited to, breakfast, lunch, and dinner menus; dessert menus; beverage menus; children's menus; other specialty menus; electronic menus; and menus on the Internet. The proposed definition would also provide that menus may be in different forms, e.g., booklets, pamphlets, or single sheets of paper and that menu boards include those inside a restaurant or similar retail food establishment as well as drive-through menu boards at restaurants or similar retail food establishments.

In the proposed rule, we stated that given the importance for all consumers to have access to nutrition information when making order selections, "primary writing" should be interpreted from a consumer's vantage point (76 FR 19192 at 19202). For example, while a printed menu may be the "primary writing" of a restaurant used by a customer ordering food while dining inside the restaurant itself, a menu mailed as a flyer to another customer's home could be the "primary writing" of the restaurant used by that customer ordering take-out or delivery from the same restaurant. Both the printed menu and the menu flyer would meet the definition of "menu" or "menu board" under proposed § 101.11(a).

In the following paragraphs, we discuss comments on this proposed definition. We have revised the definition by replacing the term "restaurant or similar retail food establishment" with "covered establishment" in three locations in the definitions for clarity (see explanation in section VI.I). We are also including factors used to determine whether a writing is or is part of the primary writing from which a consumer makes an order selection.

(Comment 40) Many comments supported the proposed definition and agreed that "primary writing" should be interpreted from the perspective of consumers, so that each writing of the establishment that is the primary writing used by consumers in making order selections would be considered a menu or menu board. Several comments asserted that consumers need to see calorie information when making order selections in order for the information to be useful to them. One comment noted that Congress did not intend for covered establishments to only provide calorie declarations on a single medium in each establishment, as evidenced by the fact that section 4205 of the ACA requires calorie declarations on drive-through menu boards and menus and menu boards located inside establishments. Another comment suggested that we emphasize that any list or display of a standard menu item that is primary to the consumer placing an order would constitute a menu or menu board.

One comment considered that a single store that has multiple menus or menu boards should be able to select the menu on which the calories must be disclosed. For example, a single store might have more than one menu board—with one such board being handwritten and highlighting specific special options. As long as every food offered for sale in the establishment is listed on one menu board and that menu board includes the necessary information, the comment considered that requiring calories on that one menu board should be sufficient. Alternatively, the comment suggested that the calorie declaration be required on the "menu board of prominence," which the comment considered to be the menu board from which the order is placed.

Another comment similarly asserted that covered establishments must post the required information on the menu used most often rather than on all menus. Alternatively, the comment suggested that we provide an exemption for menus not commonly used by customers. In support of its suggestion, the comment pointed out that the statute uses the singular term "writing" and not a plural term. The comment stated that 90 percent of pizza customers order over the phone or the Internet or may order from memory. The comment asserted that to require nutrient information on every menu, menu board, Internet menu, or other writing is expensive, time consuming, and burdensome. The comment stated that it already uses in-store brochures to provide nutrition information to the small percentage of in-store customers. Although each franchisee in the applicable chain is required to carry certain menu items, the comment considered that each franchisee has the latitude to add items to the menu. Because the franchisee can add menu items to its menu, the comment asserted that it would be costly to a franchisee to change menu boards, because the franchisee will be required to order new menu boards and request calorie information for the new menu items.

One comment referred to an "industry proposal" for posting calories only on menus and menu boards that have the highest percentage of sales for that particular establishment, e.g., Web sites used for Internet ordering and paper menus for phone ordering. This comment was opposed to any such proposal. The comment asserted that this approach would be an unfair business advantage for certain restaurants because it would allow some restaurants to provide calorie declarations on less expensive menus such as paper take-out menus or Internet Web sites while others would have to provide calorie declarations for more expensive in-restaurant menus and menu boards. The comment also expressed concern that any requirement for a covered establishment to declare calories on only the menus that listed substantially all menu items would exclude children's menus and dessert menus.

(Response 40) We agree with the comments in support of the proposed definition. We disagree that the required information should only be posted on the menu or menu board most often used by consumers in a covered establishment, the "menu board of prominence," or only on the menus and menu boards that have the highest percentage of sales for a particular covered establishment. The critical factor is whether written material is or is part of the primary writing of a covered establishment from which a customer makes an order selection. It is not a matter of physical prominence of a menu, or the proportion of customers who order from a menu. Some consumers may want to select from a subset of standard menu items sold in the covered establishment. For example, if a consumer wanted to order only a dessert, he or she may ask for a dessert menu. As raised by one comment, if calorie information is listed only on the dinner menu, the consumer would not have access to the calorie information for the desserts if he or she is ordering from the dessert menu. As we stated in the proposed rule, given the importance for all consumers to have access to nutrition information when making order selections, we believe that the term "primary writing" should be interpreted from a consumer's vantage point (76 FR 19192 at 19202).

In addition, in the proposed rule, we tentatively concluded that a "menu" or "menu board" includes any writing of the covered establishment that is the primary writing from which a consumer makes an order selection (76 FR 19192 at 19201). We affirm this conclusion. The "primary writing" of an establishment can include more than one form of written material, such as a paper menu, a delivery menu, and a menu board; the critical factor is whether the written material is or is part of the primary writing of a covered establishment from which a customer makes an order selection. Further, we clarify that determining whether a writing is or is part of the primary writing from which a consumer makes an order selection depends on a number of factors, including whether the writing, such as a paper menu, delivery menu, or sign, lists the name of a standard menu item (or an image depicting the standard menu item) and the price of the standard menu item, and whether the writing can be used by a consumer to make an order selection at the time the consumer is viewing the writing (e.g., the writing is posted at the cash register in a covered establishment, or the writing lists the phone number or email address of a covered establishment for purposes of placing an order).

Accordingly, a writing of a covered establishment that contains the name (or image) and price of a standard menu item, and that can be used by a consumer to make an order selection from the establishment at the time the consumer is viewing the writing would be a menu or menu board regardless of whether, for example, the writing is not the menu used most often by consumers. Another writing, such as a poster on a storefront, a banner or billboard located along a road or highway, or a tray-liner or table-tent at a quick-service restaurant, could be considered a "secondary" writing within this context and would not meet the definition of a "menu or menu board," provided that such writing does not contain the name (or image) and price of a standard menu item, and cannot be used by a consumer to make an order selection at the time the consumer is viewing the writing.

We interpret the comment asserting that section 403(q)(5)(H)(xi) of the FD&C Act uses the singular term "writing" in defining the term "menu or menu board" as raising the question of what Congress intended "primary writing" to mean within the context of section 403(q)(5)(H)(xi) of the FD&C Act. In construing section 403(q)(5)(H)(xi) of the FD&C Act, FDA is confronted with two questions. First, has Congress directly spoken to the precise question presented (Chevron step one)? (Chevron, U.S.A., Inc. v. NRDC, Inc., 467 U.S. 837, 842 (1984).) If the "intent of Congress is clear," an Agency "must give effect to the unambiguously expressed intent of Congress." (Id. at 843.) However, if "Congress has not directly addressed the precise question at issue," and the statute is "silent or ambiguous with respect to the specific issue," then our interpretation of the term "primary writing" will be upheld as long as it is based on a "permissible construction of the statute (Chevron step two). (Chevron, 467 U.S. at 842-43; FDA v. Brown & Williamson Tobacco Corp, 529 U.S. 120, 132 (2000).) To find no ambiguity, Congress must have clearly manifested its intention with respect to the particular issue. (See e.g., Young v. Community Nutrition Institute, 476 U.S. 974, 980 (1986).)

We have determined that, in enacting section 403(q)(5)(H)(xi) of the FD&C Act, Congress did not speak directly and precisely to the meaning of "primary writing" within the definition of "menu or menu board." In conducting the Chevron step one analysis, we began with the language of section 403(q)(5)(H)(xi) of the FD&C Act. (See e.g., Touche Ross & Co. v. Redington, 442 U.S. 560, 568 ("[A]s with any case involving the interpretation of a statute, our analysis must begin with the language of the statute itself.").) The term "primary writing" is not defined in section 403(q)(5)(H) of the FD&C Act or elsewhere in the FD&C Act. In general, a term that is undefined in a statute carries its ordinary meaning. (See e.g., Perrin v. United States, 444 U.S. 37, 42 (1979) ("A fundamental canon of statutory construction is that, unless otherwise defined, words will be interpreted as taking their ordinary contemporary, common meaning.").) One common definition of the term "writing" is "something written, especially (a) meaningful letters or characters that constitute readable matter . . . (b) a written work, especially a literary composition" (Ref. 20). Similarly, another common definition of the term "writing" is "something written: As (a) letters or characters that serve as visible signs of ideas, words, or symbols; (b) a letter, note, or notice used to communicate or record; (c) a written composition." (Ref. 21; see also Ref. 22).

One common definition of the term "primary" is "first or highest in rank or importance; principal" (Ref. 23; see also Refs. 24 and 25). Another common definition of the term "primary" is "functioning or transmitting without intermediary: Direct" (Ref. 25; see also Ref. 24).

Where, as here, the statutory language on its face does not clearly establish Congressional intent, it is appropriate to also consider other traditional tools of statutory construction, including other language in the section, the language, design, and purpose of the statute as whole, and legislative history. (See e.g., Pharmaceutical Research & Manufacturers of America v. Thompson, 251 F.3d 219, 224 (D.C. Cir. 2001); Davis v. Michigan Department of Treasury, 489 U.S. 803, 809 (1989); Martini v. Federal National Mortgage Association, 178 F.3d 1336, 1345 (D.C. Cir. 1999).) The other language in section 403(q)(5)(H)(xi) of the FD&C Act indicates that the writing at issue is writing of the establishment "from which a consumer makes an order selection." Further, other provisions within section 403(q)(5)(H) of the FD&C Act indicate that requirements apply to more than one form of writing within a covered establishment. (See sections 403(q)(5)(H)(ii)(I) and (II) of the FD&C Act.) In addition, a general purpose of section 4205 of the ACA is to make calorie and other nutrition information available to consumers in a direct and accessible manner to enable consumers to make informed and healthful dietary choices. Lastly, the legislative history does not suggest that Congress intended to limit the term to only one writing of the establishment.

Having determined that the meaning of "primary writing" in section 403(q)(5)(H)(xi) of the FD&C Act is ambiguous, we have determined that the final rule's interpretation of "primary writing" is a permissible construction of the statute (Chevron step two). In conducting the Chevron step two analysis, the same tools of statutory construction are available as those for the step one analysis.

First, the interpretation in the final rule is consistent with the plain meaning of the statute (Ref. 26). (See also Perrin v. United States, 444 U.S. 37, 42 (1979).) Under the final rule, a "primary writing" is "something written," such as letters or characters on a sign or board. Further, determining whether the "writing" is "primary," meaning of the most relevance or importance within this context or functioning without intermediary, or direct, depends on a number of factors, including whether the writing lists the name of a standard menu item (or an image depicting the standard menu item) and the price of the standard menu item, and whether the writing can be used by a consumer to make an order selection at the time the consumer is viewing the writing. In developing these factors, we considered other language in section 403(q)(5)(H)(xi) of the FD&C Act, specifically that the writing of the establishment is one "from which a consumer makes an order selection." We also considered other language within section 403(q)(5)(H) of the FD&C Act, including sections 403(q)(5)(H)(i) and (ii)(I) and (II) of the FD&C Act, which together require a covered establishment to post calorie and other information on a menu and menu board. Further, in considering the general purpose of the section 4205 of the ACA, we determined that construing the term "primary writing" within the meaning of section 403(q)(5)(H)(xi) of the FD&C Act so as to include more than one form of writing, dependent on specific factors, would better serve the purposes of section 4205.

For all of these reasons, § 101.11(a) continues to specify that a menu or menu board is defined as the primary writing of the restaurant or similar retail food establishment from which a consumer makes an order selection.

In response to the comment regarding costs related to adding new menu items to a menu or menu board, we first note that section 403(q)(5)(H)(ii) of the FD&C Act requires covered establishments to declare calories on menus and menu boards for standard menu items listed on such menu and menu boards. Therefore, to the extent a covered establishment adds a new standard menu item to the establishment's menu or menu board, the establishment would be required to declare calories on the menu or menu board for the new standard menu item. Further, a covered establishment that decides to add a new menu item to a menu or menu board has already decided to incur the cost of redesigning or replacing the menu or menu board for such change—i.e., to display the new standard menu item. In this situation, the additional cost to the establishment is the cost for determining the calorie information that must be declared for the new standard menu item.

Regarding costs related to determining nutrition information for standard menu items, we note that this rule also provides flexibility in order to minimize such costs. As discussed in section XVIII, section 403(q)(5)(H)(iv) of the FD&C Act provides that a restaurant or similar retail food establishment must have a reasonable basis for its nutrient content disclosures. As also discussed in section XVIII, this rule provides that a covered establishment can satisfy the requirements of 403(q)(5)(H)(iv) of the FD&C Act by various means, including use of nutrient databases, cookbooks, laboratory methods, and other reasonable means, including the use of Nutrition Facts on labels on packaged foods that comply with the nutrition labeling requirements of section 403(q)(1) of the FD&C Act and § 101.9, FDA nutrient values for raw fruits and vegetables in Appendix C of part 101 (21 CFR part 101), or FDA nutrient values for cooked fish in Appendix D of part 101 (see § 101.11(c)(1)). In addition, this rule provides that a covered establishment can satisfy the requirements of 403(q)(5)(H)(iv) of the FD&C Act by relying on nutrition information for a standard menu item determined by the establishment's corporate headquarters or parent entity (see § 101.11(c)(3)(i)(F), (c)(3)(iii)(D), and (c)(3)(iv)(D)). In some cases, a corporate headquarters or parent entity could decide to maintain a nutrient database and use it to determine nutrition information for specialty standard menu items offered for sale by one or a few individual establishments in the chain. Therefore, this rule provides flexibility for covered establishments in order to minimize costs while also helping to ensure that calorie and other nutrition information is made available to consumers in a direct and accessible manner to enable consumers to make informed and healthful dietary choices.

(Comment 41) A few comments appeared to believe that the proposed rule would require covered establishments to post or otherwise have menu boards for disclosing calorie information. These comments asked for other options for disclosing calories. One comment suggested that large menu boards should not be required because they will obscure the consumers' view of the preparation of their food and thereby create a food safety issue. One comment suggested that we consider "technological solutions" instead of menu boards, e.g., use of a kiosk near the point of sale. The comment also suggested that we provide flexibility to cover alternative sources such as a daily feature board.

One comment asked us to provide flexibility for facilities that operate in locations too small to display a menu board by allowing establishments to choose among several different options for display methods. As one alternative to the traditional menu board, the comment asked us to permit the use of a display terminal to provide nutrition information for menu items or allow "menu identifiers" (a term the comment did not define) at the point of selection, and to permit nutrition information to be displayed adjacent to the food item in cafeteria and buffet type settings.

(Response 41) Some comments may have misinterpreted the proposed rule. We did not propose to require that covered establishments post or otherwise have menu boards. Rather, within this context, we proposed to define the terms "menu" and "menu board," based on the statutory definition at section 403(q)(5)(H)(xi) of the FD&C Act, and to provide direction regarding what information must be disclosed on menus and menu boards for covered establishments that have menus and menu boards. That proposed definition relies on the concept of a primary writing. If an electronic display is the primary writing of the covered establishment from which a customer makes an order selection, it would satisfy our definition of a menu or menu board. As such, electronic menus may be used by covered establishments, and we have retained electronic menus as an example of menus in the definition of menu or menu board in § 101.11(a).

Standard menu items offered for sale in covered establishments with cafeteria- and buffet-type settings are most likely foods on display or self-service foods. As discussed in section XVII.B, for a food on display or a self-service food, section 403(q)(5)(H)(iii) of the FD&C Act and § 101.11(b)(2)(iii) require covered establishments to place a sign adjacent to the food listing calories per displayed food item or per serving. This rule provides flexibility for covered establishments by providing a number of options for meeting the requirements of section 403(q)(5)(H)(iii) of the FD&C Act and § 101.11(b)(2)(iii). For example, covered establishments are permitted to declare calories for a food on display or a self-service food by posting calorie declarations on signs adjacent to the food, on a sign attached to a sneeze guard, or on a single sign or placard (§ 101.11(b)(2)(iii)(A)). Therefore, this rule provides flexibility, as requested by some comments, for covered establishments to choose among several options for declaring calorie information for standard menu items, including self-service foods or foods on display in cafeteria and buffet-type settings.

(Comment 42) In the proposed rule, we noted that many consumers order restaurant-type food from restaurants or similar retail food establishments over the phone or Internet. We tentatively concluded that if consumers can order from a covered establishment online, over the phone, or by fax, using a writing of the covered establishment on the Internet as the primary writing from which he or she makes his or her order selection, then the writing on the Internet is a menu for the purposes of section 403(q)(5)(H) of the FD&C Act (76 FR 19192 at 19202). Some comments asked us to keep in mind the need to keep up with technology and not have a rigid standard.

(Response 42) The definition of "menu or menu board" clearly specifies that menus may be in different forms and does not establish a standard for the technology used on a menu or menu board. The definition lists a number of examples of primary writings that may be menus or menu boards, including electronic menus and menus on the Internet, that are not meant to be all-inclusive, as indicated by use of the terms "including, but not limited to" before the examples. Because a menu or menu board is defined as the primary writing of the covered establishment from which a customer makes an order selection, the definition is adequate to capture methods and media other than those specifically listed in that definition, so long as such methods and media otherwise satisfy the criteria in the definition.

(Comment 43) Several comments noted that some local zoning laws do not permit restaurants with drive-through windows to build larger menu boards. These comments expressed concern about how to comply with the new requirements for menu boards in light of State or local size restrictions. One comment asked us to provide more flexibility for compliance, including permitting the use of a pamphlet next to the drive-through menu board. Some comments suggested that we allow nutrition information on a large poster adjacent to the menu board.

A few comments supported the use of stanchions (i.e., free-standing boards that are not connected to the menu board and are often placed near drive-through menu boards) to post calorie information. One comment maintained that restaurants and similar retail food establishments have a vested interest in customer satisfaction in the context of drive-through windows and have concluded that clear and organized space, presented within the framework of a known brand, is the most critical success factor in presenting information to consumers on menu boards. This comment considered that stanchions adjacent or close to menu boards are "complete thoughts" if the information is relevant, well organized, and clearly marked, and that such stanchions will help consumers with their menu choices. The comment considered that in many cases information on stanchions is more clear and conspicuous than on menu boards. The comment noted that calorie information is provided on stanchions in some jurisdictions that require nutrition labeling on menus and menu boards, including Montgomery County (Maryland), New York City, Philadelphia, and certain counties in New York. The comment maintained that the current use of stanchions in some jurisdictions is evidence of its effectiveness, and noted that some States and localities permit stanchions because information is hard to read on already crowded drive-through menu boards.

A comment from a quick-service restaurant chain asserted that stanchions are less costly to update and replace than menu boards. The chain had conducted a consumer survey of customers who purchased food from the chain's drive-through windows in 13 of the chain's restaurants that use stanchions, as permitted in King County, Washington, and submitted a report of this survey to the docket for this rule (Ref. 27). For the 128 customers surveyed, the comment reported that 92 percent felt it was easy to find calories, 98 percent felt calories were easy to understand, 95 percent thought the stanchion location was clearly visible to consumers, 95 percent noted nothing blocked view of stanchion, and 76 percent felt they had adequate time to review before ordering.

One comment considered that while "the statute" refers to menus and menu boards, it also gives us authority to define those terms. (We assume this comment is referring to section 4205 of the ACA.) The comment stated that we could include stanchions as a method to communicate calorie information that is clear and conspicuous.

Several comments agreed with our tentative conclusion that stanchions inadequately convey calorie information. The comments asserted that it is challenging for consumers to read different information in different locations at a drive-through window especially when trying to read the information from a car, where consumers have limited mobility and a limited field of vision. The comments also asserted that, even with different zoning laws, drive-through menu boards have enough room for calories, although photos and other marketing information may need altering. One comment pointed out that separate stanchions would not comply with section 403(q)(5)(H)(ii) of the FD&C Act, which requires that calories be on the menu board itself.

(Response 43) We disagree that the rule should provide for declaration of calorie information in pamphlets or on posters or stanchions, rather than on the menu board at a drive-through in a covered establishment. In the proposed rule, we tentatively concluded that stanchions inadequately convey calorie information because a situation in which customers need to look to one board (the menu board) for important food-selection information, such as price, and another (the stanchion) for calories, is likely to be more difficult for customers attempting to use the declared calorie information at the point of selection (76 FR 19192 at 19206). We also tentatively concluded that this is particularly true in the drive-through context, where customers have a restricted field of vision from their car windows, and may have a relatively short time to consider the menu board prior to ordering, because customers often cannot view the full menu while waiting in line. As discussed further in the following paragraphs, the comments provide insufficient basis for us to conclude otherwise, and as a result, we affirm our conclusion from the proposed rule.

In addition, section 403(q)(5)(H)(ii)(II)(aa) of the FD&C Act requires the number of calories contained in standard menu items to be disclosed on the menu board itself. Section 403(q)(5)(H)(xi) of the FD&C Act defines "menu" or "menu board" as "the primary writing of the restaurant or similar retail food establishment from which a customer makes an order selection." Because a stanchion is a free-standing board that is not connected to a drive-through menu board and therefore typically is not used by consumers to make order selections, we do not consider it to meet the definition of "menu" or "menu board" as defined in this rule and section 403(q)(5)(H)(xi) of the FD&C Act. Accordingly, we concluded that a stanchion cannot be the means by which a covered establishment discloses calorie declarations on menus and menu boards as required under section 403(q)(5)(H)(ii) of the FD&C Act and this rule.

We considered the consumer survey results provided with one comment and did not find the information adequate to overcome the concerns we raised in the proposed rule regarding the use of stanchions (Ref. 28). Although the participants expressed favorable impressions of the stanchions, the survey data:

- Did not provide a comparison with other calorie displays, including calorie declarations on drive-through menu boards without stanchions;

- Did not show whether participants would have more or less favorable impressions of calorie declarations on drive-through menu boards without stanchions.

- Only showed that the participants liked the display and not whether the display was useful for them in making their order selections; and

- Did not assess the use of stanchions in situations where the consumer needs to make quick decisions because other consumers are in the drive-through line behind them.

For all of the reasons discussed in response to this comment, this rule does not provide for declaration of calories in a pamphlet or on a stanchion at a drive-through of a covered establishment as a means of satisfying the requirement that the number of calories contained in a standard menu item be disclosed on the menu and the menu board, as required by section 403(q)(5)(H)(ii) of the FD&C Act and § 101.11(b)(2)(i).

(Comment 44) Some comments asserted that the proposed rule allows the Secretary to amend the nutrition information that must be disclosed and that this will further burden restaurants to replace drive-through and interior menu boards multiple times.

(Response 44) We interpret the comments as referring to section 403(q)(5)(H)(vi) of the FD&C Act. Under section 403(q)(5)(H)(vi) of the FD&C Act, the Secretary (and, by delegation, FDA) may, by regulation, require the disclosure of a nutrient, other than a nutrient required under section 403(q)(5)(H)(ii)(III) of the FD&C Act, in the written nutrition information that is available to consumers upon request if FDA determines that the nutrient information should be disclosed for the purpose of providing information to assist consumers in maintaining healthy dietary practices. If this is indeed what the comments mean, the comments appear to have confused section 403(q)(5)(H)(vi) of the FD&C Act with the requirements in section 403(q)(5)(H)(ii)(I)(aa) related to the disclosure of calories on a menu or menu board. The statutory authority in section 403(q)(5)(H)(vi) of the FD&C Act for FDA to require disclosure in the written nutrition information of a nutrient other than one required under section 403(q)(5)(H)(ii)(III) of the FD&C Act does not address the calories declarations that must be on a menu or menu board.

(Comment 45) In the proposed rule, we stated that we recognize that some establishments may send menus as a form of advertising. We tentatively concluded that advertisements for food fall outside the scope of section 4205 of the ACA. However, take-out and delivery menus, which include all or a significant portion of items offered for sale and serve as the primary writing from which consumers make their order selections, would be menus under the proposed rule (76 FR 19192 at 19201).

Several comments considered that the proposal did not adequately distinguish between menus and menu boards and advertisements or promotional material. One comment considered that it is not appropriate to require calorie disclosure in advertising, such as a postcard announcing a new restaurant that has pictures of a few sample dishes. However, the comment also considered that when the advertising is the menu itself and can be used as the "primary writing" a customer uses to make an order, calorie disclosure should be required. The comment recommended that the test be whether customers can use the menu as a primary writing for making their selection, not the way in which the menu is presented or delivered to the customers by the restaurant or similar retail food establishment. One comment asked us to clarify that calorie disclosure should be on any menu regardless of whether the menu also serves as a marketing tool. One comment stated that any list of covered food items that is the primary vehicle from which a customer places his or her order constitutes a menu. The comment noted that in some instances, an in-store sign that looks like an advertisement (e.g., promotional poster) for a menu item is the primary vehicle from which the customer orders the menu item when the menu item is not included on the menu but is included only on that sign. This comment asked us to make clear that a sign listing a menu item that is only listed on that sign makes it a menu board.

One comment asked us to make clear that covered menus include individualized order sheets used at certain restaurants. Another comment asked us to make clear that take-out menus are included and suggested that a take-out menu be added as an example to the definition in the regulation.

Some comments asked us to make a clear statement that advertisements and promotional material such as table top stands, newspaper advertisements and flyers, tray liners and point of purchase marketing materials are not menus, even if they list some names and prices. One comment noted that, in the proposed rule, we tentatively concluded that "advertisements for food fall outside the scope of section 4205" but did not include this statement in the proposed definition. The comment asserted that we hinted at potential grounds for excluding some menus from coverage, when we stated that "take-out and delivery menus, which include all or a significant portion of items offered for sale and serve as the primary writing from which consumers make their order selections, would be menus under the proposed rule" (76 FR 19192 at 19202; emphasis added by comment). The comment expressed concern that, without specific language in the final regulation that advertisements are not menus and thus fall outside the scope of section 4205 of the ACA, the terms "menu" or "menu board" could be construed to encompass materials that list menu items but that are in fact used as advertisements. The comment maintained that this clarity is needed to ensure consistent enforcement. The comment also recommended that we expand on our statement that such promotional materials are menus subject to the menu labeling requirements if they "include all or a significant portion of items offered for sale." The comment asserted that limiting labeling requirements, for example, to only menus listing more than a certain percentage of standard menu items sold by the restaurant would have the practical effect of limiting the number of pieces covered, excluding many promotional items (such as door hangers and pizza box tops) and creating an objective standard that could guide both restaurant behavior and enforcement. The comment considered that requiring calorie disclosures on promotional material is especially burdensome for some of the franchises who pay for this promotional material.

One comment stated that circular advertisements should not be menus. Another comment recommended that grocery store signs that highlight the attributes of a food in the store not be considered a menu or menu board. One comment supported including nutrition information on any food advertisement that makes a health claim.

(Response 45) As discussed previously in this document, the term "menu" or "menu board" includes any writing of the covered establishment that is the primary writing from which a consumer makes an order selection. As discussed in Response 40, determining whether a writing is or is part of the primary writing from which a consumer makes an order selection depends on a number of factors, including whether the writing, such as a take-out menu, sign, or poster, lists the name of a standard menu item (or an image depicting the standard menu item) and the price of the standard menu item, and whether the writing can be used by a consumer to make an order selection at the time the consumer is viewing the writing (e.g., the writing is posted at the cash register in a covered establishment, or the writing lists the phone number or email address of a covered establishment for purposes of placing an order). Accordingly, a writing of a covered establishment that contains the name (or image) and price of a standard menu item, and that can be used by a consumer to make an order selection from the establishment at the time the consumer is viewing the writing would be a menu or menu board regardless of whether, for example, the writing is mailed to a consumer's home or is posted inside a covered establishment. In contrast, written material of an establishment that does not satisfy this criteria, such as a poster on a storefront, a coupon or other promotional material, banners, tray liners, billboards, and stanchions, could be considered a "secondary writing" of an establishment.

We recognize that, in the proposed rule, we tentatively concluded that take-out and delivery menus would be considered menus within the meaning of section 403(q)(5)(H)(xi) of the FD&C Act to the extent that such menus include all or a significant portion of items offered for sale (76 FR 19192 at 19201). However, we are not affirming this conclusion for a number of reasons. First, we agree with the comment asserting that the critical factor should be whether the take-out or delivery menu is or is part of the primary writing from which a consumer makes an order selection, not the way in which the menu is presented or delivered to consumers.

Second, as discussed previously in this document, in this rule we clarified the factors to be considered in determining whether a writing is or is part of the primary writing from which a consumer makes an order selection, and these factors help clarify whether a writing constitutes a menu or menu board or an advertisement or promotional material, as requested by several comments. Further, in light of these factors, if we were to conclude that delivery or take-out menus would only be considered menus if they included all or a significant portion of items offered for sale, that conclusion would be inconsistent with how we will be determining whether other written material constitutes a primary writing of an establishment from which a consumer makes an order selection, particularly since consumers can use take-out and delivery menus to make order selections in generally the same way as they would use dine-in menus.

In addition, menus vary in size and selection. A covered establishment that has a single menu for daily use, including menu offerings for breakfast, lunch, and dinner, may nonetheless have separate take-out menus directed only to breakfast, lunch, or dinner. We see no reason to treat a take-out menu that only includes menu offering for breakfast any differently than we would treat a breakfast menu used by consumers to order and consume breakfast while seated at the establishment.

For these reasons, in this rule we are not affirming the proposed rule's tentative conclusion that take-out and delivery menus would be considered menus within the meaning of section 403(q)(5)(H)(xi) of the FD&C Act to the extent that such menus include all or a significant portion of items offered for sale. Instead, in this document we identify factors we would use to determine whether a writing is the primary writing from which a consumer makes an order selection—i.e., the name (or image) and price of the standard menu item food and a means to make an order selection at the time the consumer is viewing the writing. Accordingly, determining whether a writing is a menu or menu board does not depend on how many items are listed. If a writing constitutes a menu or menu board within the meaning of section 403(q)(5)(H)(xi) of the FD&C Act and § 101.11(a), it must contain the information required under section 403(q)(5)(H) of the FD&C Act and § 101.11(b), regardless of the number of items on that menu or menu board.

Any written material that is or is part of the primary writing from which a consumer makes an order selection, whether it is an individualized order sheet or a take-out menu, would be a menu for purposes of this rule if it includes the name (or image) and price of a standard menu item and a means by which a consumer can make an order selection from the establishment at the time the consumer is viewing the writing. Providing calorie and other required information on menus and menu boards will make such information available to consumers in a direct and accessible manner to enable consumers to make informed and healthful dietary choices.

Using these factors, other writings of a covered establishment, such as newspaper ads, circular advertisements, banners, or postcards that announce a new restaurant and provide pictures of sample dishes generally would not be menus or menu boards. Although it is possible that such writings could include the name (or image) and price of standard menu items, they generally would not provide a means by which a consumer can make an order selection at the time the consumer is viewing the writing and therefore such a writing would not constitute a primary writing from which a consumer makes an order selection within the meaning of section 403(q)(5)(H)(xi) of the FD&C Act. Likewise, a sign in a grocery store that highlights attributes of a standard menu item (e.g., by the name or image of the menu item), without including the price, would not be a menu or menu board.

While a writing may constitute a menu or menu board, not all of the menu items listed on such writing would require calorie declarations. For example, if the requirements of section 4205 of the ACA do not apply to a food (e.g., as a daily special, temporary menu item, or customary market test item), a covered establishment would not be required to declare calories or other nutrition information for such food under this rule, meaning that a writing listing a daily special or temporary menu item would not be required to bear a calorie declaration for such item. Further, as discussed later in this document (see Response 79), for certain "mix and match" situations, where the menu or menu board describes an opportunity for a consumer to combine standard menu items for a special price (e.g., "Combine Any Sandwich with Any Soup or Any Salad for $8.99"), and the calories for each standard menu item, including each size option if applicable, available for the consumer to combine are declared elsewhere on the menu or menu board, a covered establishment would not be required to declare the calories for such item (see § 101.11(b)(2)(i)(A)(6)(iv)).

The comment supporting nutrition information on any food advertisement that makes a health claim is outside the scope of this rule, which establishes requirements for declaring nutrition information for standard menu items offered for sale in establishments covered by the requirements of section 4205 of the ACA. We note, however, that material that constitutes food labeling within the meaning of section 201(m) of the FD&C Act would be subject to the requirements in § 101.10. Under section 201(m) of the FD&C Act, the term "labeling" means all labels and other written, printed, or graphic matter (1) upon any article or any of its containers or wrappers, or (2) accompanying such article.

(Comment 46) One comment recommended that menu labeling requirements apply to airline magazines that include menus.

(Response 46) In the proposed rule, we tentatively concluded that most airplanes would not satisfy the definition of "restaurant or similar retail food establishment" because, in general, they do not present themselves to the public as restaurants, nor are they likely to meet the floor space (or revenue) threshold. As discussed in section VI.D, under the definition of "covered establishment" established in this rule airplanes are not covered establishments that must comply with the rule. Therefore, the nutrition labeling requirements of this rule do not apply to airline magazines that include menus.

VIII. Comments and FDA Response on the Proposed Definition of Terms Related to Foods Covered by the Rule (Proposed § 101.11(a))

A. Restaurant Food and Restaurant-Type Food

As discussed in section VI.C, after considering comments, we are deleting the proposed definition of "restaurant food" and establishing a revised definition of "restaurant-type food" that better reflects the food most like the food offered for sale in restaurants. We discussed these changes to two terms related to foods covered by the rule within section VI because the definition of "restaurant-type food" established in this rule is one of several terms related to the scope of establishments covered by the rule.

B. Standard Menu Item

Proposed § 101.11(a) would define "standard menu item" as a restaurant or restaurant-type food that is routinely included on a menu or menu board or routinely offered as a self-service food or food on display. In the following paragraphs, we discuss comments on this proposed definition. We are finalizing it without change, except to revise "restaurant or restaurant-type food" to "restaurant-type food" to conform with our deletion of the term "restaurant food" throughout the rule (see section VI.C).

(Comment 47) Several comments supported the proposed definition. One comment opposed the proposed definition because it is "incomplete" and misunderstands the meaning of "standard" within the context of a chain of 20 or more restaurants and similar retail food establishments doing business under the same name and offering for sale substantially the same menu items. The comment argued that it is not the regularity with which a menu item is sold at a given restaurant that renders the item "standard" within the context of a restaurant chain; rather, it is the fact that the menu item is offered across many establishments in the chain, in substantially the same form, and is prepared according to the same recipe and using the same ingredients. The comment maintained that when foods are standardized, nutrition information can be derived. On the other hand, according to the comment, if foods do not have a common recipe, nutrition information would be determined case-by-case, which is impractical and cost prohibitive. The comment suggested the following definition: "A menu item that appears on the menus of substantially all restaurants in a chain that uses the same general recipe and that is prepared in substantially the same way with substantially the same food components, even if the name of the menu item varies."

The comment also recommended that, for a chain that prints a single standardized menu for all its restaurants or establishments or for those in a given region, the term "standard menu item" be interpreted to refer to menu items that appear on those centrally printed and distributed menus. The comment maintained that adopting this definition would harmonize the terms "standard menu item" and "covered establishment" and ensure that the requirements apply to the foods that are subject to the type of standardization that would allow them to be consistently prepared. The comment also requested that a covered establishment be allowed but not required to provide the nutrition information in writing at the point of sale for menu items offered for sale in only some establishments in a chain if we decide to include such menu items within the definition of standard menu item in the final rule. Otherwise, the comment considered that a chain retail food establishment would have to include, in nutrition brochures, information on many menu items that are sold in a small percentage of stores, which could be confusing and costly.

(Response 47) We disagree that the definition of "standard menu item" should be based on whether the menu item is offered across substantially all of the establishments within the chain, in substantially the same form, and is prepared according to the same recipe and using the same ingredients. Section 403(q)(5)(H)(i) of the FD&C Act provides, in relevant part, that "in the case of food that is a standard menu item that is offered for sale in a restaurant or similar retail food establishment that is part of a chain with 20 or more locations doing business under the same name . . . and offering for sale substantially the same menu items, the restaurant or similar retail food establishment shall disclose the [required] information. . . .". The statutory language does not indicate that a menu item must be offered for sale in all of the restaurants or similar retail food establishments within a chain in order for it to be a "standard menu item" at a particular covered establishment. Indeed, it would be burdensome and impractical for establishments and inspectors to continually evaluate all of the menu items offered by a chain to determine which items are offered by all establishments in the chain in order to determine whether a given menu item is a standard menu item subject to requirements of this rule. In addition, we have no evidence that it would be impractical and cost prohibitive to require covered establishment to provide the nutrition required by this rule for menu items that they routinely offer. We continue to believe that it is reasonable to interpret "standard menu item" to mean a restaurant-type food routinely included on a menu or menu board or routinely offered as a self-service food or food on display in a given covered establishment.

We would not object to central printing of a single, standardized menu for use by all covered establishments within a chain, provided that the centrally printed menu complies with the requirements of this rule and applicable provisions of the FD&C Act. However, if an individual covered establishment offers for sale an additional standard menu item that is not offered by every establishment in the chain and, therefore, is not included on the centrally printed menu, that establishment still must comply with all applicable requirements of this rule for that standard menu item, including where and how the nutrition information must be disclosed.

We disagree that a covered establishment would have to include, in nutrition brochures, information on many menu items that are sold in a small percentage of stores. A covered establishment need only provide the required information for the standard menu items it offers for sale.

(Comment 48) A few comments stated that grocery stores use items from other departments within the grocery store (e.g., meat department, produce department) to make its prepared food items. The ingredients for a given prepared food can vary significantly depending on the availability of items in the store. These comments argued that labeling and determining calorie information for these items would be difficult.

(Response 48) If a prepared food item varies significantly depending on what ingredients a covered establishment happens to have available, the item may not meet the definition of standard menu item. For example, if a grocery store with a hot soup bar offers a different vegetable soup every day based on whatever vegetables the store happens to have in surplus (e.g., cabbage and tomatoes soup one day, carrots and leeks the next, spinach and squash on a third day), and if none of these vegetable soups is offered for sale routinely, then none of the vegetable soups would meet the definition of standard menu item. Even if the grocery store names each version of the soup as "vegetable soup," the item would not be considered a standard menu item, because the soup's ingredients significantly differ daily.

C. Combination Meal

Proposed § 101.11(a) would define "combination meal" as a standard menu item that consists of more than one food item, for example a meal that includes a sandwich, a side dish, and a drink. The proposed definition would further provide that a combination meal may be represented on the menu or menu board in narrative form, numerically, or pictorially. Some combination meals may include a variable menu item (or be a variable menu item as defined in § 101.11(a)) where the components may vary. For example, the side dish may vary among several options (e.g., fries, salad, or onion rings) or the drinks may vary (e.g., soft drinks, milk, or juice) and the customer selects which of these items will be included in the meal.

Comments that addressed the proposed definition agreed with it. Therefore, we are finalizing it without change, except to correct a typographical error by removing an open parenthesis mark between "may include a variable menu item" and "or be a variable menu item . . ."

D. Variable Menu Item

Proposed § 101.11(a) would define "variable menu item" as a standard menu item that comes in different flavors, varieties, or combinations, and is listed as a single menu item. In the following paragraphs, we discuss comments on this proposed definition. We are finalizing it without change.

(Comment 49) Several comments considered that the term "variable menu item" does not include items listed on a menu that can be assembled in varying combinations, such as pizza. These comments suggested that the definition of variable menu item be revised to "a standard menu item that comes in different flavors, varieties, or combinations, and is listed as a single menu item. It does not include foods, beverages, or meals that are listed as separate menu items but could be combined in a variety of combinations or that are different sizes of the same menu item."

Several comments asked that we clarify that the definition for "variable menu item" does not mean different sizes. They maintained that each size should be accompanied by a calorie declaration. In contrast, one comment opposed the posting of calories for different sizes, maintaining that providing calorie information for each size would take too much space and might force the reduction in font size. This comment asked us to permit covered establishments to provide a range of calories to reflect the calorie content range from the smallest to the largest size for beverages offered as standard menu items. This comment considered that the statute provides us discretion to allow covered establishments to provide calorie information for different sized beverages using ranges, as long as the calorie information is clear and conspicuous.

(Response 49) We disagree that variable menu items do not include foods such as pizza. Our proposed definition is consistent with section 403(q)(5)(H)(v) of the FD&C Act, which expressly includes pizza as an example of a standard menu item that comes in different flavors, varieties, or combinations, but is listed as a single menu item. For example, a menu or menu board can list a pizza with a particular price and up to four toppings. This is an example of a food that comes in different varieties because the consumer has the choice of various toppings.

We agree with the comments asserting that different sizes of a standard menu item are not variable menu items, but disagree with the comment opposing the posting of calories for different sizes. Section 403(q)(5)(H)(v) of the FD&C Act provides, in relevant part, that FDA shall establish by regulation standards for disclosing the nutrient content for standard menu items that come in different flavors, varieties, or combinations, but which are listed as single menu items. When a standard menu item, including a beverage, is listed on a menu or menu board by name with different sizes, or each size has its own price, each size would constitute a standard menu item rather than a different flavor, variety, or combination, and each standard menu item must include a calorie declaration.

E. Food on Display

Proposed § 101.11(a) would define food on display as restaurant or restaurant-type food that is visible to the customer before the customer makes a selection, so long as there is not an ordinary expectation of further preparation by the consumer before consumption. In the following paragraphs, we discuss comments on this proposed definition. After considering comments, we are finalizing the definition without changes, except to revise "restaurant or restaurant-type food" to "restaurant-type food" to conform with our deletion of the term "restaurant food" throughout the rule (see section VI.C).

(Comment 50) A few comments agreed with the proposed definition. Other comments suggested modifications to the definition. Some comments recommended that the definition clarify that the food can be self-serve or served by the restaurant staff and that the food could be in the open or behind glass. The comments suggested that the following language be added to the proposed definition: "It includes food that is served by restaurant staff or self-served by customers and foods with Nutrition Facts labels that customers cannot examine without assistance. Food on display can be behind glass or other material or in an open display accessible to consumers."

(Response 50) We decline the requests to revise the proposed definition. The definition applies regardless of whether the food is self-serve or served by the restaurant staff, whether it is in the open or behind glass, or whether it has a Nutrition Facts label that can be examined by a consumer without assistance. In addition, we do not want to appear to limit the definition to only those foods described in the language suggested by the comment.

(Comment 51) One comment asserted that food on display, such as deli meats and cheeses, should be covered even if there is an expectation that there will be further preparation before consuming. A few comments asked that we clarify that foods on display and self-service food do not include fresh breads, cheese wheels, bulk olives, bulk sauces, condiments, and salads sold by the pound like "tuna salad, egg salad, chicken salad, etc." One comment recommended that grocery stores provide calories for bakery items, prepared deli foods such as salads and sandwiches, prepared meals and side dishes, freshly cooked pizza, fountain drinks, salad bars, and other foods sold for immediate consumption. One comment requested an exemption for certain food items prepared for home consumption, such as fruit slices, fruit cups, fruit salads, containers of fresh-cut fruit, fresh squeezed juices, bulk or packaged nuts, seeds, or dried fruit, and similar items that are packaged (or in the case of bulk products, are sold in containers that are available for self-packaging).

(Response 51) As discussed in section VI.C, we are establishing a revised definition of "restaurant-type food" that better reflects the food most like the food offered for sale in restaurants (see Comment 24 and Response 24). Because restaurants typically sell food that is fully prepared, deli meats and cheese generally will not meet the definition of "restaurant-type food," and therefore generally will not be covered. However, certain foods offered for sale in grocery stores that are visible to the consumer before the consumer makes a selection, such as prepared sandwiches, freshly cooked pizza, and salad and hot food bars would meet the definition of restaurant type food and do not have an ordinary expectation of further preparation by the consumer before consumption. These foods meet the definition of foods on display. Other foods commonly offered for sale by grocery stores are not within the definition of "restaurant-type food" and would not be subject to the nutrition disclosure requirements of this rule (e.g., foods such as dried fruit and nuts bought from bulk bins or cases; foods such as loaves of bread, bags or boxes of dinner rolls, whole cakes, bags or boxes of candy or cookies to be eaten over several eating occasions or stored for later use; foods such as deli salads sold by unit of weight that are not self-serve and are not intended solely for individual consumption, either prepacked or packed upon consumer request).

F. Self-Service Food

Proposed § 101.11(a) would define "self-service food" as restaurant or restaurant-type food that is available at a salad bar, buffet line, cafeteria line, or similar self-service facility and that is served by the customers themselves. Self-service food also includes self-service beverages. Comments that addressed the proposed definition supported it. We are finalizing it without changes, except to revise "restaurant or restaurant-type food" to "restaurant-type food" to conform with our deletion of the term "restaurant food" throughout the rule (see section VI.C).

G. Custom Order

Proposed § 101.11(a) would define "custom order" as a food order that is prepared in a specific manner based on an individual customer's request, which requires the restaurant or similar retail food establishment to deviate from its usual preparation of a menu item, e.g., a club sandwich without the bacon if the establishment usually includes bacon in its club sandwich. In the following paragraphs, we discuss comments on this proposed definition. We are finalizing it without change, except for two clarifications. First, we are clarifying that the deviation is from the usual preparation of a standard menu item (emphasis added). Second, we are replacing the term "restaurant or similar retail food establishment" with "covered establishment" to clarify the applicability of the definition (see the discussion in section VI.I).

(Comment 52) Several comments agreed with the proposed definition. Some comments considered that the custom order exemption should apply to custom birthday cakes and sandwiches made to order, because they have no standard preparation from which to deviate.

One comment maintained that supermarkets often preprint labels or previously affix them to packaging (e.g., a paper bag for a sandwich or bread) to improve efficiency or to save costs. Because consumers may request that toppings be added or removed from a food item that is sold in the prelabeled packaging, the comment considered that this would be a custom order that would be exempt from the menu labeling requirements. The comment asked us to clarify that the product would not be misbranded if the packaging contained nutrition information based on the standard preparation.

(Response 52) If a custom birthday cake that is made to order is not routinely included on a menu or menu board or routinely offered as a self-service food or food on display, it would not be covered by the rule, because it is not a standard menu item.

We agree that a sandwich that is made to order can be a custom order if the sandwich is prepared in a specific manner based on an individual customer's request, which requires the covered establishment to deviate from its usual preparation of a standard menu item. However, some sandwiches that are made to order can be variable menu items, depending on how the food is depicted on a menu or menu board or otherwise offered for sale. We discuss the definition of variable menu item in section VIII.D.

We also agree that if a customer asks that toppings be changed or removed from a standard menu item, and the standard menu item normally includes certain toppings, the customer's order is a custom order. In response to the question regarding the use of a preprinted label on a food product, which is subject to modification, we first note that a food order that is prepared in a specific manner based on an individual customer's request, which requires a covered establishment to deviate from its usual preparation of a standard menu item, is a custom order and is not subject to the requirements of section 403(q)(5)(H) of the FD&C Act and this rule. Nevertheless, food labeling, including nutrition labeling, for a food must be truthful and not misleading (section 403(a)(1) of the FD&C Act). If a label on a food bears nutrition information for such food that is false or is otherwise misleading, the food would be misbranded under section 403(a)(1) of the FD&C Act. Accordingly, if a custom order, such as a club sandwich without the bacon if the establishment usually includes bacon in its club sandwich, bears nutrition information in a preprinted label that is false or is otherwise misleading, such food could be misbranded under the FD&C Act. We recommend that covered establishments refrain from affixing preprinted labels on custom orders unless the information included on such labels is truthful and not misleading.

H. Daily Special

Proposed § 101.11(a) would define "daily special" as a menu item that is prepared and offered for sale on a particular day, that is not routinely listed on a menu or offered by the covered establishment, and that is promoted by the covered establishment as a special menu item for that particular day.

Comments that addressed the proposed definition agreed with it. Therefore, we are finalizing it without change, except to add "or menu board" after "not routinely listed on a menu." We inadvertently omitted "or menu board" in the proposed definition.

I. Food That Is Part of a Customary Market Test

Proposed § 101.11(a) would define "food that is part of a customary market test" as food that is marketed in a covered establishment for fewer than 90 consecutive days in order to test consumer acceptance of the product. Comments that addressed the proposed definition agreed with it. Therefore, we are finalizing it without change, except for changes to clarify that food that is part of a customary market test is food "that appears on a menu or menu board for less than 90 consecutive days" rather than food "that is marketed in a covered establishment for fewer than 90 consecutive days." These changes are consistent with section 403(q)(5)(H)(vii)(I)(cc) of the FD&C Act, our description of "food that is part of a customary market test" in the proposed rule (76 FR 19192 at 19205), and with the definition for "temporary menu item" in § 101.11(a).

J. Temporary Menu Item

Proposed § 101.11(a) would define "temporary menu item" as a food that appears on a menu or menu board for less than a total of 60 days per calendar year. Proposed § 101.11(a) would explain that the 60 days includes the total of consecutive and non-consecutive days the item appears on the menu. In the following paragraphs, we discuss comments on this proposed definition. We are finalizing it without change.

(Comment 53) Several comments agreed with the proposed definition. One comment agreed that the 60 days need not be consecutive, but considered that seasonal items (such as the pumpkin-flavored latte example we included in the proposed rule (76 FR 19192 at 19205)) should not be exempt if they are routinely offered each year.

One comment recommended that we change the definition for temporary menu item to shorten the time period from 60 to 45 days, to discourage restaurants from continuously changing menus to avoid calorie disclosure.

(Response 53) The proposed definition for "temporary menu item" focused on the explicit statutory language in section 403(q)(5)(H)(vii) of the FD&C Act, which provides in relevant part that the requirements of section 403(q)(5)(H)(i) through (vi) of the FD&C Act do not apply to "temporary menu items appearing on the menu for less than 60 days per calendar year." Accordingly, we decline to shorten the 60-day time period for temporary menu items to 45 days, as suggested by the comment, because doing so would not be consistent with section 403(q)(5)(H)(vii) of the FD&C Act. We did not propose to go beyond the language of section 403(q)(5)(H)(vii) of the FD&C Act by developing a new category of foods called "seasonal items." We disagree that seasonal items should not be exempt if they are routinely offered each year. Whether a "seasonal item" would be exempt would be determined by whether the seasonal item satisfied the definition of a "temporary menu item" as determined by the total number of consecutive and non-consecutive days per calendar year that the menu item appears on the menu or menu board.

IX. Comments and FDA Response on Proposed § 101.11(b)(1)(i)—Food Subject to the Labeling Requirements

Proposed § 101.11(b) would establish requirements for nutrition labeling of food sold in covered establishments. Proposed § 101.11(b)(1)(i) would provide that the labeling requirement would apply to standard menu items offered for sale in covered establishments. We are finalizing it without change.

Most comments we received about how the nutrition labeling requirements of the rule apply to standard menu items addressed specific labeling requirements (e.g., the provisions of § 101.11(b)(2)(i) for what must be provided on menus and menu boards), and we discuss these comments as they relate to such specific requirements. Immediately following, we discuss one comment more generally directed to the applicability of the labeling requirements of this rule.

(Comment 54) One comment recommended that foods that are preordered and picked up at a later date, such as birthday cakes, boxed lunches, deli trays, and sandwich platters, not be covered by the menu labeling requirements because they are not foods on display, standard menu items, restaurant-type foods, or ordered from a menu or menu board. The comment asserted that restaurant foods are ordered for consumption within a proximate time from when they are ordered, and the person ordering the food intends to eat a portion of the food, whereas catered foods are ordered on behalf of a larger group of people and further ahead of time.

(Response 54) The rule applies to standard menu items offered for sale in covered establishments. The rule defines standard menu item as restaurant-type food that is routinely included on a menu or menu board or routinely offered as a self-service food or food on display (see § 101.11(a)). The definition of "restaurant-type food" in § 101.11(a) captures the time when the food will be eaten relative to when it is purchased or picked up (i.e., usually eaten on the premises, while walking away, or soon after arriving at another location) but when the food is ordered in relation to when it is picked up, and how many people will share the food, have no bearing on the applicability of the rule.

X. Comments and FDA Response on Proposed § 101.11(b)(1)(ii)—Food Not Subject to the Labeling Requirements

A. The Proposed Requirements

Proposed § 101.11(b)(1)(ii) would provide that the labeling requirements would not apply to alcohol beverages; items such as condiments that are placed on the table for general use; daily specials; temporary menu items; custom orders; and food that is part of a customary market test. In sections X.B through X.E of this document, we discuss comments on this proposed provision. After considering comments, we are:

- Narrowing the proposed exemption of alcohol beverages from all of the new requirements for nutrition labeling;

- Clarifying that the exemption applies to condiments that are for general use, including those placed on the table or on or behind the counter; and

- Clarifying that the labeling requirements of paragraph (b) do not apply to self-service food and food on display that is offered for sale for less than a total of 60 days per calendar year or fewer than 90 consecutive days in order to test consumer acceptance.

B. Alcohol

1. Alcoholic Beverages

(Comment 55) Some comments agreed with our proposal that alcoholic beverages should not be covered. Some comments stated that alcoholic beverages should not be considered food within the context of menu labeling. Some comments supporting FDA's proposal to exclude alcoholic beverages referenced Alcohol and Tobacco Tax and Trade Bureau's (TTB's) oversight of alcoholic beverage labels, which includes premarket approval. One comment referred to the district court decision cited in FDA's proposed rule (76 FR 19192 at 19203), Brown-Forman Distillers Corp. v. Mathews, 435 F. Supp. 5 (W.D.Ky. 1976), as evidence that TTB has jurisdiction over the labeling of alcoholic beverages under the Federal Alcohol Administration Act (FAA Act). Another comment argued that requiring calorie declarations for alcoholic beverages will not affect obesity, because obesity is the result of years of poor diet and lack of exercise. Another comment mentioned a 2011 survey of adult consumers and stated that it showed that most consumers do not want to see calorie counts on drink menus and want to order what they want. The comment did not include or provide a reference for the survey.

In contrast, many comments argued that alcoholic beverages should be covered in the final rule. Some comments asserted that it was not the intent of Congress to exclude alcoholic beverages from the menu labeling requirements. According to these comments, Congress excluded some foods from menu labeling, but did not exclude alcoholic beverages. One comment, referring to a press release of two Senators (Ref. 29), contended that Congress rejected lobbyists who wanted to exclude alcoholic beverages.

Several comments argued that FDA has jurisdiction to require menu labeling for alcoholic beverages and not TTB. According to these comments, Congress directed FDA to require menu labeling for all food, including alcoholic beverages. Some comments maintained that FDA currently has exclusive authority to regulate labeling of certain alcoholic beverages (such as wines containing less than 7 percent alcohol by volume and some beers), and another comment stated that FDA had asserted its authority over alcoholic beverages when FDA and the Federal Trade Commission took action on caffeinated alcohol drinks. One comment maintained that in the absence of a specific prohibition or direct conflict, each Agency can regulate alcoholic beverages in line with its mandate. Another comment stated that the U.S. Supreme Court has noted, "The courts are not at liberty to pick and choose among congressional enactments, and when two statutes are capable of coexistence, it is the duty of the courts, absent a clearly expressed congressional intention to the contrary, to regard each as effective," citing Morton v. Mancari, 417 U.S. 535, 551 (1974). Thus, this comment asserted that there is no need to pick and choose between the FAA Act and section 4205 of the ACA because these statutes are capable of coexistence in that they apply to different groups and different practices.

Several comments questioned the applicability of the Brown-Forman Distillers v. Matthews case to section 4205 of the ACA and contended that Brown-Forman addressed the FAA Act and FDA's authority to impose ingredient labeling on alcoholic beverage labels, not nutrition labeling on menus.

Some comments also argued that FDA's proposed position with regard to alcoholic beverage menu labeling contrasts markedly with its position on meat and poultry menu items, the labels for which are regulated by the USDA. One comment remarked that alcohol used in non-beverage foods, such as bananas foster, would be covered under the proposed rule, so not covering alcohol in foods that are beverages would not be consistent.

Comments supported covering alcoholic beverages on public health grounds. Some comments argued that excluding alcoholic beverages is problematic because it may give the false impression that alcoholic drinks do not contribute to the overall caloric consumption of consumers, working against the underlying goal of section 4205 of the ACA. Other comments remarked that alcoholic beverages contribute a substantial portion of average total calories consumed by Americans, representing the fifth leading source of calories in American adults' diets. One comment stated that alcoholic beverages provide more calories per day on average than many of the food items required to be labeled under this law including pizza, hamburgers, and fried potatoes. Another comment argued that calories in alcoholic beverages count toward overweight and obesity just like calories in foods and other beverages.

According to some comments, if some drinks are labeled and some are not, consumers might be confused, and they would not have the information to compare beverage options and make informed choices. Comments also stated that the calorie content of alcoholic beverages can vary widely and cited studies indicating that consumers are likely to have difficulty identifying lower calorie options. Comments argued that failing to provide consumers with calorie information for alcoholic beverages will make it more difficult for them to follow the 2010 Dietary Guidelines' advice to control total calorie intake to manage body weight.

(Response 55) The final rule does not provide a general exemption for alcoholic beverages. As we stated in the proposed rule, alcoholic beverages are "food" under the FD&C Act. Section 201 of the FD&C Act defines "food" to include "articles used for . . . drink for man," "for the purposes of this Act." The nutrition labeling requirements of section 403(q)(5)(H) of the FD&C Act apply to "food that is a standard menu item." In addition, as some comments indicated, section 403(q)(5)(H)(vii) of the FD&C Act deems the requirements of section 403(q)(5)(H) of the FD&C Act inapplicable to certain foods, and alcoholic beverages are not one of them.

While section 4205 of the ACA amends section 403(q) of the FD&C Act, which generally provides nutrition labeling requirements for certain foods, the nutrition labeling requirements in section 4205 are directed specifically toward standard menu items sold in covered restaurants or similar retail food establishments. Within this context, providing nutrition information for an alcoholic beverage for which other labeling is also regulated by TTB provides the same public health benefit as providing the information for other foods. The provisions of section 4205 of the ACA do not apply to and have no effect on the labels of food products sold in packaged form, including alcoholic beverages regulated by TTB.

Thus, we conclude that the nutrient content disclosure requirements in amended section 403(q)(5) of the FD&C Act for standard menu items offered for sale in covered establishments apply to alcoholic beverages, even though the labeling of alcoholic beverage containers under the FAA Act is regulated by TTB.

FDA's decision to include alcoholic beverages in the menu labeling regulations is not inconsistent with the Brown-Forman decision, which addressed the labeling of containers of distilled spirits, wines, and malt beverages subject to the requirements of the FAA Act. This conclusion will not subject the regulated alcohol beverage industry "to 'duplication and inconsistent standards,'" a key basis for the Brown-Forman decision. (Brown-Forman at 14, citing United States v. National Ass'n of Securities Dealers, 422 U.S. 694, 735 (1975)). The requirements we are finalizing here do not directly conflict with any TTB requirements. As comments pointed out, the nutrition labeling requirements of section 4205 of the ACA do not apply to and have no effect on the labels of alcoholic beverage containers. In addition, this final rule applies to covered establishments, while the FAA Act's labeling and advertising regulations generally apply to distillers, brewers, rectifiers, blenders, producers, importers, wholesalers, bottlers, and warehousemen of alcoholic beverages (see 27 U.S.C. 205). In short, the two regulatory schemes address different labeling and different actors; they are "capable of coexistence." (See Manconi, cited previously in this document.)

We also recognize that applying this final rule to alcoholic beverages also regulated by TTB is more consistent with the inclusion of meat, poultry, and egg products that are also regulated by USDA.

From a public health perspective, we agree that requiring nutrition labeling of alcoholic beverages that are standard menu items is more likely to enable consumers to compare beverage options and make informed order selections in covered establishments. In addition, while obesity may be related to poor diet generally and a lack of exercise, calories in alcoholic beverages contribute to obesity and overweight just like calories in other foods. Alcoholic beverages contribute a substantial portion of average total calories consumed by American adults (Ref. 3). Table 2-2 in the 2010 Dietary Guidelines for Americans ("2010 Dietary Guidelines"), jointly developed and issued by HHS and the USDA, reports that alcoholic beverages rank sixth in a list of the top 25 food sources of calories among Americans ages 2 years and older, and fifth in a list of the top 25 food sources of calories among adult Americans ages 19 years and older (Ref. 3). The 2010 Dietary Guidelines also discuss alcohol in Chapter Three, entitled "Foods and Food Components to Reduce" (Ref. 3).

As to the 2011 survey mentioned in one comment, FDA is unable to draw regulatory conclusions from such a survey without being able to evaluate the survey itself.

(Comment 56) Several comments argued that providing calorie and other nutrition labeling for alcoholic beverages on menus is feasible, and one comment provided an example of a menu which included nutrient content disclosures for alcoholic beverages.

(Response 56) We agree with these comments. We see no basis for why providing calorie and other nutrient content information for alcoholic beverages on menus would be less feasible for covered establishments than providing that same information for most other standard menu items.

(Comment 57) Some comments noted that TTB and FDA currently work together through a Memorandum of Understanding (MOU) and asserted that under this MOU, TTB ensures adequate and non-misleading labeling, and FDA ensures safety. One comment that mentioned this MOU indicated that FDA should not begin to regulate the labeling of alcoholic beverages, while another comment that mentioned the MOU indicated that FDA's coverage of alcoholic beverages would not be inconsistent with the specific language of the MOU.

(Response 57) We agree that FDA's coverage of alcoholic beverages in this context does not affect the delineation of responsibilities between FDA and TTB articulated in the MOU. FDA and TTB continue to work together under the MOU, and FDA has consulted with TTB during this rulemaking.

(Comment 58) A few comments maintained that establishing menu labeling requirements for alcoholic beverages could lead to inconsistencies with TTB requirements. One comment pointed out that TTB has rulemaking underway for "serving facts" on alcoholic beverage labels and asserted that, if FDA establishes menu labeling requirements for alcoholic beverages, there could be inconsistencies between nutrition information on labels and menus.

At the time that the proposed rule was issued, alcoholic beverages subject to the labeling regulations under the FAA Act were required to include a statement of average analysis if the label or advertisement made a claim with regard to the calorie or carbohydrate content of the product, and were allowed to include a statement of average analysis for any product. The statement of average analysis listed the number of calories and the number of grams of carbohydrates, fat, and protein per serving (see TTB Ruling 2004-1). In the Federal Register of July 31, 2007 (72 FR 41860), TTB published a proposed rule to amend its regulations to require a Serving Facts statement, which would include a statement of calories, carbohydrates, fat, and protein per serving, on alcohol beverage labels. As of December 1, 2014, the TTB proposed rule has not been finalized. On May 28, 2013, TTB issued a ruling (TTB Ruling 2013-2) (Ref. 30) that allows alcohol beverage industry members to provide consumers with nutritional information on alcoholic beverage container labels by using the format of a statement of average analysis or a Serving Facts statement.

The comment stated that TTB's rulemaking should be completed before FDA takes further action or FDA should exclude alcoholic beverages from the menu labeling requirements permanently. According to another comment, the labels currently approved by TTB with a statement of average analysis apply to a small portion of the total volume of beers produced by small brewers. The comment stated that the format is not consistent with FDA's proposed rule, because TTB only requires the disclosure of calories, carbohydrates, protein, and fat, while FDA's proposed rule would require disclosure of additional nutrients. Without agreement on formats, the comment asserted, compliance with FDA proposed menu labeling could contradict TTB guidance. This comment also stated that without a final rule from TTB, beer sold in bottles and cans on display in covered establishments will not be required to bear nutrition information. Comments stated that if FDA decides to cover alcoholic beverages in its menu labeling rule, FDA should coordinate with TTB to ensure consistency.

Some comments that were against including alcoholic beverages maintained that the cost of laboratory analysis for alcoholic beverages, which they assumed would fall on the alcoholic beverage manufacturers, would be significant, especially for alcoholic beverage manufacturers that are small businesses. One comment asserted that the number of brands and styles of beer produced by small brewers varies dramatically in comparison to large brewers, and without in-house laboratories, which the comment believed large breweries would have, covering alcoholic beverages would have a disproportionate effect on small brewers. Several comments argued that sufficiently accurate calorie values for various types of alcohol are readily available from easily accessible databases, such as the USDA's National Nutrient Database for Standard Reference. One comment suggested allowing covered establishments to list estimated or approximate calorie values by category on wine lists rather than by each brand, recognizing that some types of alcoholic beverages, like red or white wines, contain substantially the same calories regardless of variety.

(Response 58) We agree with some comments and disagree with others. As previously mentioned, the nutrition labeling requirements finalized here do not apply to and have no effect on the labels of alcoholic beverage containers. In addition, the new requirements apply to covered establishments, not to alcoholic beverage manufacturers. In contrast, TTB's "Serving Facts" rulemaking would establish new requirements for disclosures on alcoholic beverage labels and would apply to alcoholic beverage bottlers and importers.

Under this final rule, covered establishments have significant flexibility in choosing a reasonable basis for their nutrient content disclosures, which can include a database such as the USDA's National Nutrient Database for Standard Reference (see § 101.11(c) and the discussion in sections XVIII and XIX). The USDA's National Nutrient Database for Standard Reference includes the categories, "alcoholic beverage, wine, table, red," "alcoholic beverage, wine, table, white," among several other general categories for alcoholic beverages. Consistent with our treatment of other standard menu items (see section XVIII of this document), we will allow covered establishments to use these entries as the bases for their nutrient content disclosures for alcoholic beverages that are standard menu items.

In addition, we recognize that statements of average analysis and nutrient content disclosures under current TTB guidance include four nutrients, and our final rule requires that covered establishments make additional nutrient content disclosures for most standard menu items. However, we do not see these differences as conflicts. Nutrient content information on alcoholic beverage labels that is required by or consistent with TTB regulations or guidance could be a reasonable basis for a covered establishment's corresponding nutrient content disclosures. In addition, many alcoholic beverages will be eligible for the simplified format (see discussion re: § 101.11(b)(2)(ii)(B)(2)). As provided in § 101.11(c)(1), covered establishments may also choose to use a database such as the USDA National Nutrient Database for Standard Reference as the reasonable basis for making their nutrient content disclosures, including disclosures for nutrients that do not currently appear on alcoholic beverage labels. This should address the comment's concerns about malt beverages or other alcoholic beverages that do not currently include nutrient information. FDA has consulted with TTB on this rulemaking and intends to continue to consult with TTB in the future.

(Comment 59) Some comments recommended that drinks that are ordered by customers at the bar and that are not listed on the menu should be exempt from this rule.

(Response 59) We agree with these comments. The final rule covers alcoholic beverages that are standard menu items that are listed on a menu or menu board. However, we are finalizing the proposed exemption for a subset of alcoholic beverages that are not listed on a menu or menu board. Specifically, § 101.11(b)(1)(ii)(B) of the final rule provides that the labeling requirements of § 101.11(b)(2)(iii) do not apply to those alcoholic beverages that are food on display. Our reasons follow. Because these reasons do not apply equally to alcoholic beverages that are self-service foods, § 101.11(b)(1)(ii)(B) of the final rule clarifies that alcoholic beverages that are self-service foods are covered.

First, it is unclear whether covered establishments could provide nutrient content disclosures for alcoholic beverages on display behind a bar that would assist consumers in making informed and healthful order selections. Covered establishments often serve such beverages in mixed drinks, and the amount of each alcoholic beverage and other mixers they serve to consumers may vary depending on the drink ordered. Section 403(q)(5)(H)(iii) of the FD&C Act requires that calories for self-service food and food on display be declared per serving or per item. Examples of other food on display include: Burrito fillings behind a counter at a burrito restaurant where burritos are made to order and salad ingredients behind a counter at a quick-service salad restaurant where salads are made to order. An employee generally adds a standard serving of each burrito filling or salad ingredient when asked by the customer, e.g., a standard measured weight of meat or a standard spoonful of beans. Nutrient content declarations based on those standardized servings are directly applicable to consumers' order selections.

Even for some foods on display that have servings that vary, e.g., ice cream (where a customer can order one, two, or three scoops) or burrito fillings (where a customer can order extra cheese), the amount the customer receives is generally a simple multiple of a base serving. Ice cream would likely be labeled per scoop and cheese would likely be labeled per standard portion, with extra cheese being double the standard portion.

In contrast, covered establishments with bottles of alcoholic beverages on display behind a bar generally serve varying amounts of alcohol and mixers depending on the establishment's recipes for the various beverages ordered. For example, at a given covered establishment, a martini recipe might have 2 ounces (oz.) of gin and 0.5 oz. vermouth; a cosmopolitan recipe might have 3.5 oz. vodka, a dash of triple sec, a dash of cranberry juice, 1 tsp of sugar, and 1 oz. of lime juice; and a grasshopper recipe might have 1 oz. white crème de cacao, 1 oz. green crème de menthe, and milk or cream to fill the glass (Ref. 31). As a result, the covered establishment does not have a standard serving on which to base a nutrient content declaration for each ingredient that will be directly applicable to all routinely ordered mixed drinks. In addition, recipes for even well-known drinks, like margaritas, may differ from one chain of restaurants to another, and consumers are unlikely to know a particular establishment's recipe while ordering (Ref. 31). It is difficult to see how a consumer would use an establishment's nutrient content disclosure on a bottle of alcohol behind a bar in choosing which mixed drink to order.

Section 403(q)(5)(H)(x)(II)(aa) of the FD&C Act requires FDA to "consider standardization of recipes and methods of preparation" and "variations in ingredients" in issuing these regulations. Therefore, in finalizing the exemption for alcoholic beverages that do not appear on menus or menu boards, we considered that recipes and methods of preparation for alcoholic mixed drinks are not standardized throughout the industry. In addition, we considered the variations of the amounts of alcoholic beverages and other mixers served in mixed drinks in a given covered establishment.

Alcoholic beverages that are on display differ from other food on display in additional relevant ways. Alcoholic beverages that are on display, particularly bottles of alcohol that are behind a bar, often appear to be on display primarily for decoration or storage, not to aid consumers in selecting among food options. This contrasts with most food that is on display, which is on display in order to aid consumers in selecting among food options (e.g., food choices at a salad bar, cookie varieties at a mall cookie counter). Once covered establishments comply with these new regulations, consumers in covered establishments who look at food on display to decide which displayed food they would like to consume will be able to consider calorie information on signs adjacent to the food and adjust their selection if they choose.

In contrast, bottles of alcoholic beverages often are displayed very close together, layered on top of each other, staged in low lighting or back lighting, or placed very high. In other words, they are displayed in a manner that does not enable consumers to easily identify the particular alcoholic beverages available to assist them in making their selections. In addition, bartenders often use bottles of alcoholic beverages under the bar—that are not on display—to mix alcoholic drinks. Finally, at many covered establishments that serve alcoholic beverages, mixed drinks and other alcoholic beverages that are not on menus or menu boards are ordered by customers sitting at tables, from which the bar could be completely out of sight.

Based on the above considerations, we are exempting alcoholic beverages that are food on display and are not self-service food. Because these considerations do not apply readily to self-service alcoholic beverages (e.g., bottles of beer in a cooler near the register at a quick service restaurant), self-service alcoholic beverages are covered by the final rule. Therefore, § 101.11(b)(1)(ii)(B) of the final rule provides that the labeling requirements of § 101.11(b)(2)(iii) for standard menu items that are self-service or on display do not apply to alcoholic beverages that are foods on display and are not self-service foods.

C. Condiments

(Comment 60) Several comments recommended that covered establishments provide calorie information for all condiments. Other comments maintained that calorie information should be provided for condiments if they are part of the standard menu item. One comment recommended that the following be added to the provision: "Condiments and sauces included as an ingredient or standard accompaniment to a menu item must be included in the nutrition information calculated for that item."

Another comment asked us to clarify that if condiments are provided for optional use, they should not be included in the calorie declaration. As an example, if a container of ketchup is provided on the side with a hamburger and the consumer can decide whether to use it, the container of ketchup should be treated the same as a bottle on the table and be exempted from calorie declaration. Another comment asked that the words "on the table" be removed from the provision and that the statute be interpreted to encompass condiments and other items kept behind the counter for general use. This comment explained that its establishment does not typically have tables as most of the business is take-out, and the condiments are kept behind the counter and available to the consumer upon request.

One comment suggested that the exemption for condiments include only those self-serve items that are calorie free or that have a Nutrition Facts label. Another comment recommended that self-serve restaurants have the flexibility to determine which items can reasonably be considered condiments for general use, noting that many of its restaurants have an extensive "spice bar" that contains dozens of different spices, seasonings, and other condiments that any customer can use, regardless of that customer's order or food selections. The comment maintained that the regulation should be clear that all spices and seasonings fall in this exempt category.

(Response 60) We are clarifying the exemption for condiments. Section 403(q)(5)(H)(vii)(I)(aa) of the FD&C Act provides that the requirements of section 403(q)(5)(H) of the FD&C Act do not apply to "items that are not listed on a menu or menu board (such as condiments and other items placed on the table or counter for general use)." We affirm our tentative conclusion in the proposed rule that, given the phrase "for general use," it is reasonable to interpret section 403(q)(5)(H)(vii)(I)(aa) of the FD&C Act to apply to foods, such as many condiments, that are available for use by any customer in the covered establishment, regardless of the customer's particular order or food selection (76 FR 19192 at 19205). For example, it is reasonable to apply section 403(q)(5)(H)(vii)(I)(aa) of the FD&C Act to maple syrup that is provided in a bulk container or bottles of ketchup that are available for any customer to add to his or her food.

However, we agree that the calorie declaration for a standard menu item must include the number of calories in the condiment if the condiment is used as a component in the standard menu item, as usually prepared and offered for sale. In such situation, the nutrient declarations for the standard menu item in the written nutrition information required by section 403(q)(5)(H)(ii)(III) of the FD&C Act and § 101.11(b)(2)(ii) must also include the nutrient amounts from the condiment because the condiment is used as a component in the standard menu item. The exemption in section 403(q)(5)(H)(vii)(I)(aa) of the FD&C Act does not apply to condiments that are part of a standard menu item, as the standard menu item is usually prepared and offered for sale. For example, if a covered establishment ordinarily offers for sale burgers containing ketchup and mayonnaise added by the establishment, the ketchup and mayonnaise would be part of the standard menu item as usually prepared and offered for sale, and the calorie declaration for the standard menu item would include the calories in the ketchup and mayonnaise. Likewise, if a covered establishment ordinarily provides each customer who orders pancakes with a single serving container of maple syrup, the maple syrup would be part of the standard menu item as usually prepared and offered for sale, and the calorie declaration for the standard menu item would include the calories in the single serving container of maple syrup. Similarly, as noted previously in this document, in these situations, the nutrient declarations for the standard menu item in the written nutrition information required by section 403(q)(5)(H)(ii)(III) of the FD&C Act and § 101.11(b)(2)(ii) must also include the nutrient amounts from the condiment because the condiment is used as a component in the standard menu item.

We see no difference between a condiment brought to the table for general use and a condiment kept behind the counter for general use (and then provided to a customer who requests it), provided that such condiments are not listed on the menu or menu board separately or as part of a standard menu item. Therefore, we agree that condiments that are behind the counter for general use are exempt from the nutrition labeling requirements of section 403(q)(5)(H) of the FD&C Act under section 403(q)(5)(H)(vii)(I)(aa) of the FD&C Act. For clarity, we have revised § 101.11(b)(1)(ii) to explicitly provide that the labeling requirements in paragraph (b) do not apply to items such as condiments that are for general use, including those placed on the table or on or behind the counter. (Emphasis added.) As revised, § 101.11(b)(1)(ii) includes condiments placed "on" the counter in accordance with section 403(q)(5)(H)(vii)(I)(aa) of the FD&C Act and in order to take into account varying business practices.

We disagree that the exemption for condiments should include only those self-serve items that are calorie free or that have a Nutrition Facts label. The exemptions under § 101.11(b)(1)(ii) are based on the language of section 403(q)(5)(H)(vii) of the FD&C Act. Section 403(q)(5)(H)(vii) of the FD&C Act generally provides that the nutrition labeling requirements of section 403(q)(5)(H) of the FD&C Act do not apply to certain foods, including certain condiments. Section 403(q)(5)(H)(vii) of the FD&C Act does not qualify such exemptions based on the caloric content of the food or the fact that some food would be available in packaged form that provides a Nutrition Facts label. However, we note that under § 101.11(b)(2)(iii)(C), a covered establishment would not be required to provide the written nutrition information required by section 403(q)(5)(H)(ii)(III) of the FD&C Act and § 101.11(b)(2)(ii) for a self-service food or food on display that is a packaged food insofar as it bears nutrition labeling information required by and in accordance with § 101.11(b)(2)(ii) and the packaged food, including its label, can be examined by a consumer before purchasing the food.

We also note that spices and seasonings (such as crushed dried peppers) are considered condiments that are exempt from the requirements of section 403(q)(5)(H) of the FD&C Act under section 403(q)(5)(H)(vii)(I)(aa) of the FD&C Act, provided that they are for general use by customers regardless of their particular order selection.

D. Daily Specials, Temporary Menu Items, Custom Orders, and Food That Is Part of a Customary Market Test

(Comment 61) Several comments agreed with the proposed exemption for daily specials. One comment disagreed with the proposed exemption because the burden to calculate the calories and other nutrition information is not so great for daily specials to justify this exemption. The comment maintained that consumers often buy what is on sale and that excluding daily specials from the requirements of section 403(q)(5)(H) of the FD&C Act would undermine the purpose of the statute.

One comment opposed the proposed exemption for temporary menu items because temporary menu items represent a large portion of what is ordered on a single day at some establishments.

Several comments agreed with the proposed exemption for food that is part of a customary market test. One comment opposed the proposed exemption because chain restaurants test market their menu items carefully before they mass market menu items and the determination of the nutrient content should be part of that process. The comment asserted that disclosing the calorie content of the food may impact the consumer's decision to purchase the food and may impact the establishment's decision whether to include that food on the regular menu.

(Response 61) We are retaining in § 101.11(b)(1)(ii) the exemptions for daily specials, temporary menu items, custom orders, and food that is part of a customary market test. Section 403(q)(5)(H)(vii) of the FD&C Act specifically exempts such items from the requirements of section 403(q)(5)(H) of the FD&C Act regardless of the factors identified by the comments, such as how the burden to calculate calories for these items compares to the burden to calculate calories for standard menu items; the tendency of consumers to buy what is on sale; and whether a chain restaurant could determine nutrition information.

Section 403(q)(5)(H)(vii) of the FD&C Act generally provides that the nutrition labeling requirements of section 403(q)(5)(H) of the FD&C Act do not apply to certain foods, including daily specials, temporary menu items appearing on the menu for less than 60 days per calendar year, custom orders, and food that is part of a customary market test appearing on the menu for less than 90 days under terms and conditions established by FDA. Accordingly, § 101.11(b)(1)(ii) provides that the labeling requirements of § 101.11(b) do not apply to such foods and § 101.11(a) defines the terms for such foods. We note that, as discussed in Response 62, self-service food and food on display that are temporary menu items or part of a customary market test, but do not appear on a menu, are also exempt from the requirements of section 403(q)(5)(H) of the FD&C Act because these foods are not standard menu items.

However, neither section 403(q)(5)(H) of the FD&C Act nor this rule would prevent a covered establishment from voluntarily declaring calories or providing written nutrition information for condiments, daily specials, temporary menu items, or food that is part of a customary market test.

Regarding daily specials, we note that we would not consider an item that is offered every week on a particular day (e.g., the Monday special) to be a "daily special" because it is being routinely offered for sale (i.e., every Monday). In addition, we would not consider a standard menu item, as defined in this rule, to be a "daily special" if it is offered at a discounted price on a particular day (e.g., a turkey club sandwich that is a standard menu item and normally costs 5 dollars, but is specially advertised as costing only 4 dollars on Fridays).

(Comment 62) In the proposed rule (76 FR 19192 at 19205), we noted that self-service food and food on display that do not appear on menus or menu boards would not be considered temporary menu items or food that is part of a customary market test. Therefore, even if a self-service food or food on display that does not appear on a menu or menu board is only offered by a covered establishment for a limited time, such as a pumpkin spice muffin available only in November, we tentatively concluded that the nutrition information declaration requirements in section 403(q)(5)(H) of the FD&C Act would still apply.

Several comments that addressed the exemption in proposed § 101.11(b)(1)(ii) for temporary menu items and food that is part of a customary market test considered that this exemption should apply to self-service food and food on display even though such foods may not "appear[ ] on a menu" as described in section 403(q)(5)(H)(vii) of the FD&C Act. These comments said that Congress excluded temporary menu items and customary market test items from the nutrition labeling requirements of section 403(q)(5)(H) of the FD&C Act because it recognized that restaurants should be able to test products (many of which fail and are discontinued quickly) without incurring the significant costs associated with changing their menu and compiling nutritional information. The comments considered that this same reasoning applies to temporary menu items and customary market test items offered in self-service restaurants (whether the restaurant displays items on a menu, menu board, or individual signs). The comments asserted that for buffet-type restaurants, there would be significant costs in attempting to improve and change their menus for temporary menu items and food that is being market tested and that these costs would not be incurred by other kinds of non-buffet-type restaurants.

(Response 62) We agree with these comments that the statutory exemptions for temporary menu items appearing on the menu for less than 60 days per calendar year and customary market test items appearing on the menu for less than 90 days apply to self-service foods and foods on display that fall into those categories, as defined in § 101.11(a). We also agree that a self-service food and food on display that does not appear on a menu or menu board but otherwise meets the definition for temporary menu items or food that is part of a customary market, in that the food is offered for sale in a covered establishment for less than a total of 60 days per calendar year or fewer than 90 consecutive days in order to test consumer acceptance, should not be required to comply with the requirements of section 403(q)(5)(H) of the FD&C Act and § 101.11. The requirements of section 403(q)(5)(H) of the FD&C Act and § 101.11 apply to foods that are standard menu items. However, self-service foods and foods on display that do not appear on a menu or menu board, but otherwise meet the definitions for temporary menu items or food that is part of customary market test, along with the foods described in section 403(q)(5)(H)(vii) of the FD&C Act, do not meet the definition for a standard menu item in § 101.11(a) because such self-service foods and foods on display are neither "routinely included on a menu or menu board" nor "routinely offered as a self-service food or food on display." Like temporary menu items or food that is part of a customary market test appearing on a menu or menu board, as described in section 403(q)(5)(H)(vii) of the FD&C Act, self-service foods and foods on display that do not appear on a menu or menu board but otherwise meet the definitions for temporary menu items or food that is part of a customary market are offered for a limited time and are subject to variation and discontinuation depending on the seasonality and consumer response. Thus, these foods, like the foods described in section 403(q)(5)(H)(vii) of the FD&C Act, are not standard menu items and the requirements of this rule do not apply to such foods.

For these reasons, we are modifying § 101.11(b)(1)(ii)(A). First, we are specifying in § 101.11(b)(1)(ii)(A) that the labeling requirements in paragraph (b) do not apply to foods that are not standard menu items. Second, we are specifying in § 101.11(b)(1)(ii)(A)(1) that such foods that are not standard menu items include items such as condiments that are for general use, including those placed on the table or on or behind the counter; daily specials; temporary menu items; custom orders; and food that is part of a customary market test. Third, we are specifying in § 101.11(b)(1)(ii)(A)(2) that such foods that are not standard menu items also include self-service food and food on display that is offered for sale for less than a total of 60 days per calendar year or fewer than 90 consecutive days in order to test consumer acceptance.

E. Additional Comments on Food That Is Part of a Customary Market Test

(Comment 63) Some comments asked us to clarify that if a food is tested in more than one location, the 90-day period is applied to each location. These comments maintained that it is common for restaurants and similar retail food establishments to conduct iterative tests to evaluate the performance of a menu item and change the menu in light of test results. For example, the results of iterative tests may lead to "changes in product makeup, including size, shape, taste profile, and preparation," with accompanying changes to the underlying nutrient content. The comment asked us to clarify that a food that changes in such a manner during a market test is a new food, and the 90-day period would begin again. One comment asked us to confirm that a market test may be conducted in multiple locations and that the 90-day period starts when the testing begins in a particular location.

(Response 63) As we discussed in the proposed rule (76 FR 19192 at 19205) and as suggested by the comments, in some cases, a chain of restaurants and similar retail food establishments may test a new product in different locations within the chain and in more than one region of the country at different times. We conclude that a "customary market test," for the purposes of § 101.11, refers to a test in a single covered establishment. Therefore, we agree with the comments that the 90-day period for the food that is part of a customary market test applies to each covered establishment that offers for sale food that is part of a customary market test.

Further, we recognize that restaurants and similar retail food establishments may change the foods that they are market testing in an iterative process. Therefore, we agree that if a food changes in ways such as those noted in the comments (e.g., changes in product makeup, including size, shape, taste profile, and preparation), it would be a new food and the 90-day period would begin again. We would consider the food to be a new food if it is not made with the same general recipe or same ingredients or otherwise has a significant change in the nutrient profile during the market test. For example, we would consider a soup prepared without meat, and a soup prepared with added sausage, to be different foods and would expect differences between the nutrient profiles of these different foods.

XI. Comments and FDA Response on Proposed § 101.11(b)(2)(i)(A)(

Proposed § 101.11(b)(2)(i)(A)(1) to (b)(2)(i)(A)(3) would require that covered establishments declare the number of calories contained in each standard menu item listed on the menu or menu board, as usually prepared and offered for sale in the following manner:

- The number of calories must be listed adjacent to the name or the price of the associated standard menu item, in a type size no smaller than the name or the price of the associated standard menu item, whichever is smaller, in the same color, or a color at least as conspicuous as the name of the associated standard menu item, and with the same contrasting background as the name of the associated standard menu item (proposed § 101.11(b)(2)(i)(A)(1)).

- The calories must be declared to the nearest 5-calorie increment up to and including 50 calories and to the nearest 10-calorie increment above 50 calories, except that amounts less than 5 calories may be expressed as zero (proposed § 101.11(b)(2)(i)(A)(2)).

- The term "Calories" or "Cal" must appear as a heading above a column listing the number of calories for each standard menu item or adjacent to the number of calories for each standard menu item. If the term "Calories" or "Cal" appears as a heading above a column of calorie declarations, the term must be in a type size no smaller than the smallest type size of the name or price of any menu item on that menu or menu board in the same color or a color at least as conspicuous as that name or price and in the same contrasting background as that name or price. If the term "Calories" or "Cal" appears adjacent to the number of calories for the standard menu item, the term "Calories" or "Cal" must appear in the same type size and in the same color and contrasting background as the number of calories (proposed § 101.11(b)(2)(i)(A)(3)).

In the following paragraphs, we discuss comments on these proposed provisions. After considering the comments, we are:

- Revising § 101.11(b)(2)(i)(A) to specify that in the case of multiple-serving standard menu items, the calorie declaration must be for the whole menu item as listed on the menu or menu board, as usually prepared and offered for sale (e.g., "pizza pie: 1600 calories"), or per discrete serving unit as long as the discrete serving unit (e.g., pizza slice) and total number of discrete serving units are declared on the menu or menu board, and the menu item is usually prepared and offered for sale divided in discrete serving units (e.g., "pizza pie: 200 cal/slice, 8 slices").

- Revising § 101.11(b)(2)(i)(A)(1) to provide additional flexibility for the contrasting background used for the calorie declaration;

- Making a conforming editorial change to the requirement for the color used for the calorie declaration for grammatical consistency; and

- Making an editorial correction for clarity to insert "the type size of" between "no smaller than" and "the name or the price" in § 101.11(b)(2)(i)(A)(1).

(Comment 64) Many comments regarding the proposed requirement that the number of calories contained in each standard menu item listed on the menu or menu board be declared as usually prepared and offered for sale addressed the discussion in the proposed rule regarding how the calorie labeling requirements on menus and menu boards would apply to multiple-serving foods that are standard menu items (76 FR 19192 at 19203-19204). Many comments agreed with the view we expressed in the proposed rule that section 403(q)(5)(H) of the FD&C Act requires that calories be declared for standard menu items regardless of how many servings are included in the item (76 FR 19192 at 19203). The comments asserted that servings vary by product and by portions taken by consumers. One comment considered that if a menu item is to be shared, it would be easier for consumers to determine how many people will share the item and divide the calories accordingly than for the restaurant to choose how many servings are in a menu item. The comment said that we should not allow restaurants to choose how many servings are in a menu item.

Many other comments opposed listing the calories for the entire standard menu item and instead supported the listing of calories per serving. Some comments asserted that listing calories per serving would be less confusing, would be consistent with calorie declarations on packaged food, and would not require consumers to do a calculation. One comment agreed with our determination that a multiple-serving food is a standard menu item but disagreed with our tentative conclusion that the calorie declaration should be for the entire multiple-serving food because providing calories for the entire multiple-serving food would not be helpful and would be detrimental for those who need the information per serving (e.g., diabetics). A few comments asked us to provide an option to permit either the declaration of calories for the entire multiple-serving menu item, or the declaration of the number of servings and the calories per serving. As an example, one comment suggested that a restaurant selling a four-serving family-style platter of pasta could comply either by disclosing that the whole menu item contains 2,000 calories, or by disclosing that the menu item consists of 4 servings, 500 calories per serving.

One comment pointed out that if we required calorie declaration for an entire multiple-serving food, nutrition information would be inconsistent in some instances. For example, a cheesecake from a display case would have different nutrition information than the same cheesecake in prepackaged form, because the first would list calories for the entire item whereas the second would list calories per serving. One comment suggested that, for foods that are not appetizers or desserts that are intended to serve more than one person, calorie disclosure should include the number of persons intended to be served and the calorie content per serving.

A few comments recommended that calories for pizza be listed per slice. One comment reported that it received complaints when it provided calorie information for the entire listed pizza. The comment provided a report of consumer research showing that 60 percent of consumers preferred calorie information per slice. The report of this survey was submitted with the comment (Ref. 32). Some comments referred to our previous statements that nutrition information should be declared per serving. For example, in our proposed rule on "Food Labeling: Serving Sizes," we stated that for "[f]oods in large discrete units," "the household measure most meaningful for these products is a fraction of the whole unit." (56 FR 60394 at 60410, November 27, 1991). Another comment referred to statements in our 2008 "Guidance for Industry: A Labeling Guide for Restaurants and Other Retail Establishments Selling Away-From-Home Foods (the 2008 restaurant labeling guide) (Ref. 10) that generally the nutrition information should be presented on a per serving basis. For example, the 2008 restaurant labeling guide states that "[i]t is especially important that the basis be declared when a food is available in more than one size serving (e.g., pizza that is available whole and byslice). . . . The restaurant may provide additional information, such as `8 slices per medium 16-inch pizza, 1 slice contains . . .' to help consumers put nutrition information in context."

Other comments urged us to clarify that a covered establishment can voluntarily provide nutrition information per serving. These comments suggested that we revise the rule to indicate that fact. These comments suggested adding the following to § 101.11(b)(2)(i)(A): "(5) For items that could serve more than one person, such as a large pizza or a bucket of chicken, calories must be listed per standard menu item as offered for sale and listed on the menu or menu board or as placed on display. In addition, restaurants and similar retail food establishments may also voluntarily provide nutrition information per serving."

(Response 64) Listing calories for multiple-serving standard menu items as usually prepared and offered for sale by a covered establishment is consistent with section 403(q)(5)(H) of the FD&C Act. As discussed in the proposed rule, section 403(q)(5)(H) of the FD&C Act requires covered establishments to disclose calorie information for standard menu items as usually prepared and offered for sale, regardless of how many servings are included in the menu item (76 FR 19192 at 19203).

Based on the comments that supported calorie declarations for multiple-serving standard menu items "per serving," the complexity of consumer eating habits and preferences described by the comments, and the variety of ways that covered establishments may choose to usually prepare and offer their foods for sale, we have revised the rule's calorie declaration requirements for multiple-serving standard menu items on menus and menu boards.

Where a multiple-serving standard menu item is usually prepared and offered for sale divided in discrete serving units (e.g., slices of pizza), we are allowing covered establishments to provide the calorie declaration per discrete serving unit, subject to some additional requirements. If a covered establishment declares calories for a multiple-serving standard menu item per discrete serving unit, the establishment must also declare the discrete serving unit and the total number of discrete serving units in the menu item on the menu or menu board so that the consumer can make a fully-informed decision before selecting the item.

We are allowing calorie declarations per discrete serving unit for multiple-serving standard menu items that are usually prepared and offered for sale divided in discrete serving units because such division will likely enable consumers to easily identify the discrete serving unit (e.g., pizza slice) and therefore keep track of the number of serving units consumed. Pizza slices that come in a pie, or breadsticks that come in a bunch (e.g., "pizza pie: 200 cal/slice, 8 slices;" "breadsticks: 150 cal/stick, 5 sticks") are examples of multiple-serving standard menu items that are usually prepared and offered for sale divided in discrete serving units. If consumers share such a menu item, the discrete serving units provide a distinct division along which portions can be divided, thereby allowing consumers to keep track of calories consumed by either adding or multiplying the per discrete serving unit calorie declaration based on the number of serving units consumed. Providing the number of calories per discrete serving unit and the total number of discrete serving unit contained in the menu item for multiple-serving standard menu items that are usually prepared and offered for sale divided in discrete units enables consumers to determine the number of calories they may actually consume and therefore enables consumer to make informed dietary choices.

However, where a multiple-serving standard menu item is not usually prepared and offered for sale divided in discrete serving units, covered establishments must declare calories for the entire menu item listed on the menu or menu board, as usually prepared and offered for sale. We disagree with the comment that said a calorie declaration for a whole multiple-serving standard menu item would be unhelpful or detrimental. If consumers decide to share a multiple-serving standard menu item, they can divide the total number of calories by the number of individuals sharing it. We clarify—as one comment suggested—that for multiple-serving standard menu items that are not usually prepared and offered for sale divided in discrete serving units, we would not object if a covered establishment decided to voluntarily declare calories per serving, in addition to the calories for the entire standard menu item.

(Comment 65) A few comments recommended that calories be declared per reference amount customarily consumed (RACC) or by household measure. A RACC represents the amount of food customarily consumed at one eating occasion (§ 101.12 (21 CFR 101.12)). A few comments considered that listing calories per serving based on the RACC would be consistent with the labeling of packaged food. One comment noted that customers are used to seeing information per serving even though actual consumption may not be aligned with the RACC.

(Response 65) We assume that "household measure" refers to measures such as "cups" or "tablespoons." RACCs represent the amount of food customarily consumed at one eating occasion and are calculated for a variety of foods purchased by consumers in establishments such as grocery stores (see § 101.12). RACCs are based on data set forth in national food consumption surveys and other sources of information on serving sizes of food, including serving sizes used in dietary guidance recommendations or recommended by other authoritative systems or organizations, serving sizes used by manufacturers and grocers, and serving sizes used by other countries (§ 101.12(a)). We developed RACCs as the basis for determining serving sizes for specific products for the purpose of declaration of nutrition information on product labels.

We disagree that calories for standard menu items should be declared per RACC or by household measure. Section 403(q)(5)(H) of the FD&C Act requires covered establishments to disclose the number of calories contained in a standard menu item "as usually prepared and offered for sale." Although many standard menu items may have an associated RACC, others may not. Even if some standard menu items have an associated RACC, each covered establishment is free to choose the amount of food offered for sale in its standard menu items, and section 403(q)(5)(H) of the FD&C Act does not require covered establishments to prepare and offer standard menu items in particular amounts, such as RACCs.

(Comment 66) Some comments considered that calories should be declared for each size of a menu item (such as "upgrades" or "upsized options" and "downsized options") offered on menus and menu boards. Some comments linked the requirement to declare calories for different sizes to different prices—e.g., by considering that calories must be declared for any size option that has a distinct price on the menu or menu board. Some comments specifically addressed fixed combination meals and considered that calories should be declared for fixed combination meals available in multiple sizes.

One comment asked us to allow the restaurant to list calories for a 6-inch version of a sandwich and provide a statement on the menus and menu boards that the 12-inch sandwich is double that amount.

(Response 66) The calorie labeling requirements of § 101.11(b)(2)(i)(A) apply to each standard menu item listed on the menu or menu board, as usually prepared and offered for sale. Thus, if a standard menu item (such as fries or onion rings) is listed on the menu or menu board in more than one size (such as "small" and "large"), the menu or menu board must provide calories for each size, following the format requirements of § 101.11(b)(2)(i)(A)(1), (b)(2)(i)(A)(2), and (b)(2)(i)(A)(3). Likewise, if a fixed combination meal (i.e., a meal consisting of components that are not subject to a consumer's selection, such as a burger and fries) is listed on the menu or menu board in more than one size (e.g., a hamburger with small fries or large fries), the menu or menu board must provide calories for each size of the fixed combination meal, also following the format requirements of § 101.11(b)(2)(i)(A)(1), (b)(2)(i)(A)(2), and (b)(2)(i)(A)(3).

If a 6-inch sandwich and a 12-inch sandwich are both standard menu items listed on a menu or menu board, or are on display in a covered establishment, the establishment must disclose the number of calories for each sandwich size, following the format requirements of § 101.11(b)(2)(i)(A)(1), (b)(2)(i)(A)(2), and (b)(2)(i)(A)(3) or § 101.11(b)(2)(iii) as applicable, unless the sandwich is exempt from the nutrition labeling requirements under section 403(q)(5)(H)(vii) of the FD&C Act.

(Comment 67) One comment interpreted the phrase "as usually prepared" within "as usually prepared and offered for sale" in proposed § 101.11(b)(2)(i)(A) to be a "standard formula," "recommended formula," "standard build," or any other term that means a predetermined method of preparation designed to ensure that all menu offerings are nutritionally consistent and uniform throughout all covered establishments in a chain.

One comment agreed that the number of calories for a standard menu item should be measured based on how the standard menu item is usually prepared and offered for sale, but expressed concern about build-as-you-go menu items. The comment explained that, a covered establishment might post the number of calories for a build-as-you-go menu item as an "undressed" sandwich (the comment did not define this term), giving the false impression that the sandwich has fewer calories than it may actually contain as prepared by the covered restaurant and then consumed by a customer. This comment contended that this type of sandwich should be considered a variable menu item with calories posted as a range (i.e., in accordance with proposed § 101.11(b)(2)(i)(A)(4)) that includes the undressed sandwich and the fully built one, because there is standardization with respect to the specific amount of each particular food item or condiment that consumers can add to the build-as-you-go menu item. As evidence for this view, the comment referred to the standard extra charge for items such as an extra scoop of guacamole.

(Response 67) We agree that "standard build" or "recommended formula" is consistent with the term "as usually prepared and offered for sale." However, it is the build that is standard to any given covered establishment, rather than recommendations or standards by or from the chain as a whole, that dictates the nutrition information that would be required to be declared for standard menu items in a particular covered establishment.

Regarding the comment expressing concern about build-as-you-go menu items, we first note that a build-as-you-go menu item, such as a sandwich with the option of adding different fixings, that is a standard menu item, likely would be considered a variable menu item. As discussed previously in this document (see sections VIII.B and VIII.D), § 101.11(a) defines the terms, "standard menu item" and "variable menu item." A variable menu item is defined in § 101.11(a) as a standard menu item that comes in different flavors, varieties, or combinations, and is listed as a single menu item. A variable menu item is one type of standard menu item. In the proposed rule, we provided examples of "standard menu items"—e.g., a hamburger, a combination meal, a specific type of pizza (e.g., deluxe pizza), potato salad that is routinely offered at a salad bar, pancakes that are routinely offered at a buffet, and pudding that is routinely offered at a cafeteria line (76 FR 19192 at 19203). We also provided examples of variable menu items—i.e., foods that may have flavoring options (e.g., a milkshake that is available in vanilla, chocolate, or strawberry flavors) or topping options (e.g., pizza prepared with a selection of toppings) (76 FR 19192 at 19204). In the following paragraphs, we provide additional examples relevant to build-as-you-go menu items and explain how the calorie labeling requirements of § 101.11(b)(2)(i)(A) would apply.

A standard menu item that is listed on a menu or menu board that is not a variable menu item, in that it does not come in different flavors, varieties, or combinations that are listed as a single menu item, (e.g., a turkey and Swiss cheese sandwich on whole wheat bread with mustard), would be subject to the calorie declaration format requirements of § 101.11(b)(2)(i)(A)(1) to (b)(2)(i)(A)(3), but would not be subject to the additional format requirements for variable menu items (proposed § 101.11(b)(2)(i)(A)(4)), established in this rule as § 101.11(b)(2)(i)(A)(4) through (b)(2)(i)(A)(8); see the discussion of the additional format requirements for variable menu items in section XII). However, a standard menu item that comes in different flavors, varieties, or combinations, and is listed as a single menu item on a menu or menu board (e.g., a "turkey and cheese sandwich," with different options for the type of bread (e.g., whole wheat or white), cheese (e.g., Swiss, provolone, cheddar), fixings (e.g., onions, lettuce, tomato), and condiments (mustard, ketchup, mayonnaise)) would be a variable menu item subject to both the general calorie declaration format requirements of § 101.11(b)(2)(i)(A)(1) to (b)(2)(i)(A)(3) for all standard menu items and the additional format requirements for variable menu items as applicable in § 101.11(b)(2)(i)(A)(4) through (b)(2)(i)(A)(8).

(Comment 68) Several comments agreed with proposed § 101.11(b)(2)(i)(A)(2) and the flexibility in proposed § 101.11(b)(2)(i)(A)(3) to permit the abbreviation "Cal" for calories.

Several comments addressed the placement provisions for the calorie declarations in proposed § 101.11(b)(2)(i)(A)(1) and (b)(2)(i)(A)(3). A few comments agreed that the number of calories be posted next to the name or price of the menu item (proposed § 101.11(b)(2)(i)(A)(1)) and that the term "Calories" or "Cal" be next to the number of calories (proposed § 101.11(b)(2)(i)(A)(3)). One comment found that customers in its restaurants confused calorie declarations with price declarations and noted that declaring calories in the same font, size, and contrast as the price would create confusion, even if the color is different.

Another comment from a chain restaurant found that consumers in its restaurants were confused when calories were posted next to the name of the menu item and thought the number of calories was the order number; to address this confusion, the restaurant put the number of calories after the price and in a different color, font, and size. This comment emphasized its 3 years of experience with posting calorie declarations and provided examples of its menu boards to demonstrate how it communicates calorie information about its menu offerings. This comment agreed that calorie information should be listed in a manner that allows the customer to easily identify the calories associated with a particular menu item, but disagreed that listing calories adjacent to a menu item is the only way (or even the best way) for customers to understand the information associated with their menu choice. This comment asserted that it had specifically learned from practical application and guest feedback that this generally is not the most useful method of providing caloric information. This comment suggested that the rule require a logical and clear association between the menu item and calorie declaration, but provide flexibility for how that logical and clear association occurs.

(Response 68) We appreciate receiving the sample menu boards from the comment as a means of sharing experience with us. However, we are retaining in § 101.11(b)(2)(i)(A)(1) the requirement that the number of calories be listed adjacent to the name or the price of the associated standard menu item. This requirement is consistent with section 403(q)(5)(H)(ii)(I)(aa) of the FD&C Act, which requires that the calorie declaration be "adjacent to the name of the standard menu item, so as to be clearly associated with the standard menu item." Placing calorie declarations adjacent to the names of standard menu items provides a clear and logical association between the standard menu item and the calorie declaration and helps to ensure that consumers are able to see the declarations. In addition, § 101.11(b)(2)(i)(A)(3) provides that the term "Calories" or "Cal" must appear as a heading above a column listing the number of calories for each standard menu item or adjacent to the number of calories for each standard menu item. As such, § 101.11(b)(2)(i)(A)(3) helps to further ensure that the calorie declaration is clearly associated with a particular standard menu item, and the required use of the term "Calories" or "Cal" will help inform consumers that the number listed refers to calories. Section 101.11(b)(2)(i)(A)(1) also provides flexibility by requiring a covered establishment to declare calories adjacent to either the name or the price of the standard menu item. This flexibility is consistent with what one comment described doing in a restaurant. As finalized, § 101.11(b)(2)(i)(A)(1) also provides sufficient flexibility to accommodate different types of menus and menu boards and the various ways that standard menu items may be listed on menus and menu boards. Specifically, in this rule § 101.11(b)(2)(i)(A)(1):

- Provides flexibility to use a color "at least as conspicuous" as that of the name of the associated standard menu item and, thus, allows for the use of a different color;

- Provides flexibility to use a contrasting background "at least as conspicuous" as that used for the name of the associated standard menu item and, thus, allows for the use of a different contrasting background (see Response 73);

- Provides flexibility to use a type size "no smaller than the type size of the name or price" of the associated standard menu item and, thus, allows for the use of a different type size; and

- Does not restrict the font style.

We also note that the sample menu boards of the chain restaurant provided in the comment generally followed the provisions of the proposed rule in terms of type size and placement of calorie declarations. For example, the menu boards listed calorie declarations adjacent to the names of standard menu items in a type size no smaller than the name or the price of the associated standard menu item, whichever is smaller, in a column with a heading "Calories." Therefore, while the comment opposed the requirement that calorie declarations be placed adjacent to the names of standard menu items on menus and menu boards, the menu boards of the chain restaurant, nevertheless, generally used the same method of calorie declaration on menus and menu boards as required by this rule.

(Comment 69) In the proposed rule, we tentatively concluded that some packaged foods offered for sale in covered establishments are covered by the menu labeling requirements (see 76 FR 19192 at 19217, proposed § 101.11(b)(2)(iii)(C)). For example, a covered establishment may list "chips" on its menu board, referring to packaged bags of chips that are available as self-service foods or foods on display within the establishment. In this situation, the establishment would be required to disclose on the menu board calorie information for the packaged chips. In addition, if a covered establishment lists on its menu or menu board a combination meal that includes a packaged food, the establishment would be required to disclose the total calorie information for the combination meal, including the packaged food.

One comment agreed with requiring the total calorie information of a combination meal that includes a packaged food to include the calories for the packaged food. Another comment disagreed that calories should be declared on a menu or menu board for packaged foods, particularly packaged soft drinks.

(Response 69) As required by section 403(q)(5)(H) of the FD&C Act, covered establishments must provide calorie information for all standard menu items, including foods that are packaged. In addition, sections 403(q)(5)(H)(ii)(I)(aa) and (II)(aa) of the FD&C Act requires that covered establishments disclose the number of calories contained in a standard menu item, "as usually prepared and offered for sale." As such, we agree that a covered establishment that lists on its menu or menu board a combination meal that includes a packaged food must disclose the total number of calories in the combination meal, including the calories for the packaged food.

(Comment 70) One comment stated that the total calorie declaration for a standard menu item must include all ingredients of a standard menu item, as it is usually prepared and offered for sale, e.g., for a teaspoon of sugar added to oatmeal and salad dressings served on or with salad.

(Response 70) We agree that the total calorie declaration for a standard menu item must include all ingredients of the standard menu item, as it is usually prepared and offered for sale, e.g., for a teaspoon of sugar added to oatmeal and salad dressings served on or with salad. As with the scenario discussed in Response 69 for a combination meal that includes a packaged food, doing so is required by section 403(q)(5)(H) of the FD&C Act and by sections 403(q)(5)(H)(ii)(I)(aa) and (II)(aa) of the FD&C Act.

(Comment 71) One comment suggested that we require that covered establishments provide the Reference Daily Intakes (RDIs) of calories, fat, cholesterol, and "salt" on menus and menu boards. The comment acknowledged that there is no RDI for sugar, but requested that it nonetheless be included on menus and menu boards. The comment also recommended that menus and menu boards only list percent Daily Value (DV) of calories, fat, cholesterol, sugar, and "salt" and not list vitamins and minerals because "too many details may lead to information overload and defeat the purpose."

(Response 71) We disagree with the comment's suggestions, and we are not requiring covered establishments to include RDIs or percent DVs for certain nutrients on menus and menu boards. On menus and menu boards, we are requiring the number of calories contained in standard menu items, as usually prepared and offered for sale, and a succinct statement concerning suggested daily caloric intake, as required by sections 403(q)(5)(H)(ii)(I) and (II) of the FD&C Act. The succinct statement will adequately enable the public to understand, in the context of a total daily diet, the significance of the caloric information provided on menus or menu boards. We further note that percent DVs cannot be expressed for sugar or calories because Daily Reference Values (DRVs) have not been established for these nutrients. (See § 101.9(c)(9), which lists DRVs for fat, cholesterol, sodium, and other food components.) The term Reference Daily Intake (RDI) applies to a vitamin or mineral but does not apply to calories, fat, cholesterol, sugar, or salt. (See § 101.9(c)(8)(iv), which lists the RDIs for vitamins and minerals that are essential for human nutrition.) For the Nutrition Facts Label, the amount of a nutrient is calculated as a percentage of the RDI or DRV, as appropriate, and expressed using the same term—i.e., percent DV. Because "salt" can be either a general term applicable to substances such as calcium chloride or potassium chloride, or a synonym for the specific food substance "sodium chloride," and because nutrition information generally is directed to information about the sodium content of food, we considered the request of the comment to be directed to the declaration of percent DV for "sodium" rather than to "salt."

(Comment 72) A few comments agreed with the proposed requirement (in proposed § 101.11(b)(2)(i)(A)(1)) that the type size for the calorie disclosure be no smaller than the name or the price of the associated standard menu item, whichever is smaller. Other comments considered that the proposed type size requirements are too prescriptive and recommended that we require only that the type size be "clear and conspicuous." One comment stated that restaurants located in one State have already complied with a clear and conspicuous standard; therefore, to move to a type size no smaller than the smaller of the name or price of the menu item would require changes. Another comment asked us to provide guidance that if the calorie declaration is as large as the name, price, or description of the menu item, whichever is smaller, it is presumptively clear and conspicuous and complies with section 4205 of the ACA, rather than require a specific font size relative to the price or name; as an alternative, the type size of the calorie declaration could be the same size as the description of the menu item (rather than the name of the menu item) (emphasis added). One comment recommended that any required minimum type size for the calorie declaration be half the size of the name or price, whichever is smaller. Another recommended that the calorie declaration be the same size and font as either the name or price.

A few comments recommended that we require that the calorie declaration be at least as large as (or no smaller than) the name or price, whichever is larger. One comment recommended that the type size of the calorie declaration be no less than 10 point font on menus and no less than 22 point font on menu boards or a type size equal to the type size of the food listed.

(Response 72) We are retaining the type size requirements for the calorie declaration without change. We disagree that the requirements for the type size of the calorie declaration are too prescriptive. Some type size requirements suggested in the comments would be more restrictive than what we proposed. This would be true for those comments specifying a type size at least as large as (or no smaller than) the name or price, whichever is larger; a type size the same as the type size of the name or price; a type size the same size as the description of the menu item; or a specific type size. Such type size requirements would not take into consideration the various types and sizes of menus and menu boards that may be used in covered establishments. We have concerns that a type size that is half the size of the name or price, whichever is smaller, would result in a calorie declaration that is not clear and conspicuous and, therefore, not compliant with sections 403(q)(5)(H)(ii)(I) and (II) and 403(f) of the FD&C Act. Sections 403(q)(5)(H)(ii)(I) and (II) of the FD&C Act require, in relevant part, that calorie declarations required on menus and menu boards be clear and conspicuous and clearly associated with the corresponding standard menu item. Further, section 403(f) of the FD&C Act provides that a food shall be deemed misbranded "if any word, statement, or other information required by or under authority of this Act to appear on the label or labeling is not prominently placed thereon with such conspicuousness (as compared with other words, statements, designs, or devices, in the labeling) and in such terms as to render it likely to be read and understood by the ordinary individual under customary conditions of purchase and use." The calorie declaration specified in § 101.11(b)(2)(i)(A)(1) is tied to the name and price of the standard menu item, which typically are included on menus and menu boards and are two primary features of a menu or menu board typically used by consumers to make order selections. The type size requirements for calorie declarations balance the statutory requirements of sections 403(q)(5)(H)(ii)(I) and (II) and 403(f) of the FD&C Act that calorie declarations be clear and conspicuous with the mandate in section 403(q)(5)(H)(x)(II)(aa) of the FD&C Act to consider space on menus and menu boards and, thus, provide flexibility for different covered establishments.

(Comment 73) A few comments discussed the proposed requirements (in proposed § 101.11(b)(2)(i)(A)(1)) for the color and contrasting background of the calorie declaration. Some comments suggested changes to the proposed requirements for color and contrasting background. One comment emphasized that some menus and menu boards may have different contrasting background colors and provided two suggestions to accommodate such menus and menu boards. One suggestion was that we require that the calorie declaration have the same contrasting background, or a background at least as contrasting as the background used for the name of the associated standard menu item on the menu or menu board. As an alternative, the comment suggested that we could require that the calorie declaration have a background at least as contrasting as that used for the price and that menus using the same contrasting background as the price of the standard menu item will be presumed to comply.

One comment asserted that the color and contrast requirements are too restrictive and maintained that many menu boards have a variety of colors to enhance customer experiences. One comment suggested that the color of the calorie declaration should not be fainter or less obvious than that of the other items on the menu. Another comment asked us to permit the calorie declaration to be in the same color as the subtext that lists ingredients. One comment that opposed the proposed requirement for color asserted that "the eye becomes overwhelmed" when all copy is the same size and color, and the consumer misses the information or gives up looking for the information. This comment requested flexibility in color and "weight of calorie information" (a term the comment did not define). This comment also asked us to clarify whether "type" is limited to font type (e.g., Arial) or whether it also includes text effects (e.g., bold, italics, color).

One comment stated that the proposal was written with menu boards in mind and noted that some restaurants use translites (lighted boxes) where the name and price are in "oversized type" for marketing purposes. It asked us to permit the use of "reverse type" (which is white or light colored type printed on a dark background) and varied backgrounds if translites are used.

(Response 73) We have revised the contrasting background portion of § 101.11(b)(2)(i)(A)(1) to require that the number of calories be in the same contrasting background, or a background at least as contrasting as that used for the name of the associated standard menu item. We agree that this revision provides additional flexibility related to the prominence requirements to take into account that there may be different backgrounds on a single menu or menu board.

We disagree that the color requirements of the calorie declarations should be revised. Section 403(q)(5)(H)(ii) of the FD&C Act requires that the calories be disclosed in a clear and conspicuous manner and clearly associated with the standard menu item. Further, section 403(f) of the FD&C Act provides that a food shall be deemed misbranded "if any word, statement, or other information required by or under authority of this Act to appear on the label or labeling is not prominently placed thereon with such conspicuousness (as compared with other words, statements, designs, or devices, in the labeling) and in such terms as to render it likely to be read and understood by the ordinary individual under customary conditions of purchase and use." Requiring the calorie declaration to be in the same color, or in a color at least as conspicuous as the color of the name of the associated standard menu item helps ensure that the calorie declarations are clear and conspicuous, prominently placed on the menu or menu board with such conspicuousness as compared to other words on the menu or menu board and likely to be read and understood by the ordinary individual under customary conditions of purchase and use, and clearly associated with the standard menu item. However, to match the grammatical construction of the revised requirement for the contrasting background used for the calorie declaration, we are making a conforming editorial change to require that the color used for the calorie declaration be in the same color, or a color at least as conspicuous as that used for the name of the associated standard menu item (emphasis added).

In addition, we are not requiring calorie declarations to be in a specific font or to include particular text effects because we recognize that menus and menu boards come in a variety of sizes and include different fonts and type sizes. We are providing flexibility by taking into consideration the space on menus and menu boards (see section 403(q)(5)(H)(x)(II)(aa) of the FD&C Act), along with the fonts and type sizes already in use by the covered establishments, while also establishing requirements that help ensure calorie declarations are disclosed in a manner that is clear and conspicuous and that otherwise satisfies the requirements of applicable sections of the FD&C Act.

We would not object to reverse type and varied backgrounds on translites, provided that the calorie declarations are clear and conspicuous and satisfy the requirements of applicable sections of the FD&C Act and § 101.11. Calorie declarations on translites would be subject to the same general requirements as disclosures on other types of menu boards, as specified in § 101.11(b)(2)(i)(A).

(Comment 74) Some comments asked us to require a comma for declaring more than 1,000 calories because consumers are accustomed to seeing a comma in numbers of one thousand or greater. The comments suggested that we revise proposed § 101.11(b)(2)(i)(A) to include a new subparagraph to state "(4) Calorie numbers over 1,000 must include a comma after the thousands place."

(Response 74) We would not object to the voluntary use of a comma for calorie declarations of 1,000 or more, but decline to revise the rule to require a comma. The requirements we have established in § 101.11(b)(2)(i)(A) adequately ensure that calorie declarations are disclosed in a clear and conspicuous manner, as required by section 403(q)(5)(H) of the FD&C Act, and render the calorie declarations likely to be read and understood by the ordinary individual under customary conditions of purchase and use, as required by section 403(f) of the FD&C Act. A covered establishment may choose to declare numbers over 1,000 with or without a comma.

(Comment 75) One comment suggested that we accommodate vision-impaired consumers by providing for alternate menus and availability of other nutrition information. This comment asserted that vision-impaired consumers suffer more from hypertension, heart problems, and diabetes.

(Response 75) We recognize that vision-impaired consumers should have access to nutrition information for standard menu items in covered establishments. However, we are only implementing the nutrition labeling requirements specified in section 403(q)(5)(H) of the FD&C Act, at this time. Covered establishments may voluntarily provide visually impaired individuals with nutrition information for standard menu items in a way that is accessible to them. For example, we would not object to a covered establishment providing nutrition information for standard menu items through a Braille menu or a menu that gives information about menu items orally, in addition to providing nutrition information in accordance with § 101.11.

XII. Additional Format Requirements That Apply When Declaring Calories on Menus and Menu Boards for Variable Menu Items, Combination Meals, and Toppings (Final § 101.11(b)(2)(i)(A)(

A. Proposed Format for Declaring Calories for Variable Menu Items

Section 403(q)(5)(H)(v) of the FD&C Act requires FDA to establish by regulation standards for determining and disclosing the nutrient content for variable standard menu items that are listed as a single menu item "through means determined by the Secretary, including ranges, averages, or other methods." (See the discussion of the definition of the term "variable menu item" in section VIII.D) In the proposed rule, we considered five options for implementing this statutory provision, and selected Option 2 (76 FR 19192 at 19207-19209). Consistent with Option 2, proposed § 101.11(b)(2)(i)(A)(4) would require, in relevant part, that for variable menu items, the calories must be declared as a range, in the format "xx-yy" where "xx" is the caloric content of the lowest calorie variety, flavor, or combination, and "yy" is the caloric content of the highest calorie variety, flavor, or combination. The other options we considered were as follows:

- Option 1. Single value; either in the form of an average (obtained by summing up the calorie content of all options and then dividing by the number of options) or a median of all options (obtained by determining the "middle" number of calories from the list of options).

- Option 3. Hybrid combining averages and ranges; declaration of a single average value for variable menu items whose calorie ranges fall within specified bounds and declaration of a range for variable menu items whose calorie ranges fall outside those bounds.

- Option 4. If only 2 options are available for an item (e.g., a sandwich with fries or with fruit), provide both numbers with a forward slash between (e.g., 450/350). If three or more options are available, provide the range in calories.

- Option 5. If only 2 options are available for an item (e.g., a sandwich with fries or with fruit), provide both numbers with a forward slash between (e.g., 450/350). If three or more options are available, use one of the hybrid approaches outlined in Option 3.

We also proposed specific requirements that would apply when a variable menu item appears on the menu or menu board and is a self-service food or food on display, and there is no clearly identifiable upper bound to the range, e.g., all-you-can-eat buffet. In the following paragraphs, we discuss comments on these proposed provisions. After considering these comments, we have revised the provisions to:

- Require Option 4 instead ofOption 2;

- Specify additional format requirements that apply when declaring calories on menus and menu boards for variable menu items, combination meals, and toppings (§ 101.11(b)(2)(i)(A)(4) through (b)(2)(i)(A)(7)); and

- Redesignate the requirements that apply to a variable menu item when there is no clearly identifiable upper bound to the range of calories to § 101.11(b)(2)(i)(A)(8) and clarify that such item is otherwise exempt from the requirements of § 101.11(b)(2)(i)(A) for what must be provided on menus and menu boards.

B. Decision To Require Option 4

(Comment 76) Several comments supported our proposal to require Option 2 because they considered that ranges provide more detailed information. Several comments addressed one or more of the other four options we described. One comment stated that the use of ranges does not require customers to make calculations as would be the case for medians and means. This comment asserted that declaring calories in mixed options and hybrids would be confusing because consumers would need to understand why and when a single value (e.g., mean) is used rather than a range. One comment asserted that if single calorie values for each flavor and size were used rather than ranges, the menu board would be unreadable and consumers would be confused by too much information or would ignore the information. Another comment asserted that without a range, a single value calorie declaration for a variable menu item would be false.

Other comments supported the use of hybrid approaches (such as in Options 3 and 5) that would provide calorie information in both ranges and averages. One comment recommended that § 101.11(b)(2)(i)(A)(4) be revised to include specific exceptions that would limit the use of ranges—i.e., (1) very low or no calorie beverages should be listed separately from other beverages; (2) the mean must be used for menu items that come in different flavors, varieties, or combination meals if all options are within 40 calories of each other and all of the options contain fewer than 400 calories, or if all options are within 80 calories of each other and one or more options contain more than 400 calories; and (3) if there is a fixed or default option for a combination meal, calories should be posted for that option. This comment explained that it suggested the 40-calorie range because 40 calories is used as the basis for low calorie claims, and that it suggested a cut-off of 400 calories because 400 is 20 percent of a 2,000 calorie diet and is high according to our labeling principles.

One comment recommended that a covered establishment be able to declare one range for a variable menu item that comes in different sizes only if the difference between the upper and lower limits is less than 5 percent. This comment did not explain the basis for its recommendation to use 5 percent to limit the use of ranges.

One comment stated a preference for Option 4, but also requested that we limit the use of calorie ranges, within the constraints of Option 4. This comment considered that ranges are not particularly useful to customers in putting their choices into context. Several other comments opposed Option 4 because they considered that it would be confusing.

(Response 76) After considering all five options in light of the totality of the comments and the advantages and disadvantages of each option as described in the proposed rule (76 FR 19192 at 19207 through 19209), we are requiring Option 4, rather than Option 2, as the format for declaring calories for variable menu items on menus and menu boards.

Option 4 is similar to proposed § 101.11(b)(2)(i)(A)(4) in that it continues to provide for the declaration of calories using a range, which some comments supported. However, Option 4 also provides for the use of a different communication tool—i.e., a slash (e.g., 110/230)—that is more tailored to a situation in which there are only two options available for a variable menu item. Using a slash instead of a dash (e.g., 110-230) better reflects the fact that there are only two options for a variable menu item available (see the discussion in 76 FR 19192 at 19209), and more accurately informs consumers about the calories for each of the two options, whereas using a range represented by a dash is more appropriate when there are more than two options. As we discussed in the proposed rule, we recognize that in some instances, a calorie range may be so wide that a consumer may still need the calorie information for the particular menu item before he or she can make a fully informed purchase decision (76 FR 19192 at 19209). For example, the potential calorie range for a variable menu item that is offered for sale with the option of adding toppings (e.g., pizza) may be very wide. We are establishing specific requirements for such variable menu items when the toppings are listed on a menu or menu board in § 101.11(b)(2)(i)(A)(5), in part to address the potentially large variation in calories and to provide more specific calorie information to consumers regarding their order selections.

In general, however, we agree with the comments that use of a range is less confusing than hybrids and single values where consumers may not understand how a single value is derived if a median or mean is used. Requiring a range for variable menu items where three or more options are available gives consumers a consistent format across such variable menu items and may allow covered establishments to save some space on menus and menu boards.

We disagree that we should limit the use of ranges to calorie declarations for variable menu items where the difference between the upper and lower limits is less than 5 percent. While this approach may provide for smaller range variations, such limitations likely would require additional calorie declarations on menus and menu boards and significant redesigns of menus and menu boards. Taking into consideration the space on menus and menu boards and the fact that calorie declarations for individual variable menu items will be included in the written nutrition information required under section 403(q)(5)(H)(ii)(III) of the FD&C Act and § 101.11(b)(2)(ii), we are not requiring limits on the use of ranges where the difference between the upper and lower limits is less than 5 percent, at this time. Further, the comment provided no basis to use 5 percent to limit the use of ranges.

For these reasons, we have revised § 101.11(b)(2)(i)(A)(4) to require Option 4 for the declaration of calories on the menu or menu board for variable menu items. Requiring the declaration of calories of each option for a variable menu by using a slash where only two options are available will reduce or limit the number of times that calories are declared as a range, as requested by some comments, while also providing specific calorie information about each option. If there are three or more options available, the calories must be provided in a range in the format "xx-yy," where "xx" is the caloric content of the lowest calorie variety, flavor, or combination, and "yy" is the caloric content of the highest calorie variety, flavor, or combination. The use of a slash to declare calories for each option for a variable menu item where only two options are available and the use of a range where three or more options are available satisfy the requirements of section 403(q)(5)(H)(v) of the FD&C Act.

We have revised § 101.11(b)(2)(i)(A)(4) to specify, in subparagraphs (b)(2)(i)(A)(4) through (b)(2)(i)(A)(7):

- Specific requirements that apply to individual variable menu items (§ 101.11(b)(2)(i)(A)(4));

- Specific requirements that apply to a variable menu item that is offered for sale with the option of adding toppings listed on the menu or menu board (§ 101.11(b)(2)(i)(A)(5));

- Specific requirements that apply to a combination meal (§ 101.11(b)(2)(i)(A)(6)); and

- Specific format requirements for declaring calories for an individual variable menu item, a combination meal, and toppings as a range, if applicable (§ 101.11(b)(2)(i)(A)(7)).

We discuss these specific requirements in sections XII.C through XII.F.

We note that variable menu items that are self-service food or food on display are subject to the calorie declaration requirements, in § 101.11(b)(2)(iii), for food that is self-service or on display, as discussed in section XVII.B.

C. Requirements That Apply to Individual Variable Menu Items (Final § 101.11(b)(2)(i)(A)(4))

(Comment 77) One comment stated that the proposed rule suggests that a calorie range is only appropriate when a general term such as "soda" is used for a set of beverages, but not when specific flavors or brands are also named. The comment considered that the proposed rule therefore would require a calorie declaration for each specific size or each specific brand of a beverage listed on the menu. The comment referred to a discussion in the proposed rule (76 FR 19192 at 19216) where we compared individually listed beverages to individually listed flavors of ice cream and indicated that calorie declarations must be provided on menus and menu boards for the individually listed flavors. The comment contended that there is not enough space to list the calorie content for each size of each beverage offered for sale in the required type size. The comment also stated that this requirement will force covered establishments to refrain from listing the beverage options.

(Response 77) We are establishing in § 101.11(b)(2)(i)(A)(4)(i) through (b)(2)(i)(A)(4)(iii) requirements for declaring calories on the menu or menu board for individual variable menu items. First, we are establishing in § 101.11(b)(2)(i)(A)(4)(i) the principle, discussed in the proposed rule, that calorie declarations must be provided on menus and menu boards for the individually listed flavors (76 FR 19192 at 19216). Section 403(q)(5)(H)(v) of the FD&C Act provides, in relevant part, that FDA shall establish by regulation standards for disclosing the nutrient content for standard menu items that come in different flavors, varieties, or combinations, but which are listed as a single menu item through means determined by FDA, including ranges, averages, or other methods. Accordingly, § 101.11(b)(2)(i)(A)(4)(i) specifies that when the menu or menu board lists flavors or varieties of an entire individual variable menu item (such as soft drinks, ice cream, doughnuts, dips, and chicken that can be grilled or fried), the calories must be declared separately on the menu or menu board for each listed flavor or variety.

We acknowledge the comment's concern about space on menus and menu boards. However, a covered establishment could group together varieties or flavors that have the same number of calories (after rounding in accordance with § 101.11(b)(2)(i)(A)(2)) and declare the calories for that group as a single calorie declaration, specifying that the calorie declaration represents the calorie amount for each individual flavor or variety (e.g., "Diet Lemon Lime or Diet Cola (0 cal); Cola or Lemon Lime (150 cal)"). We have revised § 101.11(b)(2)(i)(A)(4)(i) to include this option for grouping flavors and varieties that have the same calorie amounts. We discuss in more detail the specific requirements for calorie declarations for self-service beverages in section XVII.E.3.

Flavors or varieties of variable menu items such as soft drinks, ice cream, doughnuts, dips, and chicken are not always listed on the menu or menu board. When the menu or menu board does not list flavors or varieties for an entire individual variable menu item, and only includes a general description of the variable menu item (e.g. "soft drinks"), § 101.11(b)(2)(i)(A)(4)(ii) specifies that the calories must be declared for each option with a slash between the two calorie declarations where only two options are available (e.g., "150/250 calories") or as a range in accordance with the requirements of § 101.11(b)(2)(i)(A)(7) where more than two options are available (e.g., "100-250 calories"). As discussed in section XII.F, § 101.11(b)(2)(i)(A)(7) specifies the format requirements for declaring calories as a range.

Some menus or menu boards describe flavors or varieties for only part of an individual variable menu item (such as different types of cheese offered in a sandwich). To address these types of variable menu items, § 101.11(b)(2)(i)(A)(4)(iii) specifies that when the menu or menu board describes flavors or varieties for only part of an individual variable menu item (such as different types of cheese offered in a grilled cheese sandwich (e.g., "Grilled Cheese (Cheddar or Swiss)")), the calories must be declared for each option with a slash between the two calorie declarations where only two options are available (e.g., "450/500 calories") or as a range in accordance with the requirements of § 101.11(b)(2)(i)(A)(7) where more than two options are available (e.g., "450-550 calories").

D. Requirements That Apply to a Variable Menu Item That Is Offered for Sale With the Option of Adding Toppings Listed on the Menu or Menu Board (Final § 101.11(b)(2)(i)(A)(5))

(Comment 78) A few comments recommended that the calories either be declared as a range as proposed or be declared for the basic preparation of the item together with a separate calorie declaration for each topping. These comments supported separate calorie declarations for sauces and dressings served on the side.

One comment appeared to believe that covered establishments must list a range providing calories for pizzas with no toppings and pizzas with everything on them. The comment asserted that this calorie range would be too wide and "useless." The comment also asserted that measuring toppings is not an "exact science." The comment recommended that calories be disclosed on menus and menu boards for the standard build pizzas but not for toppings, because the nutrient information for the toppings would be required in the written nutrition information. However, the comment suggested that a single calorie listing for all toppings as a range from lowest to highest would be appropriate if we require calorie disclosures for pizza toppings on menus and menu boards.

One comment recommended that ranges not be the only option for pizza. The comment asserted that pizzas can have up to 34 million combinations with a range as wide as 1,610 calories. The entity submitting the comment said it had received complaints from consumers in one jurisdiction where calorie information for pizza is provided by a range and found that the customers questioned the usefulness of a wide range of calories for a whole pizza. This comment stated that some jurisdictions have attempted to address this problem by requiring that the covered establishments list calories per each component or topping. The comment asserted that listing calories for each component or topping would not be useful for pizza because each topping has a different portioning based on the size of the pizza and the total number of toppings on the pizza. The comment explained that the amount of an individual topping selection (e.g., pepperoni, sausage, mushrooms, green peppers) added to a pizza is reduced based on the total number of individual toppings selections ordered. For example, a one-topping medium pizza where ham is the topping may have 10 grams of ham per slice (adding 10 calories from the ham per slice) whereas a medium pizza with ham as a topping and three other toppings may have 6 grams of ham per slice (adding 5 calories from the ham per slice). Therefore, the comment contended that individual labeling of toppings would lead to large calorie ranges that would not be useful information for the consumer. This comment stated that under one State law, pizza is a custom order and nutrition information is not required for toppings. The comment maintained that the best way to make calorie declarations for pizza is to declare calorie information for the standard build and provide calorie information for other customizations in a brochure or an online calculator.

One comment noted that, in the proposed rule, we discussed the possibility of listing calories for both the standard preparation of pizza and for each topping (76 FR 19192 at 19207) but did not codify this as we did for the written nutrition information. One comment asked us to clarify that calories should be listed for each separate pizza topping. Another comment recommended that calories for items such as pizzas and sundaes be posted for the standard preparation only if calories for each topping or option are also listed.

(Response 78) In § 101.11(b)(2)(i)(A)(5)(i) through (b)(2)(i)(A)(5)(iv), we are specifying format requirements that apply to a variable menu item that is offered for sale with the option of adding toppings listed on the menu or menu board. Doing so is consistent with section 403(q)(5)(H)(v) of the FD&C Act, responds to the comments making specific suggestions for how to declare calories for toppings such as those used on pizza and sundaes, and acknowledges some of the unique characteristics of such toppings (e.g., that the amount of each topping added to a menu item such as pizza may decrease with the total number of toppings ordered).

As noted by the comments, the proposed rule acknowledged that some comments received in response to the 2010 docket notice recommended that the calorie information for items such as pizza be displayed for the standard preparation of the item, with the standard preparation of the item clearly noted on the menu, menu board, or food tag or next to the food on display. The calorie content for each additional food component would then be displayed on the menu, menu board, food tag, or next to the food on display for each food component (76 FR 19192 at 19207). In light of these comments to the 2010 docket notice and the comments received to the proposed rule, § 101.11(b)(2)(i)(A)(5)(i) specifies that when the menu or menu board lists toppings that can be added to a menu item (such as pizza or ice cream), the calories must be declared for the basic preparation of the menu item as listed (e.g., "small pizza pie," or "single scoop ice cream"). Section 101.11(b)(2)(i)(A)(5)(ii) specifies that the calories must be separately declared for each topping listed on the menu or menu board (e.g., pepperoni, sausage, green peppers, onions on pizza; fudge, almonds, sprinkles on ice cream), and the menu or menu board must specify that the calories are added to the calories contained in the basic preparation of the menu item. For example:

Ice Cream Scoop: 300 cal
Toppings	Added cal
Almonds	25
Fudge	50

Furthermore, a covered establishment could group toppings that have the same calorie amounts (after rounding in accordance with § 101.11(b)(2)(i)(A)(2)), and declare the calories for such toppings as a single calorie declaration adjacent to the toppings, specifying that the calorie declaration represents the calorie amount for each individual topping (e.g., "Red Peppers or sweet onions (adds 10 cal);" "Red peppers, sweet onions (adds 10 cal per topping)"). We have revised § 101.11(b)(2)(i)(A)(5)(ii) to include this option for grouping toppings that have the same calorie amounts.

We note that if the general term, "toppings" is used on a menu or menu board, but the individual toppings are not listed, then the format requirements of § 101.11(b)(2)(i)(A)(4)(ii) would apply (i.e., the calories must be declared for each option with a slash between the two calorie declarations where only two options are available (e.g., "150/250 calories") or as a range where more than two options are available (e.g., "100-250 calories").

Foods such as pizza and ice cream are often offered for sale in different sizes (e.g., a small, medium, or large pizza pie, and ice cream dishes that contain one, two, or three scoops of ice cream). As mentioned by a comment, the amount of a topping added to a variable menu item may vary based on the size of the variable menu item ordered by a consumer. The calorie content of each topping will likely vary accordingly, depending on the size of the variable menu item ordered. To account for the potential variability in calorie content of each topping based on the size of the variable menu item ordered, § 101.11(b)(2)(i)(A)(5)(iii) specifies that the calories for the basic preparation of the menu item must be declared for each size of the menu item, and the calories for each topping listed on the menu or menu board must either be declared separately for each size of the menu item, or declared using a slash between the two calorie declarations for each topping where only two sizes of the menu item are available (e.g., "adds 150/250 cal") or as a range for each topping in accordance with the requirements of paragraph (b)(2)(i)(A)(7) of the rule where more than two sizes of the menu item are available (e.g., "adds 100-250 cal"). If a slash between two calorie declarations or a range of calorie declarations is used, the menu or menu board must indicate that the variation in calories for each topping arises from the size of the menu item to which the toppings are added. For example:

Plain Pizza Pie: Small (12") 500 cal * Medium (14") 750 cal * Large (16") 1000 cal
Toppings	Added cal	Small	Med	Large
Pepperoni	200	300	400
Sausage	250	350	450
Green Peppers	15	20	25

or

Plain Pizza Pie: Small (12") 500 cal * Medium (14") 750 cal * Large (16") 1000 cal
Toppings	Added cal(S/M/L pie)
Pepperoni	200-400
Sausage	250-450
Green Peppers	15-25

In the proposed rule, we requested comment on complexities that may be raised by certain variable menu items, such as those offered for sale with the option of adding toppings (such as pizza or ice cream) (76 FR 19192 at 19209). As mentioned by the comments, the amount of a topping added to a variable menu item, and therefore the calorie content of each topping, may vary not only based on the size of the menu item, but also based on the total number of toppings ordered by a consumer. Specifically, the amount of each topping added to a variable menu item may decrease as the total number of toppings ordered by a consumer increases.

Therefore, to address this complexity, we have established a specific calorie declaration requirement in § 101.11(b)(2)(i)(A)(5)(iv) for variable menu items offered for sale with the option of adding toppings listed on the menu or menu board, where the amount of the topping included on the basic preparation of the menu item decreases based on the total number of toppings ordered (such as sometimes is the case with pizza toppings). In such situation, the calories for each topping listed on the menu or menu board must be declared as single values representing the calories for each topping when added to a one-topping menu item, and the menu or menu board must specify that the calorie declaration is for the topping when added to a one-topping menu item. The following table provides an example of calorie declarations that would satisfy the requirements of § 101.11(b)(2)(i)(A)(5)(i) through (iv):

Plain Pizza Pie: Small (12") 500 cal * Medium (14") 750 cal * Large (16") 1000 cal
Toppings	Added cal(single topping S/M/L pie)
Pepperoni	200-400
Sausage	250-450
Green peppers	15-25

Structuring the requirement in this way helps ensure that consumers are given accurate and consistent information about the calories of each topping that are added to the calories contained in the basic preparation of the menu item. We would not object if a covered establishment voluntarily includes a statement on the menu or menu board explaining how the calories per topping might fluctuate if ordering multiple toppings; for example, for a pizza pie, the statement might say, "Calories per topping may decrease as the number of toppings per pizza increases."

In § 101.11(b)(2)(i)(A)(5)(i) through (b)(2)(i)(A)(5)(i v), we are establishing requirements for declaring calorie information for variable menu items with toppings listed on a menu or menu board, and specifying the format and manner of such declarations, as required by sections 403(q)(5)(H)(v) and (x)(II)(bb) of the FD&C Act. Because the requirements in § 101.11 (b)(2)(i)(A)(5)(iii) and (b)(2)(i)(A)(5)(iv) address the potential variability in calorie content of each topping based on the size of the menu item, and the total number of toppings ordered, the required calorie declarations will provide accurate calorie information to consumers regarding the calorie content of each topping they order. In addition, the requirement in § 101.11(b)(2)(i)(A)(5)(iii) for toppings added to menu items that come in different sizes provides covered establishments with flexibility to choose one of two options that best fits their establishments and menus and menu boards. Allowing covered establishments to use a range for each topping to represent the added calories across various sizes of the menu item may save some space on menus and menu boards while still providing the necessary calorie information for consumers to make informed dietary choices.

We disagree that pizza with toppings generally would be a custom order for the purposes of this rule and that nutrition information is not required for such foods for a number of reasons. First, the requirements of section 403(q)(5)(H) of the FD&C Act and this rule apply to standard menu items. This rule defines a standard menu item as restaurant-type food that is routinely included on a menu or menu board or routinely offered as a self-service food or food on display. To the extent a pizza with toppings meets the definition of a standard menu item, the requirements of section 403(q)(5)(H) of the FD&C Act and § 101.11(b) would apply to such pizza.

Second, while section 403(q)(5)(H)(vii) of the FD&C Act exempts from the nutrition labeling requirements of section 403(q)(5)(H) of the FD&C Act items that are custom orders, a pizza with toppings that meets the definition of a standard menu item would not be a custom order within the meaning of § 101.11. Under the definition of "custom order" in § 101.11(a), a custom order is a food order that is prepared in a specific manner based on an individual consumer's request, which requires the covered establishment to deviate from its usual preparation of a menu item. For example, if a covered establishment offers a "Meat Lovers" pizza containing ground meat and sausage as a standard menu item, and a customer orders a "Meat Lover's" pizza without sausage, that order could be considered a custom order. In contrast, a pizza with toppings routinely listed on the menu or menu board of a covered establishment would meet the definition of a standard menu item, and toppings can be added to a pizza as part of the establishment's usual preparation of the menu item.

Third, pizza is explicitly identified in section 403(q)(5)(H)(v) of the FD&C Act as a variable menu item for which the nutrition information must be disclosed. If Congress had meant for pizza, including pizza with toppings, not to be covered by the requirements of section 403(q)(5)(H) of the FD&C Act, it would not have had reason to specifically include pizza as an example of the foods described in section 403(q)(5)(H)(v) of the FD&C Act.

We also disagree that calorie declarations for different toppings should not be required on menus or menu boards because these calorie declarations will be provided in the written nutrition information or can be provided in a brochure. When toppings are listed on a menu or menu board, consumers can use such information to make order selections. Accordingly, when toppings are listed on a menu or menu board, a covered establishment must declare calories for each topping on the menu or menu board in accordance with § 101.11(b)(2)(i)(A)(5)(ii) through (b)(2)(i)(A)(5)(iv). Requiring calorie declarations for toppings when they are listed on the menu or menu board helps to inform consumers' decisions by providing the calorie content of menu items before consumers make their order selections. Further, providing such information will enable consumers to make informed and healthful dietary choices.

E. Requirements That Apply to a Combination Meal (Final § 101.11(b)(2)(i)(A)(6))

(Comment 79) Some comments recommended that, when practicable, calorie amounts for all components of a variable menu item that is a combination meal be listed on the menu or menu board. One comment provided an example of a variable menu item for a pancake combination meal with a choice of bacon strips or pork sausages to accompany pancakes, eggs, and hash browns. In the comment's example, the calories for the two options ranged from 1,200 to 1,420 calories, and the comment stated that the covered establishment could list the calories as "Two pancakes (600 calories) served with two eggs (200 calories), hash browns (300 calories) and your choice of 2 bacon strips (100 calories) or 2 pork sausages (320 calories)."

A few comments acknowledged that ranges are a better mechanism for presenting calorie information about variable menu items that are combination meals than are medians or means, but also pointed out that ranges have a disadvantage in that they do not sufficiently convey the necessary information to the consumer. One comment maintained that its consumer research shows that calorie ranges are confusing and not informative for variable menu items. Another comment recommended that if calorie ranges are used, the calories for the menu options that are included in that range must be disclosed, either on the menu, through signs for foods on display, or through the device used to provide the other written nutrition information required in section 403(q)(5)(H)(ii)(III) of the FD&C Act.

Another comment provided sample menu boards that offered for sale menu items in a meal described as "You Pick 2" (YP2), such as a meal consisting of a half sandwich and a half salad. For each menu item, the sample menu boards declared the number of calories in the menu item when ordered by a consumer individually and when ordered as one of the components of the "You Pick 2" meal, if available as a "You Pick 2" component (e.g., "Chicken Caesar Salad, YP2 360, Whole 720"). The comment asserted that declaring calories for each menu item individually, rather than declaring the calories for all possible combinations of its "You Pick 2" menu items in a range, was the best way to ensure that consumers have the necessary information to make choices about their calorie consumption.

(Response 79) We disagree that we should require calories to be listed on a menu or menu board for each component of a variable menu item that is a combination meal. In many cases, one or more components of a variable menu item (such as the pancakes, eggs, hash browns, bacon, and pork sausages in the comment's example) are also included on a menu or menu board as standard menu items, and the calories for such components would already be on the menu or menu board when this is the case. However, we would not object if a covered establishment voluntarily lists the calories for each component of a variable menu item that is a combination meal, provided that the covered establishment also complies with the format requirements for declaring calories for variable menu items on menus and menu boards in § 101.11(b)(2)(i)(A)(4) through (b)(2)(i)(A)(7).

Section 403(q)(5)(H)(v) of the FD&C Act provides, in relevant part, that FDA shall establish standards for disclosing the nutrient content for standard menu items that come in different flavors, varieties, or combinations, but which are listed as a single menu item through means determined by FDA, including ranges, averages, or other methods. Accordingly, § 101.11(b)(2)(i)(A)(6)(i) through (b)(2)(i)(A)(6)(iii) require calorie declarations for combination meals. Consistent with our selection of Option 4 for declaring calories for variable menu items generally (see discussion in section XII.B), § 101.11(b)(2)(i)(A)(6)(i) specifies that when the menu or menu board lists two options for menu items in a combination meal (e.g., a sandwich with a side salad or chips), the calories must be declared for each option with a slash between the two calorie declarations (e.g., "350/450 calories"). Section 101.11(b)(2)(i)(A)(6)(ii) specifies that when the menu or menu board lists three or more options for menu items in a combination meal (e.g., a sandwich with chips, a side salad, or fruit), the calories must be declared as a range in accordance with the requirements of § 101.11(b)(2)(i)(A)(7) (e.g., "350-500 calories").

As such, the requirements for calorie declarations for combinations meals in § 101.11(b)(2)(i)(A)(6)(i) through (b)(2)(i)(A)(6)(iii) are consistent with the view of comments asserting that ranges are a better mechanism for presenting calorie information than are medians or means. The requirements in § 101.11(b)(2)(i)(A)(6)(i) through(b)(2)(i)(A)(6)(iii) also address the concerns of other comments that ranges do not sufficiently convey the necessary information to the consumer by limiting the use of a range to combination meals with three or more options, and providing specific calorie information about each option of a combination meal where only two options are available. In addition, we find that the small sample size (n = 127) of the consumer research submitted with one comment limits it as support for the comment's assertion that calorie ranges are confusing and not informative for variable menu items (Ref. 33). Further, although this small study suggests possible consumer preference among different declaration formats, it does not provide evidence about how consumers understand and use the formats (Ref. 33).

Immediately following, in Response 80, we discuss the third provision we are establishing in § 101.11(b)(2)(i)(A)(6) regarding the format of declaring calories on the menu or menu board for combination meals—i.e., for "upsize" and "downsize" options for combination meals.

Regarding the "You Pick 2" meal described by one comment, we note that the sample menu board provided by the comment had a separate section describing an opportunity for a consumer to combine standard menu items for a special price, such as by combining any half sandwich with any half salad. The comment's sample menu board declared the number of calories for each standard menu item available for consumers to combine for a special price (e.g., "Chicken Caesar Salad, YP2 360, Whole 720"). Generally, the calories for a combination meal must be declared as a range in accordance with § 101.11(b)(2)(i)(A)(7) as required by § 101.11(b)(2)(i)(A)(6)(ii) if the menu or menu board lists three or more options for the menu items in the combination meal. However, in the sample menu boards provided by the comment, the section describing an opportunity for a consumer to combine standard menu items merely informed consumers of a special price when standard menu items separately listed on the menu board, each with declared calories, are combined in a "mix and match" situation. In this type of "mix and match" situation, as displayed in the sample menu board provided by the comment, a consumer would have the calorie information for each standard menu item available for the consumer to combine before he or she selects one or more standard menu items. Because the covered establishment would be providing calorie declarations for each standard menu item available for the consumer to combine on the menu or menu board that would be visible to consumers when making order selections, and taking into consideration space on menus and menu boards, we agree with the comment that requiring the disclosure of additional calorie ranges in such a situation, particularly where there are a large number of combinations available, likely would not be necessary. For these reasons, in this type of "mix and match" situation, where the menu or menu board describes an opportunity for a consumer to combine standard menu items for a special price (e.g., "Combine Any Sandwich with Any Soup or Any Salad for $8.99"), and the calories for each standard menu item, including each size option as described in § 101.11(b)(2)(i)(A)(6)(iii) if applicable, available for the consumer to combine are declared elsewhere on the menu or menu board, we would not require a covered establishment to also declare the calories for the combination in a range. To make this clear, § 101.11(b)(2)(i)(A)(6)(iv) of the final rule specifies that where the menu or menu board describes an opportunity for a consumer to combine standard menu items for a special price (e.g., "Combine Any Sandwich with Any Soup or Any Salad for $8.99"), and the calories for each standard menu item, including each size option as described in § 101.11(b)(2)(i)(A)(6)(iii) if applicable, available for the consumer to combine are declared elsewhere on the menu or menu board, the requirements of § 101.11(b)(2)(i)(A)(6)(i), (ii), and (b)(2)(i)(A)(6)(iii) do not apply.

In establishing § 101.11(b)(2)(i)(A)(6)(iv), we have considered space on menus and menu boards and how to minimize the burden on covered establishments to comply with this rule while ensuring that the requirements of section 403(q)(5)(H) of the FD&C Act and other applicable sections of the FD&C Act are satisfied and nutrition information for standard menu items is made available to consumers in a direct and accessible manner. Further, our approach to this "mix and match" situation is similar to our approach to a situation where a covered establishment includes packaged food (such as chips) as part of a combination meal. As discussed later in this document (see section XVII.H), a packaged food that is a food on display that bears Nutrition Facts information, including the nutrition information specified in section 403(q)(5)(H)(ii)(III) of the FD&C Act and § 101.11(b)(2)(ii) satisfies the calorie disclosure requirement for self-service food or food on display in section 403(q)(5)(H)(iii) of the FD&C Act and § 101.11(b)(2)(iii), so long as a consumer is able to examine the calorie information on the label prior to purchase.

(Comment 80) As another example of complexities that may be raised by certain variable menu items, we noted in the proposed rule that some menus with combination meals list an option to increase the size of components of those meals for a discounted additional price (76 FR 19192 at 19209). "Add 25 cents to Upgrade to Large Fries & Large Drink" is an example of such an option. We stated that we were considering whether those listings should be labeled with the number or range of calories they add to the standard combination meal, and requested comment on this issue.

Several comments responded to this request for comment. In general, these comments considered that calories should be declared for each size of a menu item (such as "upgrades" or "upsized options" and "downsized options") offered on menus and menu boards. Some comments linked the requirement to declare calories for different sizes to different prices—e.g., by considering that calories must be declared for any size option that has a distinct price on the menu or menu board. Some comments addressed combination meals, including fixed combination meals and combination meals that are variable menu items and considered that calories should be declared for fixed or variable combination meals available in multiple sizes.

(Response 80) We previously addressed comments directed to standard menu items other than variable menu items when the menu or menu board lists an option to change the size of the standard menu item (see Response 66). Here, we focus on calorie declarations for "upsized options" and "downsized options" for combination meals that are variable menu items. Consistent with our selection of Option 4 (see discussion in section XII.B), § 101.11(b)(2)(i)(A)(6)(iii) specifies that when the menu or menu board includes a choice to increase or decrease the size of a combination meal, the calorie difference must be declared for the increased or decreased size with a slash between two calorie declarations (e.g., "Adds 100/150 calories," "Subtracts 100/150 calories") if the menu or menu board lists two options for menu items in the combination meal, or as a range in accordance with the requirements of § 101.11(b)(2)(i)(A)(7) (e.g., "Adds 100-250 calories," "Subtracts 100-250 calories") if the menu or menu board lists three or more options for menu items in the combination meal.

For example, if a covered establishment offers for sale a combination meal that is a variable menu item consisting of a sandwich with fries or with onion rings, and the menu or menu board includes a choice to increase the size of the fries or the onion rings, the number of calories added by the larger size must be declared using a slash (e.g., "Adds 250/300 calories") since there are only two options for menu items in the combination meal (e.g., fries or onion rings).

As another example, if a covered establishment offers for sale a combination meal that is a variable menu item consisting of a sandwich with fries, onion rings, or tater tots, and the menu or menu board includes an option to increase the size of the fries, onion rings, or tater tots, the number of calories added by the larger size must be declared as a range in accordance with the requirements of § 101.11(b)(2)(i)(A)(7) (e.g., "Adds 250-450 calories"), because there are three options for menu items in the combination meal (e.g., fries, onion rings, or tater tots).

(Comment 81) A few comments requested flexibility and recommended that the rule allow a covered establishment to choose the option for declaring calories for variable menu items that best fits its business and menu, and display calories for variable menu items in the best way, as determined by the establishment, that allows consumers to choose healthier options. One comment presented a series of specific recommendations for disclosing calories, including specific recommendations that did not fit squarely within any of the five options for disclosing calories for variable menu items discussed in the proposed rule. This comment recommended that calories for variable menu items be disclosed by (1) providing an average or range, for each size or price of the variable menu item accompanied by the term "Avg. Cal"; (2) declaring calories for the flavors, components, or toppings that make up that variable menu item elsewhere on the primary writing; or (3) displaying the calorie amount for one preset "build" of the variable menu item. Under the comment's third option, the "build" would be representative of a finished version of the typical order and could not be a rarely ordered base product to which additional fixings are added. The comment also recommended that a covered establishment declare the calories for the additional options available for the variable menu item in a separate writing (such as an electronic kiosk, a nutrition brochure, a menu addendum, a nutrition poster, or an online nutrition application) available before or at the point of sale.

For combination meals that are fixed, this comment recommended that calories be disclosed by (1) providing total calories for the fixed combination meal or (2) providing calories for each item or component of the fixed combination meal elsewhere on the primary writing. For combination meals that contain variable menu items, the comment recommended that calories be disclosed by (1) providing calories as a range reflecting the lowest and highest total meal calorie content among the variations available; (2) providing a median or average accompanied by the term "Avg. Cal" if the calories for all variations within a variable combination meal are within 20 percent of the median calorie value; (3) providing calorie information for each item of the variable combination meal elsewhere on the primary writing; or (4) providing the calories for one specified variation of the variable combination meal. A covered establishment that elects to provide calories for one specified variation of the combination meal would identify the items in the variation specified, and disclose calories for the other variations of the variable combination meal in a separate writing available at the point of sale.

(Response 81) We decline the requests of these comments to allow a covered establishment to determine the method for declaring calories for variable menu items based on factors determined by the establishment. While this rule provides flexibility where appropriate, taking into account different business practices, standard menu items, and menus and menu boards, it also provides for uniform nutrition labeling requirements to be applied in covered establishments. Such consistency was one of the primary purposes of section 4205 of the ACA (see e.g., section 4205(c)). Further, section 403(q)(5)(H)(v) of the FD&C Act specifically directs FDA to establish by regulation requirements for disclosing nutrition information for variable menu items through means determined by FDA. In addition, section 403(q)(5)(H)(x)(II)(bb) of the FD&C Act directs FDA to issue regulations specifying the format and manner of the nutrition information disclosure requirements of section 403(q)(5)(H) of the FD&C Act. This rule establishes requirements for disclosing the nutrition information required under section 403(q)(5)(H) of the FD&C Act while also providing flexibility. For example, we are establishing specific format requirements for calorie declarations for individual variable menu items, toppings listed on a menu or menu board, and combination meals (§ 101.11(b)(2)(i)(A)(4) through (b)(2)(i)(A)(7)), and we also are providing an exemption from the requirements for calorie declarations for combination meals in § 101.11(b)(2)(i)(A)(6)(i) through (b)(2)(i)(A)(6)(iii) under the circumstances described in § 101.11(b)(2)(i)(A)(6)(iv). In addition, § 101.11(b)(2)(i)(A)(3) provides flexibility on where to place the term "Calories" or "Cal" on a menu or menu board, and § 101.11(b)(2)(i)(A)(1) provides flexibility for the color and contrasting background of calorie declarations. The calorie declaration requirements for variable menu items in this rule help ensure that consumers get consistent information when ordering from different covered establishments and even when ordering within a single covered establishment. For example, the approach suggested by the comments could lead to an inconsistent presentation on the same menu or menu board within a single establishment if a covered establishment determined that one approach worked best for some of its menu items and another approach worked best for other menu items.

(Comment 82) A few comments recommended that calories for combination meals be declared for the standard, "default," or most popular build. As an example, one comment recommended that calories declared for a combination meal include the calories for fries if the meal is depicted on a menu board as including fries. As another example, the comment recommended that calories declared for a combination meal include the calories in a full-calorie drink if more than 50 percent of a covered establishment's combination meals are sold with a full-calorie drink. One comment considered that the standard or default is the meal depicted that accounts for more than a majority (51 percent) of the sales for that meal.

(Response 82) We disagree with the comments in part. A combination meal, including those described by the comments, could be listed on a menu or menu board as a variable menu item, meaning that it could be listed as a single menu item that comes in different flavors, varieties, or combinations. Where a combination meal is listed on a menu or menu board as a variable menu item, the meal would not have a typical "default build" because some components that make up the meal (e.g., hamburger, fries or onion rings, soft drink) come in different flavors, varieties, or combinations that consumers are able to select. Section 403(q)(5)(H)(v) of the FD&C Act requires, in relevant part, that FDA establish by regulation standards for disclosing the nutrient content for variable menu items, through means determined by FDA, including ranges, averages, or other methods. Accordingly, we have established the requirements for calorie declarations for variable menu items that are combination meals in § 101.11(b)(2)(i)(A)(6)(i) through (b)(2)(i)(A)(6)(iii). These calorie declaration requirements communicate the variability of calorie content in the combination meal to consumers by providing the calorie information for each option when there are only two options available or in a range when there are three or more options available. In contrast, the methods for declaring calories for combination meals that are variable menu items suggested by the comments would not inform consumers that the calorie content of their order selection may vary based on the options selected in the combination meal.

Where a combination meal is not listed on a menu or menu board as a variable menu item, but is instead listed as a menu item that comes in only one flavor, variety, or combination, the combination meal would have a "default build." As with a combination meal that comes in different sizes, in this situation, § 101.11(b)(2)(i)(A) requires a covered establishment to provide the number of calories contained in the combination meal listed on the menu or menu board, as usually prepared and offered for sale. (See discussion about fixed combination meals offered for sale in different sizes in Response 66.)

F. Format Requirements for Declaring Calories for an Individual Variable Menu Item, a Combination Meal, and Toppings as a Range, if Applicable (Final § 101.11(b)(2)(i)(A)(7))

As discussed previously in this document (see section XII.B), we are revising § 101.11(b)(2)(i)(A)(4) to require Option 4. One such revision (established in § 101.11(b)(2)(i)(A)(7)) specifies the format requirements that must be followed when declaring calories as a range. Under § 101.11(b)(2)(i)(A)(7), calories that are declared as a range must be in the format "xx-yy," where "xx" is the caloric content of the lowest calorie variety, flavor, or combination, and "yy" is the caloric content of the highest calorie variety, flavor, or combination. We are establishing these specific format requirements as a separate subparagraph so that the rule does not need to include this format information each time the rule requires use of a range.

G. Exception for a Variable Menu Item When There Is No Clearly Identifiable Upper Bound to the Range of Calories (Final § 101.11(b)(2)(i)(A)(8))

Proposed § 101.11(b)(2)(i)(A)(4) would require, in relevant part, that if a variable menu item appears on the menu or menu board and is a self-service food or food on display, and there is no clearly identifiable upper bound to the range, e.g., all-you-can-eat buffet, then the menu or menu board must include a statement, adjacent to the name or price of the item, referring customers to the self-service facility for calorie information, e.g., "See buffet for calorie declarations." This statement must appear in a type size no smaller than the name or price of the variable menu item, whichever is smaller, and in the same color or a color at least as conspicuous as that name or price, with the same contrasting background as that name or price.

Comments that addressed this proposed provision supported it. Therefore, we are finalizing it without change, except to:

- Redesignate it as § 101.11(b)(2)(i)(A)(8) and clarify that it is an "exception" to the requirements of § 101.11(b)(2)(i)(A) for calorie declarations that must be provided on menus and menu boards;

- Make a conforming change to § 101.11(b)(2)(i)(A) to acknowledge the exception in § 101.11(b)(2)(i)(A)(8);

- Provide the same flexibility for the contrasting background used for the statement referring customers to the self-service facility for calorie declarations as for the calorie declaration in § 101.11(b)(2)(i)(A)(1);

- Make the same conforming editorial change to the requirement directed to the color of this statement as for the calorie declaration in § 101.11(b)(2)(i)(A)(1);

- Make an editorial correction for clarity to insert "the type size of" between "no smaller than" and "the name or price."

Characterizing the provisions of § 101.11(b)(2)(i)(A)(8) as an "exception" will clarify that the requirements of § 101.11(b)(2)(i)(A)(1) through (b)(2)(i)(A)(7) do not apply when a variable menu item appears on the menu or menu board and is a self-service food or food on display, and there is no clearly identifiable upper bound to the range of calories. Providing the same flexibility for the contrasting background as for the contrasting backgrounds for calorie declarations in § 101.11(b)(2)(i)(A)(1) will provide a consistent approach to background requirements on menus and menu boards. Making the conforming editorial change to the requirement directed to the color will promote consistency in terminology in the rule.

With these changes, § 101.11(b)(2)(i)(A)(8) specifies that if a variable menu item appears on the menu or menu board and is a self-service food or food on display, and there is no clearly identifiable upper bound to the range, e.g., all-you-can-eat buffet, the menu or menu board must include a statement, adjacent to the name or price of the item, referring customers to the self-service facility for calorie information, e.g., "See buffet for calorie declarations." This statement must appear in a type size no smaller than the type size of the name or price of the variable menu item, whichever is smaller, and in the same color or a color at least as conspicuous as that used for that name or price, with the same contrasting background or a background at least as contrasting as that used for that name or price.

H. Declaring Calories Using Interactive Menus or New Technology

(Comment 83) In the proposed rule, we recognized that the Internet may allow for the use of different methods for disclosing calories, such as by providing a calorie tracker in the ordering frame to tally calories as customers make order selections (76 FR 19192 at 19209). We requested comment on whether different methods should be used for nutrient content declarations for interactive Internet menus in general (76 FR 19192 at 19209). One comment asked that we acknowledge the potential for advances in technology and establish a petition process to request alternative methods of nutrition information disclosure via technological innovations, e.g., via smart phone applications. The comment also asked us to establish a process to approve methods that reflect technological advances that we did not anticipate but that comply with the statute.

(Response 83) We are not establishing a petition process to approve future methods for calorie declarations at this time. As suggested by the comment, we specifically acknowledged that potential technological advances may allow for the use of different methods in disclosing calories in covered establishments and requested comments on such methods. To the extent that the technological advances described by the comment provide methods for declaring calorie information in accordance with section 403(q)(5)(H) of the FD&C Act and § 101.11, such methods would be permissible. We will continue to consider whether specific advances in technology may result in alternative methods for nutrient content declarations under section 403(q)(5)(H) of the FD&C Act.

Later in this document (see Comment 113 and Response 113 in section XVI.E), we address a similar comment from the perspective of new technologies for providing written nutrition information.

XIII. Additional Requirements That Apply to Beverages That Are Not Self-Service or on Display (Final § 101.11(b)(2)(i)(A)(

(Comment 84) One comment noted that the proposed rule did not address the issue of ice fill for the declaration of calories for beverages. The comment asked us to permit covered establishments to calculate calories based on their standard ice fill as long as the level of ice fill is disclosed to consumers. The comment recommended that we expressly permit, regardless of whether there is a standard ice fill, the following statement regarding ice fill: "Calorie content may vary based on the amount of ice used."

(Response 84) For beverages that are standard menu items and are dispensed by an employee of a covered establishment (and, thus, are not self-service), we acknowledge that some of the beverage would be displaced by any ice added by the covered establishment. In addition, the amount of beverage displaced may vary based on the amount and type of added ice (e.g., crushed, cubed, shaved). Whereas some covered establishments may dispense a standard beverage fill (i.e., a fixed amount that is less than the full volume of the cup per cup size), others may not. Likewise, whereas some covered establishments may have a standard ice fill (i.e., a fixed amount of ice per cup size), others may not. Accordingly, § 101.11(b)(2)(i)(A)(9) of the final rule requires that, for beverages that are not self-service, calories must be declared based on the full volume of the cup served without ice, unless the covered establishment ordinarily dispenses and offers for sale a standard beverage fill (i.e., a fixed amount that is less than the full volume of the cup per cup size) or dispenses a standard ice fill (i.e., a fixed amount of ice per cup size). If the covered establishment usually prepares and offers for sale a beverage using a standard beverage fill or dispenses a standard ice fill, the covered establishment must declare calories based on such standard beverage fill or standard ice fill. Section 101.11(b)(2)(i)(A)(9) of the final rule does not require a covered establishment to set a standard beverage fill or standard ice fill. Instead, § 101.11(b)(2)(i)(A)(9) requires the covered establishment to disclose the number of calories contained in a beverage with a standard beverage fill or ice fill "as usually prepared and offered for sale," as required by section 403(q)(5)(H)(ii) of the FD&C Act. The rule also does not specify how a covered establishment should dispense a standard beverage fill or standard ice fill. A covered establishment may choose a method that is suited to its establishment—e.g., by using equipment that automatically dispenses a volume specified by the establishment, by using cups that have markings that enable an employee to manually add a certain volume of beverage or ice, or by using a particular ice scoop.

Section 101.11(b)(2)(i)(A)(9) is consistent with section 403(q)(5)(H)(ii) of the FD&C Act, which requires covered establishments to declare on menus and menu boards the number of calories contained in standard menu items listed on such menus and menu boards, as usually prepared and offered for sale. In establishing § 101.11(b)(2)(i)(A)(9), we considered among other things, reasonable variations in serving sizes used by covered establishments, and therefore are allowing covered establishments to disclose calories based on the full volume of the cup served without ice, unless the covered establishment ordinarily dispenses and offers for sale a standard beverage fill or dispenses a standard ice fill. We do not expect that a statement that the calorie content of the beverage may vary based on the amount of ice used, such as the one suggested by the comment, will be necessary in light of the requirements of § 101.11(b)(2)(i)(A)(9).

In section XVII.D, we discuss ice fill for self-service beverages.

XIV. Comments and FDA Response on Proposed § 101.11(b)(2)(i)(B)—Succinct Statement That Must Be on Menus and Menu Boards To Provide Context About Calories in a Daily Diet

A. The Proposed Requirements

Proposed § 101.11(b)(2)(i)(B) would require the following statement designed to enable consumers to understand, in the context of a total daily diet, the significance of the calorie information provided on menus and menu boards: A 2,000 calorie daily diet is used as the basis for general nutrition advice; however, individual calorie needs may vary.

In the proposed rule, we referred to the statement in this provision as the "succinct statement" and discussed principles that should be met to help ensure that the succinct statement is designed to enable consumers to understand, in the context of a total daily diet, the significance of the calorie information provided on menus and menu boards (76 FR 19192 at 19210). These principles are:

- The succinct statement should be succinct;

- The succinct statement should be in plain language that consumers can understand;

- The total caloric value should be framed appropriately so that it is not viewed as a recommendation for daily intake for every consumer;

- The succinct statement should give consumers a means to compare the calorie declaration for a menu item to total calories; and

- The succinct statement should inform consumers that individual needs vary.

In the following paragraphs, we discuss comments on this proposed provision. After considering these comments, we are:

- Revising the succinct statement; and

- Providing for an optional succinct statement (which this document refers to as the "children's succinct statement") for use on menus and menu boards targeted to children as a substitute for, or in addition to, the succinct statement.

B. Principles for Establishing the Succinct Statement

(Comment 85) Several comments supported the principles we discussed in the proposed rule for establishing the succinct statement.

(Response 85) We acknowledge these comments.

C. Wording of the Succinct Statement

(Comment 86) In the proposed rule, we signaled an intent to conduct consumer research to evaluate consumer response to the proposed succinct statement as well as to alternative succinct statements (which we discussed in the proposal) (76 FR 19192 at 19210). One comment supported such research, but suggested that more research should be done to assess if there is a permanent behavioral change.

(Response 86) Although the proposed rule contemplated consumer research to guide the design of the succinct statement, we are foregoing such research at this time in light of the number of comments providing useful insight regarding the proposed succinct statement, related principles, and whether we should provide a succinct statement for children.

(Comment 87) Several comments supported the proposed wording of the succinct statement. Other comments opposed the proposed wording of the succinct statement. Some comments considered that the information that calorie needs vary should not be included because it is obvious, it will clutter menus and menu boards, and there is no such phrase on packaged food. Another comment expressed concern about the use of 2,000 calories in the succinct statement and recommended that the succinct statement be better phrased to emphasize "individual needs may vary," e.g., by including information that many adults need fewer than 2,000 calories. This comment opposed adding phrases about the amount of exercise needed to burn a particular number of calories. One comment asserted that the proposed succinct statement is not specific enough and recommended that it focus on suggested calorie intake rather than on a typical caloric intake.

(Response 87) We are retaining the use of 2,000 calories as an appropriate reference value to include in the succinct statement. As discussed in the proposed rule, the Nutrition Facts on packaged foods uses 2,000 calories as a reference amount on which to base recommended intake for some nutrients for individuals 4 years of age and older, and the Nutrition Facts on packaged foods have been required for nearly 20 years. Moreover, a 2,000-calorie reference value is close to the midpoint of the range of energy requirements for sedentary adults (76 FR 19192 at 19209).

We also are retaining information that individual calorie needs may vary, albeit in shortened form (calorie needs vary). As discussed in the proposed rule and emphasized by the comments, although 2,000 calories is an appropriate reference value, not everyone should eat 2,000 calories per day (76 FR 19192 at 19210). As a result, a factor that FDA considered in establishing a succinct statement was whether the succinct statement should be framed appropriately so that it is not viewed as a recommendation for daily intake for every consumer because individual calorie needs vary. For these reasons, we conclude that the succinct statement should inform consumers that calorie needs vary.

(Comment 88) Several comments suggested specific revisions to the succinct statement as follows:

- "Most adults should eat less than 2,000 calories a day, or less than 600 calories per meal." (A few comments cited New York State Department of Health focus groups that showed participants preferred per meal calorie messages over daily calorie messages. The comments stated that consumers could not calculate the distribution of a daily calorie budget between meals.)

- "2,000 calories a day is an estimate of what adults need, but individual needs vary."

- "Consumption of 2,000 calories each day is used as the basis for general nutrition advice; however, individual daily calorie needs may be higher or lower."

- "The recommended caloric intake for a day varies from ____ to ____ for adolescents and adults, from ____ to ____ for school-age children, and from ____ to ____ for preschool children above age 2 years, although diets may vary."

- "2,000 calories a day is used for general nutrition advice, but calorie needs vary."

- "A 2,000 calorie daily diet is recommended for most adults; however, individual needs vary depending on age, gender, and physical activity."

- "To maintain a healthy diet, most adults need no more than 2,000 calories per day. Caloric needs for most children and less active adults range from 1,200 to 1,600 calories." One comment noted that this statement reflects a separate range for children and recommended that the statement with the range for children be on all menus, not only children's menus.

(Response 88) We have revised § 101.11(b)(2)(i)(B) to require that the following succinct statement be posted on menus and menu boards: 2,000 calories a day is used for general nutrition advice, but calorie needs vary. Most of the suggested alternatives were variations of the succinct statement we proposed. The alternative we selected captures the principles discussed in the proposed rule in a more concise fashion than the succinct statement that we proposed.

We disagree that the succinct statement should include the amount of calories per meal because individuals can choose many different ways to distribute their caloric intake throughout the day, and simply dividing the total calories into three meals does not acknowledge this variation or give consumers flexibility to distribute their own caloric intake. In addition, section 403(q)(5)(H) of the FD&C Act applies to standard menu items offered for sale in a variety of covered establishments, including establishments that do not serve foods that may constitute meals, such as chain ice cream shops and chain pretzel vendors.

We disagree that the succinct statement required on the menu or menu board should include specific reference calorie intake values or ranges for different ages or should specify the types of factors (such as age, gender, and physical activity) that impact the caloric needs of individuals. Such details are adequately captured by the phrase "calorie needs vary" and would unnecessarily increase the wordiness of the statement (i.e., make it less "succinct"). Because the Nutrition Facts label on packaged foods has been required for nearly 20 years, and the Nutrition Facts uses 2,000 calories as a reference amount, consumers are already familiar with this single reference amount for daily calorie consumption for individuals 4 years of age and older. However, as discussed later in this document (see Comment 90 and Response 90), we are providing for the optional use of a children's succinct statement on a menu or menu board targeted to children as a substitute for, or in addition to, the succinct statement.

(Comment 89) One comment noted that "a 2,000 calorie diet" may be misleading without the terms "daily" or "per day." The comment also recommended adding a message that calorie content alone is not the only nutritional factor to consider when choosing a diet for optimal health, because a focus on calories may incorrectly lead consumers to choose options that are nutrient poor instead of nutrient rich.

(Response 89) We agree that the succinct statement should provide the context that 2,000 calories refers to a daily diet and the succinct statement we are establishing in the final rule provides this context by informing consumers that "2,000 calories a day is used for general nutrition advice." However, we disagree that the succinct statement should state that calorie content alone is not the only nutritional factor to consider. Sections 403(q)(5)(H)(ii)(I) and (II) of the FD&C Act specifically require a covered establishment to disclose the number of calories contained in standard menu items and post a "succinct statement concerning suggested daily caloric intake" on menus or menu boards. The succinct statement we are establishing in the final rule adequately enables consumers to understand, in the context of a total daily diet, the significance of the calorie information provided on the menu or menu board, as required by sections 403(q)(5)(H)(ii)(I)(bb) and (II)(bb) of the FD&C Act. By allowing consumers to compare the caloric content of a standard menu item to the reference value of 2,000 calories a day, the succinct statement will enable consumers to make informed and healthful dietary choices and highlight the potential effects of additional calorie consumption throughout the day.

Further, as required by sections 403(q)(5)(H)(ii)(III) and (IV) of the FD&C Act, a covered establishment must also provide, in a written form and upon consumer request, additional nutrition information, and post on the menu or menu board a prominent, clear, and conspicuous statement regarding the availability of this additional nutrition information. Consumers therefore will have access to additional nutrition information and are notified of the availability of this information on the menu or menu board so that they are able to use the information to make informed and healthful dietary choices.

D. Succinct Statement on Menus Targeted to Children

(Comment 90) In the proposed rule, we requested comment on whether we should require a different succinct statement on menus that are targeted to children (76 FR 19192 at 19210). One comment opposed a separate succinct statement for children and a few comments recommended such a statement. One comment recommended a separate children's succinct statement if there is a separate children's menu. Another comment recommended a different succinct statement for children's menus to inform consumers that calorie needs differ because of age, sex, or activity (the comment stated that calorie needs are about 1,000 to 1,400 calories for 2- to 3-year old children, and can be up to 2,200 to 2,700 calories for 14- to 18-year old active boys).

The comments suggested the following succinct statements for children:

- "Most children 4 to 8 years old need 1,500 calories a day, or less than 500 calories a meal."

- "The daily calorie requirement for children 4 to 8 years is about 1,500 calories, though individual needs vary."

- "Calorie needs for young children range from 1,000 to 2,000 calories per day and vary based on age and physical activity levels."

- "Most children 4 to 8 years old need about 1,500 calories a day including snacks, or fewer than 500 calories a meal."

One comment suggested that we conduct consumer research on the following succinct statements:

- "Most children 4 to 8 years old need 1,500 calories a day, or less than 500 calories a meal. Most children 2 to 3 years old need 1,200 calories a day, or less than 400 calories a meal."

- "Children need smaller food portions than adults. Calorie needs vary by child. For information on healthy eating, go to www.choosemyplate.gov."

- "Children's calorie needs vary by age and the individual child's nutrition and health status. Please consult your child's physician or health care professional."

(Response 90) We have revised § 101.11(b)(2)(i)(B) to provide for the optional use of either of the following children's succinct statements on menus and menu boards targeted to children as a substitute for, or in addition to, the succinct statement:

- 1,200 to 1,400 calories a day is used for general nutrition advice for children ages 4 to 8 years, but calorie needs vary.

- 1,200 to 1,400 calories a day is used for general nutrition advice for children ages 4 to 8 years and 1,400 to 2,000 calories a day for children 9 to 13 years, but calorie needs vary.

Under § 101.11(b)(2)(i)(B), a covered establishment may use one of these children's succinct statements on a menu or menu board targeted to children (e.g., on a standalone children's menu or menu board, or in the children's section of a general menu or menu board) as a substitute for, or in addition to, the succinct statement required in § 101.11(b)(2)(i)(B). To ensure consistency, a covered establishment that includes a children's succinct statement on a menu or menu board may only use the children's succinct statements listed in § 101.11(b)(2)(i)(B). If the covered establishment chooses not to use the children's succinct statements listed in § 101.11(b)(2)(i)(B), it must use the succinct statement required in § 101.11(b)(2)(i)(B).

We realize that many covered establishments offer food selections that may only be purchased for children under a certain age specified by the covered establishment (e.g., under 9 years). Some of these children's food selections are offered on separate children's menus, while others are included on the general menu or menu board along with items for all consumers. We have concluded that covered establishments should have the option of providing a succinct statement more relevant to children on menus and menu boards that provide food selections targeted to children. Childhood obesity is an important public health concern, and a succinct statement specifically targeted to the calorie needs of children may enable parents and children to make informed dietary choices.

We considered whether covered establishments should be required to provide both the 2,000-calorie succinct statement and an additional children's succinct statement on menus and menu boards. Sections 403(q)(5)(H)(ii)(I)(bb) and (II)(bb) of the FD&C Act require that covered establishments post on menus and menu boards "a succinct statement concerning suggested daily caloric intake . . . designed to enable the public to understand, in the context of a total daily diet, the significance of the [calorie] information" provided on menus and menu boards. (Emphasis added.) Therefore, it is reasonable to interpret these sections to only require one succinct statement on menus and menu boards, and we are providing for the optional use by a covered establishment of a children's succinct statement on menus or menu boards targeted to children. Accordingly, the rule does not require that a covered establishment that includes a children's succinct statement on a menu or menu board targeted to children also include the succinct statement required by § 101.11(b)(2)(i)(B) on that menu or menu board.

To develop the children's succinct statement, we used the 2010 Dietary Guidelines as the reference for the estimated calorie needs of children (Ref. 3). The 2010 Dietary Guidelines are based on the review of scientific evidence by a committee of scientific experts. The 2010 Dietary Guidelines provide information and advice for choosing a healthy eating pattern that focuses on nutrient-dense foods and beverages, and that contributes to achieving and maintaining a healthy weight. One goal of the 2010 Dietary Guidelines is to aid policymakers in designing and carrying out nutrition-related programs. As such, the 2010 Dietary Guidelines are well suited to serve as the reference for the estimated calorie needs of children for the purpose of this rule.

As the comments noted, there is broad variability in the daily caloric needs of children, and this variability is captured in table 2-3 in the 2010 Dietary Guidelines. Table 2-3 reports the estimated calorie needs per day by age, gender, and physical activity level. The relevant data and information in table 2-3, which we used to develop the children's succinct statement, covers four age groups (ages 2 to 3 years, 4 to 8 years, 9 to 13 years, and 14 to 18 years) and three activity levels (sedentary, moderately active, and active). Male and female children are grouped together in the group aged 2 to 3 years but reported separately in the groups aged 4 to 8 years, 9 to 13 years, and 14 to 18 years. Although most comments suggesting specific wording for the children's succinct statement focused on the calorie needs of children ages 8 and younger, some covered establishments may offer food selections targeted to somewhat older children—e.g., for "kids under 12." Therefore, we focused on estimated caloric needs for children aged 4 to 8 and children aged 9 to 13. We did not focus on the estimated caloric needs for the youngest age group (aged 2 to 3 years) and the oldest age group (aged 14 to 18 years). Although one comment suggested that we include the youngest age group (aged 2 to 3 years), we considered a number of factors and ultimately decided not to include the youngest age group (aged 2 to 3 years) and the oldest age group (aged 14 to 18 years). First, we considered space on menus and menu boards, the types of standard menu items offered in covered establishments, and different practices among covered establishments. Second, we were concerned that a children's succinct statement with four age groups would cross a reasonable threshold for one of the principles governing the succinct statement—i.e., that it be succinct. Third, we concluded that covered establishments might be deterred from voluntarily posting a children's succinct statement on menus and menu boards if such statement was not succinct. Fourth, children's menus are typically not targeted to the youngest and the oldest age groups.

In developing the specific language of the two options for the children's succinct statement, we considered the principles that apply to the succinct statement, the comments, data and information discussed in the proposed rule, and the wording established in § 101.11(b)(2)(i)(B) for the succinct statement. As with the succinct statement, we concluded that the children's succinct statement should be directed to an estimated daily caloric need rather than the amount of calories per meal.

In contrast to the succinct statement, which uses a single reference value (2,000 calories) regardless of age group, we concluded that the children's succinct statement needed to both reflect a range of calories and link that range of calories to a specific age group to adequately enable parents and possibly some children to understand the significance of the calorie information in the context of their total daily diet. We focused on estimated caloric needs for sedentary children and did not focus on additional calories consumed by active children. This is consistent with our approach to the succinct statement, where the 2,000 calorie daily diet does not take into account additional calories consumed by persons such as athletes or persons with a regular fitness regime. As with the succinct statement, the children's succinct statement addresses the differential caloric consumption associated with activity and other factors by informing consumers that "calorie needs vary."

Table 2-3 in the 2010 Dietary Guidelines reports the same estimated daily caloric needs for sedentary males and females aged 4 to 8 years (i.e., 1,200 to 1,400 calories) and, thus, we selected 1,200 to 1,400 calories as the range to include for children aged 4 to 8 years in each of the two options listed in § 101.11(b)(2)(i)(B) for the children's succinct statements. Table 2-3 in the 2010 Dietary Guidelines reports different estimated daily caloric needs for sedentary males aged 9 to 13 years (i.e., 1,600 to 2,000 calories) and sedentary females aged 9 to 13 years (i.e., 1,400 to 1,600 calories). For the option listed in § 101.11(b)(2)(i)(B) for a children's succinct statement that includes the estimated caloric needs of children aged 9 to 13 years, we simply reported the range as the lowest estimated caloric needs for sedentary males and females aged 9 to 13 years (i.e., 1,400 calories for females) and the highest estimated caloric needs for sedentary males and females aged 9 to 13 years (i.e., 2,000 calories for males). Thus, the listed option that includes the group aged 9 to 13 years reports the range of estimated caloric needs as 1,400 to 2,000 calories.

(Comment 91) One comment suggested that children's menus may benefit from a traffic light concept (e.g., green, yellow, and red signage) that indicates which foods should be eaten more or less frequently.

(Response 91) Section 403(q)(5)(H) of the FD&C Act generally requires covered establishments to provide calorie declarations for standard menu items on menus, menu boards, and signs adjacent to self-service food and food on display, and other nutrition information in a written form. Section 403(q)(5)(H) also requires covered establishments to post on menus and menu boards a succinct statement concerning daily caloric intake and a statement regarding the availability of the written nutrition information. FDA is establishing requirements to implement only what is specified in section 403(q)(5)(H) of the FD&C Act and information that is necessary for the efficient enforcement of such requirements.

E. Requirements for the Succinct Statement To Be Prominent, Clear, and Conspicuous

Proposed § 101.11(b)(i)(2)(B)(1) would require that the succinct statement be posted prominently and in a clear and conspicuous manner in a type size no smaller than the smallest calorie declaration appearing on the same menu or menu board and in the same color or in a color at least as conspicuous as the calorie declarations and with the same contrasting background as the calorie declarations. In the proposed rule, we recognized that some restaurants and similar retail food establishments may have menu boards that list very few items in very large font. We asked for comment on whether the succinct statement and statement of availability should be tied to the type size for some menus that have few items and that may be listed in large type size (76 FR 19192 at 19211).

In the following paragraphs, we discuss comments on this proposed provision. After considering these comments, we are:

- Revising the proposed provision to provide additional flexibility for the contrasting background of the succinct statement;

- Making a conforming editorial change to the requirement for the color used for the succinct statement for grammatical consistency; and

- Making an editorial correction for clarity to insert "the type size of" between "no smaller than" and "the smallest calorie declaration."

(Comment 92) One comment suggested that the size of the succinct statement be "no smaller than the menu description or what any ordinary person can read without any trouble." Due to space limitations on menus, this comment considered that the succinct statement should not be tied to the type size on menus that list relatively few items that are listed in very large type size. One comment asked us to permit a type size smaller than the smallest calorie declaration appearing on the menu or menu board due to the limited space on menu boards and the amount of text required to be included in the statement. Another comment maintained that the succinct statement takes up too much space and would force covered establishments to decrease the type size used for calories. A few comments suggested that we require the succinct statement to be no smaller than the type size most frequently used throughout the menu and in the same color and contrast, or in color and contrast at least as conspicuous and contrasting as the color and contrast most frequently used throughout the menu for the names of standard menu items.

(Response 92) We agree, in part, and disagree, in part, with these comments. As a practical matter, the type size of the succinct statement would, as requested by the comments, likely be no smaller than the menu description or what any ordinary person can read without any trouble, because § 101.11(b)(2)(i)(B)(1) requires that the type size for the succinct statement be no smaller than the smallest type size of any calorie declaration and, under § 101.11(b)(2)(i)(A)(1), the type size of the calorie declaration would be in a type size no smaller than the type size of the name or the price of the associated standard menu item, whichever is smaller. Because consumers typically view the name and/or price of a standard menu item to place an order, our decision to anchor the type size of the succinct statement to the type size of information already on the menu or menu board acts, in essence, as an objective and measurable performance standard and helps ensure, among other things, that the succinct statement will be clear and conspicuous to consumers and posted prominently, as required by sections 403(q)(5)(H)(ii) and 403(f) of the FD&C Act.

We disagree that the type size, color, and contrast should be tied to the type size, color, and contrast most frequently used throughout the menu. Section 101.11(b)(2)(i)(A)(1) provides flexibility for the type size, color, and contrasting background used for the calorie declaration (and, accordingly, § 101.11(b)(2)(i)(B)(1) provides flexibility for the type size, color, and contrasting background used for the succinct statement), by anchoring these three parameters to the name or price of standard menu items. The suggestion in this comment would establish an additional burden for a covered establishment, particularly when a covered establishment has more than one menu or menu board, to determine the type size most frequently used. The comment provided no basis, such as apparent benefit for either the restaurant or the consumer, to justify this additional burden.

However, we agree that we should provide additional flexibility for the contrasting background of the succinct statement by permitting the statement to be in a background at least as contrasting as that used for the calorie declarations. Consequently, we have revised § 101.11(b)(2)(i)(B)(1) to do so. We also are making a conforming editorial change to the grammatical construction of the requirement for the color used for the succinct statement to match the grammatical construction of the revised requirement for the contrasting background used for the succinct statement. With these changes, § 101.11(b)(2)(i)(B)(1) requires that the succinct statement be posted prominently and in a clear and conspicuous manner in a type size no smaller than the smallest type size of any calorie declaration appearing on the same menu or menu board and in the same color or in a color at least as conspicuous as that used for the calorie declarations, and with the same contrasting background or a background at least as contrasting as that used for the calorie declarations (emphasis added).

F. Placement of the Succinct Statement on Menus and Menu Boards

For menus, proposed § 101.11(b)(2)(i)(B)(2) would require that the succinct statement appear on the bottom of each page of the menu. On menu pages that also bear the statement regarding the availability of the written nutrition information required in § 101.11(b)(2)(i)(C), proposed § 101.11(b)(2)(i)(B)(2) also would require that the succinct statement appear directly above the statement of availability required in § 101.11(b)(2)(i)(C). For menu boards, proposed § 101.11(b)(2)(i)(B)(3) would require that the succinct statement appear on the bottom of the menu board, immediately above the statement of availability required in § 101.11(b)(2)(i)(C).

In the following paragraphs, we discuss comments on these proposed provisions. After considering these comments, we have revised the proposed provisions for placement of the succinct statement to provide additional flexibility for the succinct statement to appear immediately above, below, or beside the statement of availability of the written nutrition information.

(Comment 93) Several comments agreed with the proposed placement requirements for the succinct statement. One comment recommended that covered establishments be permitted to put the succinct statement on a separate sign near the menu boards because of space constraints.

(Response 93) We are not revising the rule to allow a covered establishment to post the succinct statement on a separate sign near a menu board as suggested by the comment. First, we are concerned that if a covered establishment were to post the succinct statement on a separate sign, the statement would not be posted prominently, and therefore, consumers would not be able to use the statement to understand, in the context of a total daily diet, the significance of the calorie information that is provided on the menu board. Second, this rule provides flexibility regarding posting calorie declarations and other information on menus and menu boards, including flexibility regarding the size of the calorie declarations and placement of the statement of availability of additional written nutrition information, such that covered establishments have a number of ways to satisfy the requirements based on their menus and menu boards and business operations. Lastly, sections 403(q)(5)(H)(ii)(I)(bb) and (II)(bb) of the FD&C Act require that covered establishments post the succinct statement on menus and menu boards prominently and in a clear and conspicuous manner. The comment's request would be inconsistent with the express requirements of sections 403(q)(5)(H)(ii)(I)(bb) and (II)(bb) of the FD&C Act. Later in this document, we discuss the requirements for placement of the succinct statement on small signs for self-service food and food on display that may meet the definition of a "menu" or "menu board" in section 403(q)(5)(H)(xi) of the FD&C Act, in that such signs are the primary writings of the establishment from which consumers make order selections (see the discussion of § 101.11(b)(2)(iii)(B) in section XVII.G).

(Comment 94) A few comments expressed concern about the space that the succinct statement would take on menus and the proposed requirement that the statement appear on every page, in light of other statements on menus (such as the advisory statements in our Food Code, footnotes regarding daily availability of various menu items, and footnotes referencing "net weight before cooking"). The comments asserted that menus would become cluttered. One comment asserted that the message we want to convey would "get lost in the noise at the bottom of each page." The comments agreed that the succinct statement should appear at the bottom of menus and menu boards, but asked us to clarify that it would appear only once on each menu or menu board and not on each page or panel. The comments recommended that for menus, the succinct statement must appear either on the first or last page. One comment suggested that the succinct statement need only appear on one panel of the main menu board that is visible at all times to consumers.

One comment asserted that because space is finite, adding the required succinct statement to multiple pages of a menu would lead to removal of "optional information," such as some menu offerings. This comment expressed concern that menu items, such as seafood dishes, will be dropped from menus to make room for this additional information to appear on each page of the menu. The comment noted that the 2010 Dietary Guidelines have outlined the importance of including seafood in a healthy diet, and that roughly 67 percent of the seafood consumed in the United States is consumed away from the home.

(Response 94) We disagree that the succinct statement needs to appear only once on menus. In particular, we are concerned that for large multi-paged menus, consumers may not read the entire menu and instead may turn to a specific section of the menu (e.g., the section for burgers and sandwiches). Unless the succinct statement is on the page for that particular section, it is possible that consumers could miss the succinct statement and therefore be unable to use the statement "to understand, in the context of a daily diet, the significance of the caloric information that is provided on the menu," as specified by section 403(q)(5)(H)(I)(bb) of the FD&C Act. Therefore, in § 101.11(b)(2)(i)(B)(2), we are requiring the succinct statement to appear on the bottom of each page of the menu.

However, we agree that the succinct statement needs to appear only once on a menu board, including a menu board consisting of more than one panel in one physical location (a multi-paneled menu board). For the purpose of this rule, we consider such a multi-paneled menu board to be a single menu board, provided that the entire multi-paneled menu board is visible to consumers when consumers are placing order selections for the standard menu items listed on such menu board. A multi-paneled menu board is different from a menu with multiple pages because all panels are visible to consumers when they place an order, regardless of the specific panel containing the menu item the consumer selects. A succinct statement on a single panel of a multi-paneled board is likely to be clear and conspicuous to the consumer and posted prominently, provided that the type size, color, and background of the succinct statement meet the applicable requirements in § 101.11(b)(2)(i)(B)(1) and the entire multi-paneled menu board is visible to consumers when consumers are placing order selections for the standard menu items listed on such menu board.

Regarding one comment's assertion that requiring the succinct statement to appear on each page of a menu could lead to the removal from a menu or menu board of information that a covered establishment views as optional, we note that a decision to remove "optional information" or to drop certain menu items from menus belongs to the covered establishment. The succinct statement is necessary on the bottom of each page of a menu that includes standard menu items and calorie information because the succinct statement is designed to enable consumers "to understand, in the context of a total daily diet, the significance of the caloric information that is provided on the menu," as required by section 403(q)(5)(H)(I)(bb) of the FD&C Act. However, we have also considered the space on menus and therefore provided flexibility where appropriate. For example, in addressing comments on the statement of availability of written nutrition information, we concluded that this statement of availability need appear only once on a menu or menu board. In reaching that conclusion, we considered the goals of the succinct statement and the statement of availability, which are different (see the discussion of § 101.11(b)(2)(i)(C) in section XV.C).

(Comment 95) A few comments maintained that the proposed order of the succinct statement (i.e., in relation to the statement of availability of additional written nutrition information) limits flexibility. The comments asserted that both statements could be just as clear and conspicuous if they were placed in some other way.

(Response 95) We agree with the comments, and are providing flexibility for the placement of the succinct statement in relation to the statement of availability of the written nutrition information. Consequently, we have revised § 101.11(b)(2)(i)(B)(2) and (b)(2)(i)(B)(3) to provide that on menu pages that also bear the statement of availability and on menu boards, the succinct statement must appear immediately above, below, or beside the statement of availability. In addition, as an editorial change for consistency throughout § 101.11, we have revised the cross-references within § 101.11(b)(2)(i)(B)(2) and (b)(2)(i)(B)(3) referring to the statement of availability to read "the statement required by paragraph (b)(2)(i)(C) of this section" (i.e., § 101.11(b)(2)(i)(C)). With these changes, § 101.11(b)(2)(i)(B)(2) requires that for menus, the succinct statement must appear on the bottom of each page of the menu. On menu pages that also bear the statement required by § 101.11(b)(2)(i)(C), the succinct statement must appear immediately above, below, or beside the statement required by § 101.11(b)(2)(i)(C). In addition, with these changes § 101.11(b)(2)(i)(B)(3) requires that for menu boards, the succinct statement must appear on the bottom of the menu board, immediately above, below, or beside the statement required by § 101.11(b)(2)(i)(C).

XV. Comments and FDA Response on Proposed § 101.11(b)(2)(i)(C)—Statement That Must Be on Menus and Menu Boards About Availability of Written Nutrition Information

A. Proposed Wording of the Statement of Availability

Proposed § 101.11(b)(2)(i)(C) would require the following statement regarding the availability of the additional written nutrition information required in § 101.11(b)(3)(i) on all forms of the menu or menu board: Additional nutrition information available upon request. In a correction document, we corrected the regulatory designation of the requirement for the statement of availability to be § 101.11(b)(2)(ii) rather than § 101.11(b)(3)(i) (76 FR 30050 at 30051).

One comment supported the wording of the statement of availability and no comments opposed the wording. We are finalizing the proposed wording of the statement of availability without change.

B. Requirements for the Statement of Availability To Be Prominent and Conspicuous

Proposed § 101.11(b)(2)(i)(C)(1) would require that the statement of availability be posted prominently and in a clear and conspicuous manner in a type size no smaller than the smallest calorie declaration appearing on the same menu or menu board and in the same color or in a color at least as conspicuous as the caloric declarations, and with the same contrasting background as the caloric declarations.

In the following paragraphs, we discuss comments on this proposed provision. After considering these comments, we are:

- Revising the proposed provision to provide additional flexibility for the contrasting background used for the statement of availability;

- Making a conforming editorial change to the requirement for the color used for the statement of availability for grammatical consistency; and

- Making an editorial correction for clarity to insert "type size of any" between "no smaller than the smallest" and "calorie declaration."

(Comment 96) One comment recommended that the type size of the statement of availability "be no smaller than the menu description or what any ordinary person can read without any trouble." Some comments recommended that we permit a smaller type size for the statement of availability. A few comments suggested that we require the statement of availability to be in a type size no smaller than the type size most frequently used throughout the menu. Some comments suggested that the statement of availability be in the same color or a color at least as conspicuous as the color most frequently used throughout the menu for the names of standard menu items and with the same contrasting background or a contrasting background at least as contrasting as the background most frequently used throughout the menu for the names of standard menu items.

(Response 96) These comments on the proposed requirements for type size, color, and contrasting background of the statement of availability are analogous to certain comments on the proposed requirements for the succinct statement (see Comment 92), and our response to these comments is analogous to our response to Comment 92 (see Response 92). Specifically, we disagree that a smaller type size should be used for the statement of availability for the reasons discussed in Response 92. We disagree that the type size, color, and contrasting background of the statement of availability should be tied to the type size, color, and contrasting background most frequently used throughout the menu for the names of standard menu items for the reasons discussed in Response 92. However, we agree that we should provide additional flexibility for the contrasting background of the statement of availability by permitting the statement to be in a background at least as contrasting as that used for the calorie declarations. Consequently, we have revised § 101.11(b)(2)(i)(C)(1) to do so. In addition, we are making a conforming editorial change to the grammatical construction of the requirement used for the color of the statement of availability to match the grammatical construction of the revised requirement for the contrasting background used for the statement of availability. We also are making an editorial correction for clarity to insert "type size of any" between "no smaller than the smallest" and "calorie declaration." With these changes, § 101.11(b)(2)(i)(C)(1) requires that the statement of availability be posted prominently and in a clear and conspicuous manner in a type size no smaller than the smallest type size of any calorie declaration appearing on the same menu or menu board and in the same color or in a color at least as conspicuous as that used for the caloric declarations, and with the same contrasting background or a background at least as contrasting as that used for the caloric declarations. (Emphasis added.) We conclude that the type size, color, and contrasting background requirements for the statement of availability in § 101.11(b)(2)(i)(C)(1) will help ensure that the statement of availability is prominent, clear, and conspicuous, as required by sections 403(q)(5)(H)(ii)(IV) and 403(f) of the FD&C Act.

C. Placement of the Statement of Availability

For menus, proposed § 101.11(b)(2)(i)(C)(2) would require that the statement of availability appear on the bottom of the first page with menu items. For menus with more than two pages, it would also require that the statement of availability appear either at the bottom of every page with menu items (proposed § 101.11(b)(2)(i)(C)(2)(i)), or at the bottom of only the first page with menu items, as long as a symbol (e.g., asterisk) clearly referring to the required statement appearing on the first page of the menu follows the term `Calories' or `Cal,' where the term first appears on each page after the page with the statement (proposed § 101.11(b)(2)(i)(C)(2)(ii)). For menu boards, proposed § 101.11(b)(2)(i)(C)(3) would require that the statement of availability appear on the bottom of the menu board immediately above or below the succinct statement. In the following paragraphs, we discuss comments on these proposed provisions. After considering these comments, we are:

- Revising proposed § 101.11(b)(2)(i)(C)(2) to require that the statement of availability appear on the first page of a menu with menu items and to delete the proposed provisions that would have required the statement of availability, or a symbol referring to the statement of availability, on subsequent menu pages;

- Revising both proposed § 101.11(b)(2)(i)(C)(2) and (b)(2)(i)(C)(3) to provide that the statement of availability must appear immediately above, below, or beside the succinct statement; and

- Making additional editorial changes for consistency.

(Comment 97) Some comments supported the proposed requirements for placement of the statement of availability. A few comments disagreed with our proposal that a symbol (e.g., asterisk) can be used to refer to the statement of availability on the first page, if the statement does not appear on every page. These comments considered that requiring the placement of asterisks on each subsequent page in reference to a disclosure on the first page with menu items would only confuse a reader who, upon seeing an asterisk, has been trained since elementary school to look for the associated footnote at the bottom of the page on which the asterisk appears.

A few comments expressed concern about the space that the statement of availability would take in light of other statements on menus (such as consumer advisories), and recommended that the statement of availability appear only once on the menu, either on the first or last page. The comments agreed that the statement of availability should appear at the bottom of menus and menu boards, but recommended that we require that the statement appear only once on menus and menu boards, and not on each page or panel. One comment recommended that covered establishments be able to put the statement of availability on a separate sign near the menu boards.

(Response 97) We are not revising the rule to allow a covered establishment to post the statement of availability on a separate sign near a menu board as suggested by the comment. This comment is analogous to a comment on the proposed requirements for the placement of the succinct statement (see Comment 93), and our response to this comment is analogous to our response to Comment 93 (see Response 93). Section 403(q)(5)(H)(ii)(IV) of the FD&C Act requires that covered establishments post a prominent, clear, and conspicuous statement of availability on menus and menu boards. The comment's request is inconsistent with the express statutory direction. Later in this document, we discuss the requirements for placement of the statement of availability on small signs for self-service food and food on display that may meet the definition of a "menu" or "menu board" in section 403(q)(5)(H)(xi) of the FD&C Act, in that such signs are the primary writings of the establishment from which consumers make order selections (see the discussion of § 101.11(b)(2)(iii)(B) in section XVII.G).

We agree that an asterisk referring to a statement on the first page of a menu may confuse consumers. We also agree that the statement of availability only needs to appear on one page of a menu. Unlike the succinct statement, which is designed to enable the public to understand the significance of the caloric information in the context of a total daily diet and is therefore needed on each page of a menu that includes standard menu items and calorie information, the statement of availability informs consumers that there is additional written nutrition information available on the premises of the covered establishment upon request. We believe that posting the statement of availability on one page of a menu will be adequate to achieve that goal. Consequently, we have revised § 101.11(b)(2)(i)(C)(2) to require that the statement of availability appear on the first page of a menu with menu items and to delete the proposed provisions that would have required the statement of availability, or an asterisk referring to the statement of availability, on subsequent menu pages.

(Comment 98) A few comments maintained that the proposed order of the statement of availability in relation to the succinct statement limits flexibility. The comments contended that both statements would be just as clear and conspicuous if they were to appear in some other position such as side by side or in some other place on the page.

(Response 98) For menu boards, we note that there was an inconsistency in the proposed rule between the preamble and the codified regarding the proposed order of the statement of availability in relation to the succinct statement. According to the preamble, the statement of availability would have been required to appear immediately below the succinct statement (76 FR 19192 at 19211), while in the codified text, proposed § 101.11(b)(2)(i)(C)(3) would require that the statement of availability appear on the bottom of the menu board immediately above or below the succinct statement. For both menus and menu boards, we agree with the comments and are providing additional flexibility for the placement of the statement of availability of the written nutrition information in relation to the succinct statement. We have revised proposed § 101.11(b)(2)(i)(C)(2) and (b)(2)(i)(C)(3) to provide that for menus and menu boards, the statement of availability must appear immediately above, below, or beside the succinct statement. For clarity and consistency, we are specifying the placement of the statement of availability in § 101.11(b)(2)(i)(C)(2) in relation to the succinct statement even though proposed § 101.11(b)(2)(i)(C)(2) did not do so.

XVI. Comments and FDA Response on Proposed § 101.11(b)(2)(ii)—Nutrition Information That Must Be Made Available in Written Form

A. Required Nutrients

Proposed § 101.11(b)(2)(ii) would require, in relevant part, that:

- Certain nutrition information for a standard menu item be available in written form on the premises of the restaurant or similar retail food establishment and provided to the customer upon request;

- The nutrition information be presented in the order listed and using the measurements listed, except as provided in § 101.11(b)(2)(ii)(B);

- Rounding of these nutrients be in compliance with § 101.9(c); and

- Covered establishments include the following nutrition information in the written form, as specified in § 101.11(b)(2)(ii)(A)(1) through (b)(2)(ii)(A)(11):

1. Total number of calories derived from any source (cal)

2. Total number of calories derived from the total fat (fat cal)

3. Total fat (g)

4. Saturated fat (g)

5. Trans fat (g)

6. Cholesterol (mg)

7. Sodium (mg)

8. Total carbohydrate (g)

9. Dietary fiber (g)

10. Sugars (g)

11. Protein (g)

In the following paragraphs, we discuss comments on this proposed provision. After considering these comments, we have revised the provision to:

- Replace the terms "total number of calories derived from any source" and "total number of calories derived from the total fat" with the terms "total calories" and "calories from fat";

- Provide that covered establishments may use the abbreviations allowed for Nutrition Facts for certain packaged foods in § 101.9(j)(13)(ii)(B); and

- Clarify that the information must be provided on the premises of the "covered establishment" rather than the "restaurant or similar retail food establishment" (see the discussion in section VI.I).

(Comment 99) One comment suggested that we come up with a standard list of abbreviations for the nutrients for consistency and consumer understanding. This comment pointed out that we proposed "Cal" as an abbreviation for calories but did not suggest abbreviations for the other nutrients.

(Response 99) We agree with this comment. Providing abbreviations for the written nutrition information will improve the consistency of the written nutrition information provided by different covered establishments. Therefore, we have revised § 101.11(b)(2)(ii) to provide that covered establishments may use the abbreviations allowed for Nutrition Facts for certain packaged foods in § 101.9(j)(13)(ii)(B) for the nutrient information required to be disclosed in the written nutrition information under section 403(q)(5)(H)(ii)(III) of the FD&C Act. For example, a covered establishment may use "sat fat" for saturated fat and "cholest" for cholesterol.

(Comment 100) One comment suggested that "total number of calories derived from any source" (required under section 403(q)(1)(C) of the FD&C Act) be changed to "total number of calories," which, according to the comment, is clear and concise.

(Response 100) We agree with the comment's suggestion that the term "total number of calories derived from any source" can be revised to be more concise. Specifically, we are replacing the term "total number of calories derived from any source" (which had been specified by section 403(q)(1)(C) of the FD&C Act) with "total calories." This change is consistent with how the "total number of calories derived from any source" is disclosed in the Nutrition Facts under § 101.9. For consistency, we are making an analogous revision to replace the term "total number of calories derived from the total fat" with "calories from fat." This change is consistent with section 403(q)(1)(C) of the FD&C Act, and the declaration of "total calories" and "calories from fat" will be consistent with the terms used for nutrition labeling for packaged food (see § 101.9(c)).

(Comment 101) Several comments supported the proposed nutrients that must be listed in the written nutrition information. Some comments suggested that the written nutrition information also include the weight in grams of the standard menu item. These comments considered that the weight of the standard menu item is an important indicator of portion size and allows consumers to compare similar products more easily, and that including the weight of the standard menu item would be consistent with the Nutrition Facts for packaged foods.

(Response 101) We disagree that we should require that the written nutrition information include the weight in grams for each standard menu item. Section 403(q)(5)(H)(ii)(III) of the FD&C Act specifically requires covered establishments to provide in a written form, available on the premises of the covered establishment and to the consumer upon request, the nutrition information required under clauses (C) and (D) of section 403(q)(1) of the FD&C Act. We are only requiring that covered establishments provide in the written nutrition information the nutrition information specified in section 403(q)(5)(H)(ii)(III) of the FD&C Act, along with trans fat, for standard menu items as usually prepared and offered for sale, or in the case of standard menu items that are self-service food or food on display, by displayed food item or per serving. Although the weight of a standard menu item may give some indication of portion sizes, it does not necessarily correlate with how many calories are contained in a food or with what nutrients are in a food. For example, some foods may weigh less than other similar foods but have more calories because of the source of the calories. At this time, we conclude that the written nutrition information required by § 101.11(b)(2)(ii)(A) will allow consumers to make comparisons between menu items and help inform their dietary choices. A covered establishment may voluntarily provide the weight of the standard menu item in the written nutrition information. We also note that for some foods, the weight is already provided as part of the name or description of the standard menu item on the menu or menu board, e.g., a 10-ounce steak versus a 12-ounce steak.

(Comment 102) One comment recommended that the written nutrition information include calcium, potassium, and phosphorus because patients with kidney disease may have diabetes, hypertension, or both. The comment suggested that covered establishments give information on the need to limit these nutrients and to limit sodium.

(Response 102) We disagree with these comments. Section 403(q)(5)(H)(ii)(III) of the FD&C Act requires in relevant part that covered establishments provide, in written form, the nutrition information required under clauses (C) and (D) of section 403(q)(1) of the FD&C Act. Sections 403(q)(1)(C) and (D) of the FD&C Act do not require the disclosure of calcium, potassium, and phosphorus in food labeling. Section 403(q)(5)(H)(vi) of the FD&C Act provides that "[i]f the Secretary determines that a nutrient, other than a nutrient required under [section 403(q)(5)(H)(ii)(III) of the FD&C Act], should be disclosed for the purpose of providing information to assist consumers in maintaining healthy dietary practices, the Secretary may require, by regulation, disclosure of such nutrient in the written form required under [section 403(q)(5)(H)(ii)(III) of the FD&C Act]." However, the comment did not provide any supporting information showing that the disclosure of calcium, potassium, and phosphorus in the written nutrition information will assist consumers in maintaining healthy dietary practices. At this time, we conclude that the nutrition information specified in section 403(q)(5)(H)(ii)(III) of the FD&C Act, along with trans fat information, is sufficient to assist consumers in maintaining healthy dietary practices within the context of section 403(q)(5)(H) of the FD&C Act. If we determine that other nutrient information should be disclosed in the written form required under section 403(q)(5)(H)(ii)(III) of the FD&C Act, we will make changes to such requirements as appropriate. We note that consumers who have a particular disease or health-related condition may be able to use the written nutrition information to follow advice they have received from a health care professional concerning dietary practices relevant to their conditions.

(Comment 103) One comment asked us to permit voluntary declaration of micronutrients such as vitamins and minerals.

(Response 103) We would not object to the voluntary declaration of vitamins and minerals that may be declared on the Nutrition Facts Label of a packaged food (see § 101.9(c)(8)(ii)), provided that the declaration is truthful and not misleading, as required by section 403(a)(1) of the FD&C Act.

(Comment 104) One comment recommended that if future changes are made to the Nutrition Facts of packaged foods, then the requirements for the written nutrition information should be made consistent with such changes.

(Response 104) If future changes are made to the requirements regarding the Nutrition Facts for packaged foods, we will consider whether changes should also be made to the requirements regarding the written nutrition information required by this rule.

(Comment 105) One comment recommended that the nutrient values in the written nutrition information be reviewed and updated yearly or when changes are made.

(Response 105) We agree, in part, and disagree, in part, with this comment. Under § 101.11(c), a covered establishment must have a reasonable basis for its nutrient content declarations. Under section 403(a)(1) of the FD&C Act, covered establishments must also ensure that their nutrient content declarations are truthful and not misleading. To do so, a covered establishment would need to update the written nutrition information when certain changes are made, e.g., as a result of a recipe change that affects the nutrient content of a standard menu item. However, we see no reason why nutrition information for a standard menu item must be updated on a recurring basis (such as yearly) when there are no changes to the standard menu item or its method of preparation.

(Comment 106) One comment recommended that covered establishments provide references for their nutrient values to consumers on request.

(Response 106) We are not requiring a covered establishment to provide supporting references for the nutrient values in its written nutrition information to consumers upon request. Section

403(q)(5)(H) of the FD&C Act generally requires covered establishments to provide calorie and other nutrition information for standard menu items. Further, as required by section 403(q)(5)(H)(iv) of the FD&C Act, a covered establishment must have a reasonable basis for its nutrient content disclosures. Covered establishments must also ensure that their nutrient content disclosures are truthful and not misleading in accordance with section 403(a)(1) of the FD&C Act. Section 403(q)(5)(H) of the FD&C Act does not require that covered establishments provide supporting references for their nutrient content disclosures to consumers. However, we would not object if a covered establishment provides this information voluntarily.

(Comment 107) Several comments generally agreed that trans fat must be included with the written nutrition information. Some comments expressed the view that providing information about trans fat is warranted because of concern with partially hydrogenated vegetable oils.

Comments that opposed including trans fat in the written nutrition information generally focused on the distinction between "industrial trans fat" (i.e., trans fat chemically manufactured from vegetable oils) and trans fat naturally occurring in food such as ruminant animals. Some comments expressed concern that listing such naturally occurring trans fat in the written nutrition information, particularly when it is present in small amounts, could lead to problems in States and localities that have banned the use of trans fat in restaurants, or could lead consumers to think that a covered establishment is breaking State or local law. These comments stated that eliminating the requirement to list trans fat in the written nutrition information, or limiting the listing for trans fat to industrial trans fat, would prevent such problems. Other comments expressed the view that the health effects of naturally occurring trans fat from ruminants may be different from the health effects of trans fat chemically manufactured from vegetable oils. Some comments stated that, in Europe, scientists and regulators have not singled out ruminant trans fat for pejorative labeling. Some comments stated that naturally occurring trans fats derived from high fat ruminant animal products (namely, beef and dairy products) are converted to conjugated linoleic acid, which the comments reported have been associated with health benefits. These comments considered that industrial and naturally occurring trans fat should therefore be distinguished on food nutrition labels and menus to give consumers a more accurate assessment of nutritional quality.

(Response 107) We disagree that we should require the declaration of only "industrial trans fat" in the written nutrition information. For purposes of the current Nutrition Facts label, our regulatory definitions of nutrients (such as for trans fat, total fat, or saturated fat) have traditionally been based on chemical definitions. For example, under § 101.9(c)(2)(ii), the declaration of nutrition information on the label and in labeling of a food must contain a statement of the number of grams of trans fat in a serving, defined as the sum of all unsaturated fatty acids that contain one or more isolated (i.e., nonconjugated) double bonds in a trans configuration. Analytically, this definition captures all trans fatty acid isomers that have isolated bonds, regardless of the origin of the trans fatty acid. For example, vaccenic acid (one of the most abundant trans fatty acids in ruminant fat) is included in the chemical definition of trans fat. Therefore, listing the sum of all unsaturated fatty acids that contain one or more isolated double bonds in a trans configuration regardless of the source of such trans fat is consistent with the requirements for declaring the amount of trans fat in a packaged food on the label for such food (see § 101.9(c)(2)(ii)). Further, in the rulemaking to require the declaration of trans fat, we responded to comments regarding functional or metabolic aspects of trans fatty acids (e.g., their metabolic transformations to other types of fatty acids) rather than on their actual chemical structures, including potential differences between trans fat from industrial sources and trans fat from ruminant sources. We concluded that we should define trans fat based on its chemical definition rather than any functional attributes (68 FR 41434 at 41461, July 11, 2003). The comments provided insufficient information to overturn the conclusion we previously reached about declaring trans fat on the label of packaged food.

We also decline to require the declaration of "industrial trans fat" in the written nutrition information because declaration of ruminant trans fat may lead inspectors or consumers to believe that covered establishments are violating State or local requirements in jurisdictions that ban artificial trans fat. We recognize that, in the United States, some jurisdictions, such as the State of California (Ref. 34), New York City (Ref. 35), the City of Baltimore (Ref. 36), and Montgomery County, Maryland (Ref. 37) have imposed restrictions on the use of industrial trans fat ingredients in food service establishments. However, a trans fat declaration of 0.5 grams or more for a standard menu item in the written nutrition information of a covered establishment does not necessarily mean that the covered establishment is violating a State or local requirement that prohibits industrial trans fat ingredients. So long as such standard menu item does not contain the restricted trans fat ingredients and is otherwise in compliance with the applicable State or local trans fat requirement, a trans fat declaration of 0.5 grams or more for such standard menu item could mean that the menu item contains a certain amount of naturally occurring trans fat. States and localities would be able to continue to enforce requirements restricting artificial trans fat ingredients relying on the same measures they already use to determine if establishments under their jurisdiction are using a prohibited ingredient.

We also note that we recently published a tentative determination that partially hydrogenated oils, the source of industrially produced trans fat, are not generally recognized as safe for any use in food based on current scientific evidence establishing the health risks associated with the consumption of trans fat (78 FR 67169, November 8, 2013). If this determination is finalized, we will consider whether the trans fat requirements of this rule should be amended.

B. Manner of Presentation of the Written Nutrition Information

Proposed § 101.11(b)(2)(ii) would require, in relevant part, that the written nutrition information be presented in a clear and conspicuous manner. We received several comments on this proposed provision. After considering these comments, we have revised the provision to specify that the written nutrition information must be "clear and conspicuous," including in a color, type size, and in a contrasting background that render the information likely to be read and understood by the ordinary individual under customary conditions of purchase and use.

(Comment 108) One comment supported the proposed requirements that the written nutrition information be clear and conspicuous. Some comments asked us to give more guidance on format and on the standard for the written nutrition information to be presented in a clear and conspicuous manner—e.g., that it be easy to read, have a large enough font, have a contrasting background, and not use all capital letters for the names of standard menu items. One comment recommended that we include specifications for font size.

(Response 108) We disagree that we should specify the particular type size and contrasting background that must be used in the written nutrition information, and prohibit the use of all capital letters for the names of standard menu items in the written nutrition information. Section 403(q)(5)(H)(ii) of the FD&C Act requires covered establishments to provide the written nutrition information required by section 403(q)(5)(H)(ii)(III) of the FD&C Act in a clear and conspicuous manner. As discussed later in this document (see the discussion of § 101.11(b)(2)(ii)(D) in section XVI.E), we are providing covered establishments with the flexibility to use different types of media (e.g., flyers, posters, booklets, kiosks) to provide the written nutrition information. Whether the written nutrition information is clear and conspicuous depends on the media through which a covered establishment chooses to provide the written nutrition information. For example, a specific type size and contrasting background may result in written nutrition information that is clear and conspicuous on a tray liner or brochure, but not on a poster that a consumer may view from several feet away. Thus, we are not establishing specific requirements for type size, contrasting background, or use of capital letters for the written nutrition information so that covered establishments have the flexibility to provide the written nutrition information in a clear and conspicuous manner based on the particular media through which the information is presented.

However, we agree that some guidance is needed on the requirement that the written nutrition information be provided in a clear and conspicuous manner. Section 403(f) of the FD&C Act provides that a food will be deemed to be misbranded "[i]f any word, statement, or other information required by or under authority of this Act to appear on the label or labeling is not prominently placed thereon with such conspicuousness (as compared with other words, statements, designs, or devices, in the labeling) and in such terms as to render it likely to be read and understood by the ordinary individual under customary conditions of purchase and use." Accordingly, we conclude that in order for the written nutrition information to be clear and conspicuous, the information must be presented in a manner that renders it likely to be read and understood by the ordinary individual under customary conditions of purchase and use. Specifically, we have revised § 101.11(b)(2)(ii) to require that the written nutrition information be presented in a clear and conspicuous manner, including using a color, type size, and contrasting background that render the information likely to be read and understood by the ordinary individual under customary conditions of purchase and use. We are also revising § 101.11(f) to state that a standard menu item offered for sale in a covered establishment shall be deemed misbranded under sections 201(n), 403(a), 403(f), and/or 403(q) of the FD&C Act if its label or labeling is not in conformity with paragraph (b) or (c) of the section.

(Comment 109) One comment asked us to require that standard menu items in the written nutrition information be listed in the same order as they are on menus and menu boards.

(Response 109) We disagree that we should require covered establishments to list standard menu items in the written nutrition information in the same order as on menus and menu boards. The comment provided no basis for why this particular order of listing standard menu items is the only order that would be useful to consumers. We are providing flexibility for a covered establishment to list its standard menu items in the written nutrition information in a manner that is best suited to its menu offerings, and conclude that the written nutrition information can enable consumers to make informed dietary choices regardless of the order in which the standard menu items are listed.

(Comment 110) One comment responded to our request for comment on whether to require that nutrients that are particularly important for consumers with obesity and diabetes to monitor in order to maintain healthy dietary practices (e.g., total calories, total fat, sodium, sugar) be bolded or placed in a separate table of nutritional content (76 FR 19192 at 19214-19215). This comment opposed such measures because doing so would highlight the negative aspects of food even though the food also has positive nutrients. Another comment supported the bolding of nutrients of concern to consumers with obesity and diabetes, such as saturated fat and sodium.

(Response 110) We disagree that we should decide whether to require measures for highlighting nutrient declarations important to maintain healthy dietary practices for consumers with obesity and diabetes based on a concern that doing so would highlight the "negative" aspects of a menu item even though the menu item also has "positive" aspects. However, we did not receive sufficient information in the comments to warrant adding a requirement to emphasize certain nutrients, and we are not requiring such a requirement in this rule. The requirements for the written nutrition information in § 101.11(b)(2)(ii) make nutrition information available to consumers in a direct and accessible manner to enable consumers to make informed and healthful dietary choices.

C. Nutrients in Insignificant Amounts

Proposed § 101.11(b)(2)(ii)(B) would provide that if a standard menu item contains insignificant amounts of all the nutrients required to be disclosed in § 101.11(b)(2)(ii)(A), the establishment is not required to include nutrition information regarding the standard menu item in the written form. Proposed § 101.11(b)(2)(ii)(B) would explain, however, that if the covered establishment makes a nutrient content claim or health claim, the establishment is required to provide nutrition information on the nutrient that is the subject of the claim in accordance with § 101.10. Proposed § 101.11(b)(2)(ii)(B) would provide that covered establishments may present the written nutrition information in a simplified format for standard menu items that contain insignificant amounts of six or more of the required nutrients and proposed § 101.11(b)(2)(ii)(B)(1) would define what is an insignificant amount.

We note that there is an inconsistency regarding the nutrients that must be included in the simplified format between the preamble discussion and the regulatory text in proposed § 101.11(b)(2)(ii)(B)(2). In the preamble discussion, we stated: "In addition, we are proposing that the simplified format must include information on the nutrients required in § 101.9(f)(2)(i) and (ii) (i.e., total calories, total fat, total carbohydrate, protein, and sodium)." (76 FR 19192 at 19213). However, proposed § 101.11(b)(2)(ii)(B)(2) specified that the simplified format must include information on total carbohydrates, total fat, protein, and sodium, calories from fat, and any other nutrients identified in § 101.11(b)(2)(ii)(A) that are present in more than insignificant amounts. Proposed § 101.11(b)(2)(ii)(B)(2) did not specify that the simplified format must include information on total calories, as we intended. In addition, proposed § 101.11(b)(2)(ii)(B)(2) did not make it clear that the simplified format must include calories from fat only if calories from fat are present in more than insignificant amounts, as would be consistent with § 101.9(f)(2)(ii). We have revised and redesignating § 101.11(b)(2)(ii)(B)(2) so that it contains three separate subparagraphs that more clearly communicate the requirements. As revised, § 101.11(b)(2)(ii)(B)(2) requires that the simplified format must include information, in a column, list, or table, on the nutrients specified in § 101.11(b)(2)(ii)(B)(2)(i) and (ii). Section 101.11(b)(2)(ii)(B)(2)(i) specifies that the simplified format must include information on total calories, total fat, total carbohydrates, protein, and sodium. Section 101.11(b)(2)(ii)(B)(2)(ii) specifies that the simplified format must include calories from fat and any other nutrients identified in § 101.11(b)(2)(ii)(A) that are present in more than insignificant amounts. Section 101.11(b)(2)(ii)(B)(3) specifies that if the simplified format is used, the statement "Not a significant source of _____" (with the blank filled in with the names of the nutrients required to be declared in the written nutrient information and calories from fat that are present in insignificant amounts) must be included at the bottom of the list of nutrients.

In the following paragraphs, we discuss comments on proposed § 101.11(b)(2)(ii)(B)(2). We are finalizing it without change other than to revise § 101.11(b)(2)(ii)(B)(2) to correct the discrepancy between the description of the proposed requirement in the preamble and the regulatory text and to clarify the requirements.

(Comment 111) One comment recommended that the simplified format we proposed in § 101.11(b)(2)(ii)(B)(2), when a standard menu item contains insignificant amounts of more than one-half of the nutrients required to be declared in the written nutrition information, include information on fiber. The comment contended that fiber is an important element in considering the overall nutritional value of a certain food, both in addressing obesity and diabetes. The comment stated that only knowing information on the total carbohydrates without information on the fiber will not allow consumers to make sufficiently healthy choices or will undermine their intent to do so.

(Response 111) If a standard menu item has an insignificant amount of six or more of the required nutrients, the simplified format must include information on total calories, total fat, total carbohydrates, protein, and sodium (§ 101.11(b)(2)(ii)(B)(2)(i)) as well as information on calories from fat and any other nutrient that is present in the food in more than insignificant amounts (§ 101.11(b)(2)(ii)(B)(2)(ii)). Thus, if fiber is present in a standard menu item at a level that is more than insignificant (i.e., one gram or more), the amount of fiber must appear in the simplified format. On the other hand, if an insignificant amount of fiber is present in a standard menu item, the simplified format must disclose this information through the statement, "Not a significant source of ____" (with the blank filled in with "fiber" since fiber is required to be declared in the written nutrition information) (§ 101.11(b)(2)(ii)(B)(3)). Therefore, the simplified format for the written nutrition information already must include information on fiber, and there is no need to revise proposed § 101.11(b)(2)(ii)(B) to include fiber as recommended by the comment.

D. Variable Menu Items

Proposed § 101.11(b)(2)(ii)(C) would require that, for variable menu items, the nutrition information listed in § 101.11(b)(2)(ii)(A) must be declared as follows for each size offered for sale:

(1) The nutrition information required in § 101.11(b)(2)(ii)(A) must be declared for the basic preparation of the item and, separately, for each topping, flavor, or variable component.

(2) If the calories and other nutrients are the same for different flavors, varieties, and substitutable components of the combination meal, each variety, flavor, and substitutable component of the combination meal is not required to be listed separately. All items that have the same nutrient levels could be listed together with the nutrient levels listed only once.

In the proposed rule, we considered the following options for providing the nutrition information in the written form for a variable menu item:

- Option 1. List the nutrition information for each nutrient in the variable menu item as a range.

- Option 2. List the nutrition information for each component in the variable menu item (the proposed requirement).

- Option 3. If a standard menu item only has two variations (e.g. a sandwich with fruit or with fries), provide both numbers for each nutrient in each option with a forward slash between (e.g., 450/700). If three or more options are available, provide the range in calories.

In the proposed rule, we stated that option 2 provides the consumer with all the required nutrient information for each flavor or variety of a variable item, or each component of a combination meal in a format that facilitates quick comparisons between different menu items (76 FR 19192 at 19213). In the following paragraphs, we discuss comments on this proposed provision. We are making no changes in response to these comments.

However, similar to the specific format requirements we established for declaring calories on a menu or menu board for toppings listed on a menu or menu board, where the amount of the topping on the menu item decreases based on the total number of toppings ordered, we are establishing in § 101.11(b)(2)(ii)(C)(2) specific format requirements for providing the written nutrition information for toppings if the amount of the topping included on the basic preparation of the menu item decreases based on the total number of toppings ordered for the menu item (such as is sometimes the case with pizza toppings). Section 101.11(b)(2)(ii)(C)(2) of the final rule specifies that if the amount of the topping included on the basic preparation of the menu item decreases based on the total number of toppings ordered for the menu item, the nutrients for each topping must be declared as single values representing the nutrients for each topping when added to a one-topping menu item, specifying that the nutrient declaration is for the topping when added to a one-topping menu item. The nutrients for each topping must also be declared for each size of the menu item offered for sale, as required by § 101.11(b)(2)(ii)(C). We are establishing requirements for providing the written nutrition information for variable menu items offered for sale with the option of adding toppings, and specifying the format and manner of such nutrient content disclosures, as required by sections 403(q)(5)(H)(v) and (x)(II)(bb) of the FD&C Act. Section 101.11(b)(2)(ii)(C)(2) helps ensure that consumers are given accurate and consistent information about the nutrient of each topping on a menu item. We would not object if a covered establishment voluntarily includes a statement on the written nutrition information explaining how the nutrients per topping might fluctuate if ordering multiple toppings; for example, such a statement regarding a pizza pie might say, "Nutrient values per topping may decrease as the number of toppings per pizza increases." Section 101.11(b)(2)(ii)(C)(2) is therefore consistent with the requirements for declaring calories for toppings listed on the menu or menu board, where the amount of the topping on the menu item decreases based on the total number of toppings ordered.

Because we added this requirement in § 101.11(b)(2)(ii)(C)(2) to address the potential variation in nutrient content for each topping based on the total number of toppings ordered, proposed § 101.11(b)(2)(ii)(C)(2), which allows items that have the same nutrient values to be listed together with the nutrient values listed only once, is renumbered for the final rule as § 101.11(b)(2)(ii)(C)(3). We are replacing the phrase "substitutable component" in two places in the first sentence of § 101.11(b)(2)(ii)(C)(3) with "variable component." We are making this change for consistency with the term used in § 101.11(b)(2)(ii)(C)(1). We also are replacing the phrase "nutrient levels" in two places in the final sentence of § 101.11(b)(2)(ii)(C)(3) with "nutrient values." We are making this change for consistency with § 101.11(c), which we have revised to consistently use the term "values" in the requirements for determination of nutrient content.

(Comment 112) A few comments supported option 2. Some comments opposed the use of slashes for different flavors and considered that slashes would be confusing and unclear because consumers are not used to nutrition information in restaurants.

(Response 112) We are retaining Option 2 in the rule for providing the written nutrition information for variable menu items generally. Option 2 does not specify the use of the slashes opposed by some comments.

E. Form of the Written Nutrition Information

Proposed § 101.11(b)(2)(ii)(D) would permit the written nutrition information required in § 101.11(b)(2)(ii)(A) to be provided on a counter card, sign, poster, handout, booklet, loose leaf binder, or electronic device such as a computer, or in a menu, or in any other form that similarly permits the written declaration of the required nutrient content information for all standard menu items. Proposed § 101.11(b)(2)(ii)(D) would explain that if the written information is not in a form that can be given to the customer upon request, it must be readily available in a manner and location on the premises that allows the customer/consumer to review the written nutrition information upon request.

In the proposed rule, we discussed the flexibility provided by proposed § 101.11(b)(2)(ii)(D) for the written nutrition information and requested comment on whether we should be more prescriptive in the format and manner of providing the written nutrition information in order to ensure they are useful to consumers (76 FR 19192 at 19214). We also stated that we would not object to the use of tray liners or wrappers as a means to provide nutrition information, as long as the tray liners or wrappers are available upon request to the consumers, and the tray liner or wrapper contains nutrition information for all standard menu items offered for sale at the covered establishment (76 FR 19192 at 19214).

In the following paragraphs, we discuss comments on this proposed provision. We are finalizing it without change, except for an editorial change from "written information" to "written nutrition information" in the final sentence. With this editorial change, § 101.11(b)(2)(ii)(D) will consistently use the same phrase ("written nutrition information").

(Comment 113) One comment supported our proposal to permit flexibility in how the written nutrition information would be provided but questioned the use of wrappers, arguing that it is unlikely that there would be enough room on a wrapper to list the nutrition information for all standard menu items in a covered establishment and to make the information easily readable. Another comment recommended that § 101.11(b)(2)(ii)(D) specify the media allowed for the written nutrition information, with a petition and approval process for alternate media, rather than include a "catch-all phrase" such as "any other form that similarly permits the written declaration of the required nutrient content information for all standard menu items," which was included in proposed § 101.11(b)(2)(ii)(D). Another comment recommended that we expressly recognize that Nutrition Facts labels can be used to convey the written nutrition information.

(Response 113) Section 101.11(b)(2)(ii) specifies that the written nutrition information must be provided in a clear and conspicuous manner, including using a color, type size, and contrasting background that render the information likely to be read and understood by the ordinary individual under customary conditions of purchase and use. A covered establishment could use a wrapper if the written nutrition information for all standard menu items offered for sale at the covered establishment can be presented in a clear and conspicuous manner on the wrapper, is available upon request to the consumers, in accordance with § 101.11(b)(2)(ii), and otherwise complies with the applicable sections of the FD&C Act and § 101.11(b)(2)(ii). For example, there may be enough room on a wrapper to include the written nutrition information for all standard menu items in a clear and conspicuous manner when a covered establishment offers for sale a small number of standard menu items.

In addition, § 101.11(b)(2)(ii) ensures that the written nutrition information is presented in a clear and conspicuous manner without prescribing a list of allowed media or the exact format of the written nutrition information. If we amended § 101.11(b)(2)(ii)(D) to specify the particular types of media that can be used by covered establishments to provide the required written nutrition information, as recommended by one comment, § 101.11(b)(2)(ii)(D) would limit the types of media that can be used by covered establishments, including those developed based on technological advancements. Further, § 101.11(b)(2)(ii) would need to amended every time a covered establishment sought to use a type of media not specified. Rather than specify the media allowed for the written nutrition information, we conclude that the public health goal of this rule would be better served by providing flexibility to covered establishments to use any media to provide the written nutrition information in the way that is best suited to their establishments, as long as the written nutrition information is available on the premises of the covered establishment and to the consumer upon request, is clear and conspicuous, and otherwise complies with the requirements of the applicable sections of the FD&C Act and § 101.11(b)(2)(ii). Providing such flexibility satisfies the requirements of section 403(q)(5)(H)(ii)(III) of the FD&C Act while taking into consideration the varying practices at different covered establishments. With this flexibility, the petition and approval process suggested by the comment is unnecessary.

We agree that Nutrition Facts labels can be used to provide the written nutrition information required under § 101.11(b)(2)(ii) for packaged foods, and this rule provides flexibility to do so (see the discussions of § 101.11(b)(2)(iii)(C) in Response 133, and of § 101.11(c)(1) in section XVIII).

(Comment 114) Some comments stated that the written nutrition information should not have to be provided with carry out menus. The comments recommended that carry out menus could contain a link to the covered establishment's Internet menu where the written nutrition information may be found. Another comment stated that the written nutrition information should be permitted on Internet menus but not required.

(Response 114) We agree with the comments stating that the written nutrition information should not be required with carry out menus. We are not requiring a specific manner for providing the written nutrition information, as long as the written nutrition information is available on the premises of the covered establishment and provided to the consumer upon request, is disclosed in a clear and conspicuous manner, and otherwise complies with the applicable sections of the FD&C Act and § 101.11(b)(2)(ii). If a consumer who orders from a menu such as a carry out menu or an Internet menu requests the written nutrition information, the covered establishment must provide the information to the consumer. For example, if a covered establishment delivers a menu item to a consumer, the covered establishment could deliver the written nutrition information with the menu item if the consumer requests the information. As another example, if a consumer orders from an Internet menu, a covered establishment could provide the written nutrition information on its Web site or include a link directing the consumer to a Web site providing the written nutrition information. Similarly, as suggested by the comments, a covered establishment could provide a link on carry out menus that directs consumers to a Web site providing the written nutrition information. We note that all menus, including carry out menus, and menu boards must include a prominent, clear, and conspicuous statement regarding the availability of the written nutrition information, as required by section 403(q)(5)(H)(ii)(IV) of the FD&C Act.

(Comment 115) Some comments recommended that we require that the written nutrition information be readily available upon request to consumers before ordering. The comments also recommended that the information be provided in a manner that allows consumers to compare the information between different menu items before ordering and without losing their place in line or having to leave the table. The comments stated that if the written nutrition information is not in a form that can be given to the consumer upon request, it must be readily available in a manner and location on the premises that allows the consumer to review the written nutrition information when ordering (i.e., the consumer should be able to see and review both the menu or menu board and the written nutrition information at the same time). One comment recommended that the information be provided at the place where consumers place their orders and not upon request. One comment recommended that we ensure that all consumers have access to the information. The comment maintained that information on a poster or on a computer in a fixed location may not be accessible to the mobility impaired.

(Response 115) We decline to require that covered establishments make the written nutrition information readily available to consumers where consumers place their orders rather than providing such information to consumers upon request. Section 403(q)(5)(H)(ii)(III) of the FD&C Act specifically requires covered establishments to provide the written nutrition information "to the consumer upon request." In addition, nothing in § 101.11(b)(2)(ii) would preclude consumers from requesting the written nutrition information before ordering. We disagree that the rule must require a format and manner of providing the written nutrition information that ensures that a consumer who requests written nutrition information will avoid losing a place in an ordering line or leaving a table. A covered establishment has flexibility to use a format (e.g., a poster) that may be readily seen by consumers even if they do not specifically ask to see it.

We agree that covered establishments must make the written nutrition information available to all consumers, including consumers with mobility impairment, upon request, and must ensure that the information is presented in a clear and conspicuous manner to all consumers. Section 101.11(b)(2)(ii)(D) specifically identifies formats such as on a counter card, sign, poster, handout, booklet, loose leaf binder, or electronic device such as a computer, or in a menu through which a covered establishment may provide the written nutrition information.

XVII. Comments and FDA Response on Proposed § 101.11(b)(2)(iii)—Requirements for Food That Is Self-Service or on Display

A. Applicability of § 101.11(b)(2)(i) to Food That Is Self-Service or on Display

Under sections 403(q)(5)(H)(ii)(I)(aa) and (II)(aa) of the FD&C Act, we proposed to establish requirements for the declaration of calories for standard menu items on menus and menu boards in proposed § 101.11(b)(2)(i). Under section 403(q)(5)(H)(iii), we proposed to establish requirements for the declaration of calories for self-service food and food on display in proposed § 101.11(b)(2)(iii). In the proposed rule, we tentatively concluded that when self-service foods and food on display appear on menus or menu boards, the menus or menu boards must bear the calorie declarations required by sections 403(q)(5)(H)(ii)(I)(aa) and (II)(aa) of the FD&C Act (76 FR 19192 at 19216). In other words, we tentatively concluded that self-service food and food on display that appear on a menu or menu board are subject to both requirements for the declaration of calories—i.e., the requirements in § 101.11(b)(2)(i) applicable to declaration on a menu or menu board and the requirements in § 101.11(b)(2)(iii) applicable to self-service food and food on display.

(Comment 116) One comment disagreed with our tentative conclusion that the proposed requirements for calorie declaration of standard menu items on menus and menu boards (§ 101.11(b)(2)(i)(A)) apply to food on display and self-service food that is also listed on menus and menu boards. The comment asserted that this tentative conclusion is against the plain language of section 403(q)(5)(H) of the FD&C Act and that to require covered establishments to label menu boards and display cases is unnecessary. The comment asserted that only requiring calorie labeling on signs adjacent to food on display and self-service food would provide information at the point of ordering and therefore would be more consistent with the requirement of section 403(q)(5)(H) of the FD&C Act that calorie information be provided on menus and menu boards, as defined in section 403(q)(5)(H)(xi) of the FD&C Act ("the primary writing of the . . . establishment from which a consumer makes an order selection").

(Response 116) We disagree with this comment. The plain language of section 403(q)(5)(H)(i) of the FD&C Act provides that "in the case of food that is a standard menu item . . . [the covered] establishment shall disclose the information described in subclauses (ii) and (iii)" (emphasis added). As discussed in the proposed rule, the word "and" between the references to subclause (ii) and subclause (iii) indicates that for each standard menu item, including self-service food and food on display, covered establishments must follow the requirements in section 403(q)(5)(H)(ii) of the FD&C Act as applicable and section 403(q)(5)(H)(iii) of the FD&C Act as applicable. Further, if Congress had meant for section 403(q)(5)(H)(ii) of the FD&C Act not to apply to self-service food and food on display, it could have included an exception for such foods within that section, as it did for foods described in section 403(q)(5)(H)(vii) of the FD&C Act, but it did not include such an exception. See e.g., Russello v. U.S., 464 U.S. 16, 23 (1983) ("[W]here Congress includes particular language in one section of a statute but omits it in another section of the same [statute], it is generally presumed that Congress acts intentionally and purposely in the disparate inclusion or exclusion.") (internal citations omitted). In addition, a consumer may make his or her order selection by using information provided on a traditional menu or menu board or on a sign adjacent to a self-service food or food on display. Disclosing calorie information for self-service food and food on display on traditional menus and menu boards, where such menus and menu boards list self-service food and food on display, and on signs adjacent to self-service food and food on display would help ensure that consumers are able to see the calorie declarations before making order selections and is consistent with the plain language of sections 403(q)(5)(H)(ii) and (iii) of the FD&C Act.

Therefore, when a self-service food or food on display is listed on a menu or menu board, the food is subject to both § 101.11(b)(2)(i) for declaration of calories on menus and menu boards and to § 101.11(b)(2)(iii) for foods on display.

B. Placement of Calories for Self-Service Foods and Foods on Display

Proposed § 101.11(b)(2)(iii)(A) would require that when a self-service food or food on display is already accompanied by an individual sign, adjacent to the food, that provides the food's name, price, or both, the calories per item or per serving must be provided on the sign. When a self-service food or food on display is not already accompanied by an individual sign, adjacent to the food, that provides the food's name, price, or both, the covered establishment must place a sign adjacent to each food with the number of calories per serving or per item in a clear and conspicuous manner.

In the following paragraphs, we discuss comments on this proposed provision. After considering these comments, we have revised the provision to provide more options for the declaration of calories for self-service food and food on display and to require that if the individual sign does not already include the serving, the amount of the serving on which the calories are based must also be provided on the sign, e.g., "150 calories per scoop."

We also are correcting the introductory text in § 101.11(b)(2)(iii) by inserting a hyphen between "self" and "service."

(Comment 117) Several comments supported the requirements in proposed § 101.11(b)(2)(iii). Some comments recommended that foods on display be labeled with calorie information regardless of whether the food is served by the customer or employee. Some comments asked us to clarify that a calorie declaration is also required for displayed foods such as pastries and doughnuts at bakeries and ice cream behind a glass case in an ice cream shop.

(Response 117) The definition of "self-service food" includes restaurant-type food that is served by the customers themselves, and the definition of "foods on display" includes restaurant-type food that is visible to the customer before the customer makes a selection. In general, pastries, donuts, and ice cream on display, such as behind a glass case, meet the definition of food on display. Under these definitions, the requirements in proposed § 101.11(b)(2)(iii) apply to standard menu items that are foods served by the customers themselves as well as to standard menu items that are foods such as pastries, donuts, and ice cream that are behind a glass case or in an ice cream shop and are served by an employee.

(Comment 118) Some comments requested flexibility to determine the placement of calorie information that works best for them. Some comments recommended that the calorie declaration be permitted to be placed on a single sign, or electronically via kiosks or touch screen computers, and not on all individual signs. One comment asserted that, for buffets, the layout and number of items make it difficult to display signs for hundreds of items without cluttering the space or obstructing the view. The comment also asserted that customers may inadvertently move the signs, and therefore, the calorie declaration should instead appear on counters or in display cases.

Some comments stated that buffets are unique because foods vary and change often. For example, according to one comment, a restaurant may have as many as 175 different menu items in a meal period. One comment stated that the foods are changed multiple times a day, the items may change from day to day, and the rotation of foods would create confusion if the food signs are not accurately changed with each new menu item.

One comment stated that the location and size of the food signs are affected by health and safety regulations because the food signs could lead to contamination of the food and because food signs adjacent to heated areas or grills for food items cooked to order could create a hazard. Moreover, the comment noted that multiple menu items may be simultaneously prepared to order on open grills. This comment recommended that these types of restaurants be permitted to place the calorie information on individual signs adjacent to or in close proximity to the food by using a variety of options (e.g., sneeze guards; partition or placard; menu board or placard adjacent to the buffet with all the items listed with nutrition content; pamphlet adjacent to the buffet; written or electronically displayed information using kiosks; tablet computers; or touch screen computers).

(Response 118) We agree that placing individual signs adjacent to a self-service food or food on display may pose a hazard in certain circumstances, such as when there is an open heat source (such as a grill) in close proximity to the sign that could create a fire hazard. We also agree that more flexibility is needed for foods that are constantly being replenished or changed. Therefore, to provide more flexibility and reduce the potential for a sign used to declare calories for self-service food or food on display to create a hazard, we have revised § 101.11(b)(2)(iii)(A) to allow covered establishments to declare calories for standard menu items that are self-service or on display, and the serving or unit used to determine the calorie content (e.g., "per scoop" or "per muffin"), using one of the following options:

- On a sign, adjacent to and clearly associated with the corresponding food item;

- On a sign attached to a sneeze guard with the calorie declaration and the serving or unit used to determine the calorie content above each specific menu item so that the consumer can clearly associate the calorie declaration with the standard menu item. For example, if a buffet has several menu items in the serving display case including, in particular, a broccoli and cheese casserole, the sign attached to the sneeze guard right above the broccoli and cheese casserole may declare the calories, e.g., "200 calories per scoop." If it is not clear to which food the calorie declaration and serving or unit refers, then the sign must also include the name of the food, e.g., "Broccoli and cheese casserole—200 calories per scoop;" or

- On a single sign or placard listing the calorie declaration for several menu items along with the names of the menu items, so long as the sign or placard is located where a consumer can view the name, calorie declaration, and serving or unit of a particular menu item while the consumer is selecting that item. The sign must list the names of the menu items along with their corresponding calorie declarations. For example, for a soup station, the sign or placard must list all the soups that are available at that station along with each calorie declaration, e.g., "chicken noodle soup, 125 calories per cup," "minestrone soup, 100 calories per cup." This sign may be placed on the wall behind the station, on a sign at the beginning or end of the station, or at another location so long as the consumer can read the name, calorie declaration, and serving or unit of a particular menu item while selecting the menu item.

Each option, when implemented appropriately, associates the calorie declaration with the appropriate food on display or self-service food to help ensure that consumers can see such declarations when making their selections.

(Comment 119) In the proposed rule, we stated that placing a separate sign with calorie information adjacent to a food that is already accompanied by a sign bearing its name, price, or both, could make it more difficult for consumers to clearly associate the calorie information with its corresponding self-service food or food on display (76 FR 19192 at 19215). We requested comment on whether establishments that already provide an individual sign identifying each food on display or self-service food with its name, price, or both should have the option of providing a separate individual sign for each food on display or self-service food for the calorie declaration, so long as the sign with the calorie declaration is adjacent to and clearly associated with its corresponding food.

One comment recommended that calories appear on the same sign as the name or price of the food rather than on a separate sign, because more than one sign could cause confusion.

(Response 119) We acknowledge the comment's concern, which mirrored a concern we raised in the proposed rule. However, in light of the recommendations in the comments describing the need for more flexibility in declaring calories for self-service foods and foods on display, we have concluded that there are a number of ways in which a covered establishment can comply with section 403(q)(5)(H)(iii) of the FD&C Act to provide calorie declarations for self-service foods and foods on display based on the establishment's particular operations, including the use of a separate sign placed adjacent to a self-service food or food on display that is clearly associated with the food (see Comment 118 and Response 118). Therefore, we have revised § 101.11(b)(2)(iii)(A) by removing the sentence requiring that when a self-service food or food on display is already accompanied by an individual sign, adjacent to the food, that provides the food's name, price, or both, the calories per item or per serving must be provided on the sign. In addition, we have revised § 101.11(b)(2)(iii)(A) by providing options for a covered establishment to provide calorie declarations on signs for self-service food and food on display, including the options described in Response 118. We are making these changes based on the reasons discussed in Response 118 and because we recognize that existing individual signs for these foods may be quite small and either not have enough space for the calorie declaration, or cause the sign to be so crowded that the calorie declaration may not be easily read or clear and conspicuous enough for the consumer to read the information. (See, e.g., the discussions in Comment 126 and Response 126, and in Comment 127 and Response 127, about the requirements for type size of the calorie declaration when a self-service food or food on display is already accompanied by a sign with the food's name, price, or both.)

C. Declaring Calories "Per Item" or "Per Serving"

Proposed § 101.11(b)(2)(iii)(A)(1) would specify that for purposes of § 101.11(b)(2)(iii)(A), "per item" means per each discrete unit offered for sale, for example, a bagel, a slice of pizza, a muffin, or a multi-serving food such as a whole cake. Proposed § 101.11(b)(2)(iii)(A)(2) would specify that for purposes of § 101.10(b)(2)(iii)(A), "per serving" means: (1) Per each common household measure, e.g., cup, scoop, tablespoon, offered for sale as dispensed using a serving instrument such as a scoop, ladle, cup, or measuring spoon; or (2) per unit of weight offered for sale, e.g., per half pound or pound.

In the following paragraphs, we discuss comments on these proposed provisions. After considering these comments, we are:

- Deleting "a multi-serving food such as a whole cake" from the list of examples of what the rule means by "per item." As discussed in section VI.C, the definition of "restaurant-type food" established in the rule includes food that is usually eaten on the premises, while walking away, or soon after arriving at another location, and whole cakes that are self-service food or food on display are not likely to meet this definition.

- Providing the options to declare calories "per serving instrument" or "per common household measure" in separate subparagraphs, rather than in the same subparagraph, to emphasize that these are distinct alternatives for declaration of calories "per serving."

- Revising the examples of what we mean by "per unit of weight offered for sale" to be "per quarter pound" or "per 4 ounces." We are making this change because examples of a quarter pound or 4 ounces are more likely to reflect a serving of self-service food or food on display.

- Changing § 101.11(b)(2)(iii)(A)(1) and (b)(2)(iii)(A)(2) to read "paragraph (b)(2)(iii)(A) of this section" rather than "§ 101.11(b)(2)(iii)(A)" to be more consistent with FDA's general practice. We note that the proposed rule had identified the cross-reference as "§ 101.10(b)(2)(ii)(A)." We revised this to "§ 101.11(b)(2)(iii)(A)" in the correction document, but did not identify the format change at that time.

(Comment 120) One comment suggested that the portion of the standard menu item used to calculate the calorie content also be clearly displayed in the same font, color, and size as the item name and be posted on or next to the available food on display or self-service food.

(Response 120) We agree that the serving or unit of a standard menu item that is a self-service food or food on display used to determine the calorie content for such food must be included in the calorie declaration. Without information about the serving or unit of a self-service food or food on display, the consumer would not be able to ascertain the calorie content of the amount of food that would be consumed. This would defeat the purpose of the calorie declaration. Therefore, we have revised § 101.11(b)(2)(iii)(A) to require that the calorie declaration for foods on display and self-service food include the serving or unit on which the calorie content is based. The requirements in § 101.11(b)(2)(iii)(A)(3)(ii) for font size and color will apply to the entire calorie declaration, including the serving or unit used to determine calorie content. (See the discussion of § 101.11(b)(2)(iii)(A)(3)(ii) in section XVII.E.2.)

(Comment 121) One comment asked us to allow a covered establishment to list nutrition information for standard menu items that are self-service or on display per serving size and requested clarification on how the RACC would be used in this case. The comment asked us to keep in mind that many retailers would like to align their calorie declarations for menu items with serving sizes for packaged food so as not to have two different serving sizes.

(Response 121) In Response 65 in section XI, we explained why a calorie declaration for a multiple-serving standard menu item that is not self-service or on display must declare "the number of calories contained in the standard menu item, as usually prepared and offered for sale" instead of per RACC (to the extent that there is a RACC for such standard menu item). Similarly, we disagree that a calorie declaration for a standard menu item that is a self-service food or food on display should be declared per RACC or per serving size used on packaged food, unless such RACC or serving size is the portion or serving used by the covered establishment to display or otherwise offer such standard menu item for sale. Self-service food and food on display may be portioned differently than a RACC or serving size used on packaged food. Section 403(q)(5)(H) of the FD&C Act does not require a covered establishment to prepare and offer standard menu items in particular sizes or amounts, such as RACCs or serving sizes used on packaged foods. Instead, section 403(q)(5)(H)(iii) of the FD&C Act expressly requires covered establishments to disclose the number of calories for self-service foods and foods on display "per displayed food item or per serving." Accordingly, a covered establishment may choose the portion or serving of the food that it offers for sale, and must base the calorie declaration for a self-service food or food on display per displayed item (e.g., "per muffin") or per serving (e.g., "per scoop") as offered for sale.

(Comment 122) A few comments expressed concern with portion sizes and with declaring nutrient values for items that vary in size and content (e.g., baked potato, chicken breast). Some comments asked for guidance on serving sizes for calorie declarations pertaining to foods on display. One comment asked us to clarify that the calories should be declared per item or serving as offered for sale and not for a portion of a food item that is smaller than the food offered for sale. For example, a covered establishment that offers a large muffin for sale should be required to declare calories per item (i.e., the large muffin) and should not be permitted to declare calories per serving and describe the large muffin as containing two servings.

One comment maintained that calories of foods at salad bars should be declared per cup and not per serving. Several comments asked us to require that calories be based on serving utensil sizes where possible. One comment recommended that we require the same serving size as for packaged food if no utensil is used. The comment suggested that calories be declared per cup if tongs are used for lettuce at a salad bar. The comment suggested that the rule be revised to include:

(iii) The following must be provided for food that is self-service or on display.

"(1) Calories must be provided for each standard serving size offered, e.g., each beverage cup size offered for a fountain beverage dispenser or each container size available for a deli salad.

(2) For purposes of § 101.10(b)(2)(iii)(A), "per item'" means per each discrete unit offered for sale—for example, a bagel, a muffin, a sandwich, or a multi-serving food, such as a whole cake.

(3) If the item is not sold as a discrete unit, it can be labeled per serving. For purposes of § 101.10(b)(2)(iii)(A), "per serving'" means:

(i) Per each scoop or container as dished up using the serving instrument provided, such as a ladle, cup, or measuring spoon, or per weight or container-size offered, such as a quarter pound of potato salad or a container of soup.

(ii) If the item is not served using a ladle or other measuring instrument or per container size, the item must be labeled in the common household measure closest to the Reference Amount Customarily Consumed (RACC) for that item, e.g., per cup or tablespoon."

(Response 122) We agree that a calorie declaration for a self-service food or food on display per displayed food item should be declared for the entire item as offered for sale and not based on a portion of the food item that is smaller than the food item offered for sale. For example, if a covered establishment offered a muffin for sale as a self-service food or food on display, the establishment should declare calories for the entire muffin rather than just a portion of the muffin (e.g., one-half or one-third of the muffin) because the entire muffin is the standard menu item offered for sale by the establishment.

We also agree with the comment asserting that the rule should be revised to require that when a self-service food or food on display is offered for sale per displayed food item, meaning per a discrete unit offered for sale, such as a bagel, a slice of pizza, or a muffin, the calorie declaration for such food should be based on the discrete unit offered for sale rather than another amount. In the proposed rule, we tentatively concluded that for self-service food or food on display that is displayed per item, where the item represents one serving, the calorie declaration should be per item (76 FR 19215). We affirm this conclusion.

We also agree with the comment asserting that the rule should be revised to require that when a self-service food or food on display is not offered for sale per displayed food item, the calorie declaration for such food should be based on the serving offered for sale. In the proposed rule, we tentatively concluded that for self-service food or food on display that is not displayed per item (e.g., potato salad at a buffet or ice cream at an ice cream parlor), the calorie declaration should be per serving (76 FR 19215). We affirm this conclusion.

For these reasons, we have revised § 101.11(b)(2)(iii)(A) to further specify that a covered establishment must declare calories for a self-service food or food on display per displayed food item, or if the food is not sold in a discrete unit, per serving as offered for sale. Under § 101.11(b)(2)(iii)(A)(1), "per displayed food item" means per each discrete unit offered for sale, for example, a bagel, a slice of pizza, or a muffin. Accordingly, if a covered establishment offers a food that is self-service or on display for sale in a discrete unit, such as a muffin, the establishment would have to declare calories for the food per such discrete unit offered for sale, and not based on a different amount.

As discussed in Response 65 and Response 121, we disagree that the rule should require that calories for self-service food and food on display be declared per RACC and, therefore, we are not revising § 101.11(b)(2)(iii)(A)(2) to require that an item that is not served using a measuring instrument be labeled in the common household measure closest to the RACC for that item. However, we agree that specifying that calories for a self-service food or food on display be disclosed per displayed food item, if applicable, and providing other options to declare calories "per serving instrument" and "per common household measure" in separate subparagraphs, as suggested by this same commenter, would provide a clearer framework regarding how calorie declarations must be provided for self-service foods and foods on display. Therefore, in addition to the revisions we made to § 101.11(b)(2)(iii)(A)(1) as described previously, we have revised § 101.11(b)(2)(iii)(A)(2)(i) to specify that, for the purposes of § 101.11(b)(2)(iii)(A), "per serving" means (1) per serving instrument used to dispense the food offered for sale, provided that the serving instrument dispenses a uniform amount of the food (e.g., a scoop or ladle); or (2) if a serving instrument that dispenses a uniform amount of food is not used to dispense the food, per each common household measure (e.g., cup or tablespoon) offered for sale or per unit of weight offered for sale (e.g., per quarter pound or per 4 ounces). As revised, §§ 101.11(b)(2)(iii)(A)(1), and (b)(2)(iii)(A)(2)(i) to (b)(2)(iii)(A)(2)(ii) establish a logical hierarchy for determining how to declare calories for a self-service food or food on display. For example, if a covered establishment offered a self-service food for sale in a discrete unit, such as a muffin, the establishment would have to declare calories for the muffin as a whole. If the covered establishment offered another self-service food for sale, but the food was not offered for sale in a discrete unit, such as pasta salad, the establishment would have to declare calories for the food "per serving" as defined in § 101.11(b)(2)(iii)(A)(2). Under § 101.11(b)(2)(iii)(A)(2)(i), the covered establishment would have to declare calories for the pasta salad per serving instrument used to dispense the pasta salad if the serving instrument dispensed a uniform amount of the food (e.g., per scoop or ladle). If the covered establishment used a serving instrument that does not dispense a uniform amount of the food, such as tongs, declaring calories per that serving instrument used to dispense the food would not be appropriate because the calorie declarations would not always be consistent with the amount of food dispensed, and therefore the covered establishment would look to the remaining options to declare calories, which include declaring calories per common household measure or per unit of weight offered for sale (in § 101.11(b)(2)(iii)(A)(2)(ii)). If a covered establishment offers food for sale per unit of weight, and the unit of weight offered for sale is in ounces, then it would be required to declare calories per ounce (or per some number of ounces)—i.e., using the same unit of weight (ounces) as the unit of weight offered for sale.

We disagree that we should establish specific examples of portion sizes in the rule or add details such as specifying that a "container of soup" is an appropriate portion size for soup. A covered establishment has flexibility to establish the portion sizes for standard menu items offered for sale in such establishment.

As discussed in section VI.C, the definition of "restaurant-type food" generally covers food that usually is eaten on the premises, while walking away, or soon after arriving at another location. Foods (such as whole cakes and deli salads that are sold from a display case rather than from a salad bar) that are grocery-type items that consumers usually store for use at a later time or customarily further prepare would not be included within the meaning of "restaurant-type food." Thus, we have deleted "a multi-serving food such as a whole cake" from § 101.11(b)(2)(iii)(A)(1). We decline to add "deli salad" as an example in what we mean by "per serving" because doing so could incorrectly imply that a deli salad sold at a deli counter as a grocery-type item is likely to be covered by the rule. We are adding § 101.11(b)(2)(iii)(A)(2)(iii) to specify what we mean by "per serving" for self-service beverages—i.e., per total number of fluid ounces in the cup in which a self-service beverage is served and, if applicable, the description of the cup size (e.g., "140 calories per 12 fluid ounces (small)"). See Response 125 in the next section of this document for an explanation of this new provision.

(Comment 123) One comment noted that some foods on display are offered in different flavors or varieties such as ice cream or doughnuts. The comment asked us to clarify that a covered establishment may disclose the nutrition information for such items by using a range per serving (or one of the other options being considered for other variable menu items).

(Response 123) A standard menu item on display may meet the definition for a variable menu item in § 101.11(a) when it is offered for sale in different flavors, varieties, or combinations, and is listed on a menu or menu board as a single menu item. When this is the case, the format requirements for variable menu items in § 101.11(b)(2)(i)(A)(4) through (b)(2)(i)(A)(8) would apply to calories declared on the menu or menu board. Accordingly, to the extent that standard menu items on display offered for sale in different flavors or varieties are listed as single menu items on menus or menu boards, a covered establishment would be required to declare calories on such menus and menu boards for such foods using the same methods applicable to other variable menu items, including ranges, as specified in § 101.11(b)(2)(i)(A)(4) through (b)(2)(i)(A)(8). However, when these foods are on display, they would also be subject to the requirements of section 403(q)(5)(H)(iii) of the FD&C Act and § 101.11(b)(2)(iii). For a standard menu item that is a self-service food or food on display, section 403(q)(5)(H)(iii) of the FD&C Act requires the covered establishment to "place adjacent to each food offered a sign that lists the calories per displayed food item or per serving" (emphasis added). Typically, a standard menu item that is on display is presented to the consumer as a unique menu item, in that the food is made visible to the consumer, and the consumer can see what other standard menu items are available, including other standard menu items that come in different flavors, varieties, or combinations, such as various muffins or pastries in a display case. Because these standard menu items typically are on display in a manner that allows consumers to see each menu item individually, as well as the other menu items available, including menu items offered in different flavors or varieties, the way in which these items are offered for sale is not analogous to standard menu items that come in different flavors or varieties but are listed as a single menu item on a menu or menu board. For example, a covered establishment may offer for sale different flavors of ice cream (e.g., vanilla, chocolate, strawberry) in individual containers in a display case visible to consumers. In this situation, because the consumer can see each flavor of ice cream offered for sale, the consumer should also be able to see the number of calories contained for each flavor of ice cream offered for sale. As a result, the covered establishment would be required to place a sign adjacent to each flavor of ice cream in the display case that lists the calories per each individual displayed food item or per serving in accordance with § 101.11(b)(iii).

D. Declaring Calories "Per Serving" for Self-Service Beverages

In the proposed rule, we discussed the serving size of beverages following our discussion of the declaration of calories for self-service food and food on display "per item" and "per serving" (76 FR 19192 at 19216). We recognized that covered establishments may have different sizes for beverages that are listed on the menu as small, medium, and large and stated that we were considering whether the amount of calories declared should be based on the number of ounces. In the proposed rule, we anticipated that if we adopt this view in the final rule, we would not object to the covered establishment listing the number of ounces as part of the size declaration, e.g., "140 calories per 12 ounces (small)." We requested and received comment on this issue. After considering these comments, we are establishing a new provision to specify that, for beverages that are self-service or on display, "per serving" means per total number of fluid ounces in the cup in which a self-service beverage is served and, if applicable, the description of the cup size (e.g., "140 calories per 12 fluid ounces (small)") (§ 101.11(b)(2)(iii)(A)(2)(iv)). As an operational companion to new § 101.11(b)(2)(iii)(A)(2)(iii), we also are establishing a new provision (§ 101.11(b)(2)(iii)(A)(3)(iii)) to require that calorie declarations for self-service beverages be accompanied by the term "fluid ounces" and, if applicable, the description of the cup size (e.g., "small," "medium"). (See also Response 129 in section XVII.E.3 of this document.)

(Comment 124) One comment noted that the proposed rule did not address the issue of ice fill for the declaration of calories for beverages. The comment asked us to permit covered establishments to calculate calories based on their standard ice fill as long as the level of ice fill is disclosed to consumers. The comment recommended that we expressly permit, regardless of whether there is a standard ice fill, the following statement regarding ice fill: "Calorie content may vary based on the amount of ice used."

(Response 124) We previously addressed this comment with respect to beverages that are not self-service (see the discussion of § 101.11(b)(2)(i)(A)(9) in section XIII). Under section 403(q)(5)(H)(iii) of the FD&C Act, calories for standard menu items that are self-service foods and foods on display, including "soft drinks," must be declared "per displayed food item or per serving" (emphasis added). For beverages that are self-service, the actual amount of a beverage dispensed by consumers will vary depending on the size of the cup and the amount of ice or beverage that a consumer may add to the cup. For these reasons, the provisions we are establishing in this rule for self-service beverages require declaration of calories based on the full volume of the cup (i.e., without ice), and do not provide for the declaration of calories based on a standard beverage fill or standard ice fill. (See discussion of § 101.11(b)(2)(iii)(A)(2)(iii) of the final rule immediately following.)

We would not object to a covered establishment posting a statement (at the self-service beverage dispenser, on the menu or menu board, or both) indicating that the calories for the self-service beverages may vary depending on the amount of ice dispensed (e.g., "calorie content may vary based on the amount of ice used").

(Comment 125) One comment asserted that calories for self-service beverages should not be listed for an "appropriate serving size" such as 12 ounces because this may not correspond to the sizes that are actually sold in the covered establishment.

(Response 125) We agree that the number of ounces in a beverage cup may vary between covered establishments and we agree that the rule should not establish "an appropriate serving size" for self-service beverages. We also agree that consumers should be given calorie information based on the number of ounces in the cup which the consumer uses to dispense a self-service beverage. Section 403(q)(5)(H)(iii) of the FD&C Act provides that calories for self-service foods and foods on display be declared "per displayed food item or per serving" (emphasis added). For self-service beverages, the serving units depend, in part, on the cups provided by the covered establishment to consumers for use at the self-service beverage dispenser. The actual amount of beverage dispensed by consumers will vary based on the size of the cup and the amount of beverage that a consumer dispenses into the cup. As already discussed in Response 124, the actual amount of beverage dispensed by consumers also will vary based on the amount of ice that a consumer may add to the cup, and in contrast to some non-self-service beverages offered for sale by a covered establishment, self-service beverage dispensers typically do not have a standard beverage fill or standard ice fill. In addition, for any given establishment, the cups provided for self-service beverages may be in a single size or may be in different sizes, e.g., in cups labeled "small," "medium," or "large." Further, as already noted, covered establishments may have different sizes for beverages that are listed on menus as small, medium, and large. For these reasons, we are specifying that, for self-service beverages, calories "per serving" within the meaning of section 403(q)(5)(H)(iii) of the FD&C Act must be based on the number of ounces in the cup in which the beverage is served.

Therefore, § 101.11(b)(2)(iii)(A)(2)(iii) of the final rule specifies that, for purposes of § 101.11(b)(2)(iii)(A), "per serving" means, for beverages that are self-service, per total number of fluid ounces in the cup in which a self-service beverage is served and, if applicable, the description of the cup size (e.g., "140 calories per 12 fluid ounces (small)"). As an operational companion to § 101.11(b)(2)(iii)(A)(2)(iii), we also are establishing specific format requirements applicable to the declaration of calories for self-service beverages.

Section 101.11(b)(2)(iii)(A)(3)(iii) of the final rule requires that, for self-service beverages, calorie declarations must be accompanied by the term "fluid ounces" and, if applicable, the description of the cup size (e.g., "small," "medium"). By providing the number of fluid ounces in the cup in which the self-service beverage is served and a description of the size of the cup, if applicable, along with the calories for the self-service beverage, the calorie declaration will provide necessary context regarding the amount of the beverage (i.e., the number of fluid ounces dispensed) upon which to base the number of calories for the self-service beverage. This information will enable consumers to determine how many calories are contained in a serving of the self-service beverage in a direct and consistent manner.

E. Manner of Declaring Calories for Self-Service Foods and Foods on Display

1. Increments of Calories

Proposed § 101.11(b)(2)(iii)(A)(3)(i) would require that calories for self-service food and food on display be declared to the nearest 5-calorie increment up to and including 50 calories and to the nearest 10-calorie increments above 50 calories except that amounts less than 5 calories may be expressed as zero.

We received no comments on this proposed provision and are finalizing it without change, except for an editorial change to express "nearest 10-calorie increments" in the singular (i.e., "nearest 10-calorie increment").

2. Requirements for Declaration of Calories To Be Clear and Conspicuous

Proposed § 101.11(b)(2)(iii)(A)(3)(ii) would require that if the food is not already accompanied by a sign with the food's name, price, or both, the calorie declaration, accompanied by the term "Calories" or "Cal", must appear on a sign adjacent to the standard menu item in a clear and conspicuous manner if the food is not already accompanied by a sign with the food's name, price or both. If the food is already accompanied by a sign with the food's name, price, or both, the calorie declaration and the term "Calories" or "Cal" must appear on that sign in a type size no smaller than the name or price of the menu item whichever is smaller, in the same color or a color that is at least as conspicuous as that name or price using the same contrasting background. Proposed § 101.11(b)(2)(iii)(A)(3)(ii) inadvertently included the clause "if the food is not already accompanied by a sign with the food's name, price, or both" in two locations within the provision.

In the proposed rule, we requested comment on whether additional or more specific formatting requirements are necessary (76 FR 19192 at 19215). In the following paragraphs, we discuss comments on the proposed provision. We also discuss comments in response to our specific request on whether additional or more specific formatting requirements are necessary. After considering these comments, we are finalizing it with the following changes:

- For consistency with the provisions we are establishing in § 101.11(b)(2)(iii)(A), we are specifying that the calorie declarations must include the amount of the serving on which the calories are based.

- For consistency with the provisions we are establishing in § 101.11(b)(2)(iii), we are making a series of changes to address options that a covered establishment can use to declare calories for self-service food or food on display, including the use of an additional sign even if a food is already accompanied by a sign with the food's name, price, or both.

- To provide for a consistent approach to the requirements for a contrasting background throughout the rule, we are providing additional flexibility for the contrasting background used for the calorie declaration and making a conforming editorial change to the grammatical construction of the requirement for the color used for the calorie declaration.

- As an editorial correction for clarity, we are inserting "the type size of" between "no smaller than" and "the name or price."

(Comment 126) One comment recommended that we require the calorie declaration to be clear and conspicuous but not in a type size as large as the food's name or price. The comment maintained that if these foods already have signs, there is likely no room for calorie declarations.

One comment pointed out that fountain machines have small signs or "valve decals" on which the name is placed. According to the comment these valve decals can be as small as 0.7 x 1 inches to 5.25 x 5.25 inches and these signs do not have enough space to list the calorie declarations. The comment recommended that a covered establishment not have to list the calories adjacent to the dispenser if calories for fountain drinks are listed on menus and menu boards and the written nutrition information is available, because to do so would be burdensome.

One comment asked us to allow a covered establishment to use a sign or placard placed adjacent to the fountain beverage machine that lists the calories. Another comment recommended that calorie declarations for self-serve beverages be posted on menus, menu boards, or brochures, and not at the dispensers. One comment recommended that calorie declarations be listed both on the menu boards and the dispenser for each type of beverage dispensed.

One comment noted that brand names are stylized and therefore the names of beverages may be in different type sizes. The comment maintained that tying the type size of the calories to the name of the beverage would result in differing sizes for calories, which could be confusing.

(Response 126) Section 403(q)(5)(H)(iii) of the FD&C Act requires covered establishments to place adjacent to each standard menu item that is a self-service food or food on display, including self-service beverages, a sign that lists calories per displayed food item or per serving. As discussed previously in this document (see Response 116), a covered establishment must also declare calories on a menu or menu board, and follow all applicable requirements of § 101.11(b)(2)(i) for declaration of calories on the menu or menu board, when self-service food or food on display is listed on the menu or menu board.

We acknowledge that there may be space limitations on signs used for self-service food (including valves used for self-service beverages) and foods on display. As already discussed in section XVII.B, we have revised § 101.11(b)(2)(iii)(A) to provide more options for the declaration of calories for self-service food and food on display, including the use of additional signs, signs attached to a sneeze guard, or a single sign or placard listing the calorie information for several standard menu items that are self-service or on display provided that certain conditions are met. These options provide additional flexibility for a covered establishment that offers self-service foods, including self-service beverages, to declare the calories in a manner that works best for it. For example, a covered establishment has an option to declare the calories on a sign separate from the sign containing the food's name and price, provided the calories are clearly associated with the particular food item. Doing so would no longer link the type size requirements for a self-service beverage to those for the name of the beverage. As a result, we have revised § 101.11(b)(2)(iii)(A)(3)(ii) to provide that if a calorie declaration for a self-service food or food on display is provided on a sign that includes the food's name, price, or both, the calorie declaration, accompanied by the term "Calories" or "Cal" and the amount of the serving or displayed food item on which the calorie declaration is based, must be in a type size no smaller than the type size of the name or price of the food, whichever is smaller, in the same color, or a color that is at least as conspicuous as that used for the name or price, using the same contrasting background, or a background at least as contrasting.

(Comment 127) One comment addressed the different proposed requirement for self-service food and food on display depending on whether the food is already accompanied by a sign with the food's name, price, or both. If the food is already accompanied by such a sign, the comment said that the proposed provision would be prescriptive with respect to type size, color, and contrast requirements for the calorie declarations, whereas if the food is not already accompanied by such a sign, the proposed provision would be less prescriptive by merely requiring that calorie declarations be "clear and conspicuous." The comment asked us to revise the rule to establish the less prescriptive requirement that the calorie information be clear and conspicuous regardless of whether the food is accompanied by a sign with the name or price of the food. The comment considered that a prescriptive requirement linked to type size, color, and contrast requirements of the food's name, price, or both would be misleading because it would imply that the number of calories in a food, which is just one attribute of the food, is as important as the name of a food.

One comment stated that the type size of calorie declarations should be no smaller than the name or price, whichever is larger. Another comment stated that the calories for food on display should be permitted to be displayed in a font that is smaller than the font size of the name of the menu item. (By "menu item," we assume that the comment means the food's name, price, or both.) One comment suggested that the provision be revised to include "The calorie information on the sign must be readable from the point where consumers are choosing their food, and it must be readily apparent which sign labels which item, both by proximity and by including the name of the product on the sign."

(Response 127) We disagree that we should require the type size of the calorie declaration for food on display to be no smaller than the type size of the name or price, whichever is larger. All other requirements of this rule that anchor a type size to information already presented to consumers allow a covered establishment to use a type size no smaller than (rather than no larger than) the type size of the information already presented, and the comment provided no basis for why the rule should have a different standard for calorie declarations on signs for food on display and self-service food.

We also disagree that calories for food on display and self-service food should be permitted to be displayed in a font that is smaller than the font size of the name or price of the menu item. Because consumers need to see the name and price to place an order, anchoring the type size of the calorie declaration to the type size of information already on the sign acts, in essence, as an objective and measurable performance standard for whether a disclosure is clear, conspicuous, and prominent. Thus, we do not agree that a smaller type size should be used for the calorie declaration, because doing so would no longer provide for such an objective and measurable performance standard. Therefore, we are retaining the type size requirements for the calorie declaration for food on display and self-service food that are already accompanied by individual signs. However, to be consistent with changes we are making to other provisions of the rule, we have revised § 101.11(b)(2)(iii)(A)(3)(ii) to provide additional flexibility for the contrasting background of the calorie declaration by permitting the calorie declaration to be in a background at least as contrasting as that used for the name or price of the menu item. We also are making a conforming editorial change to the grammatical construction of the requirement for the color used for the calorie declaration to match the grammatical construction of the revised requirement for the contrasting background used for the calorie declaration. We also are making an editorial correction to insert "the type size of" between "no smaller than" and "the name or price."

No comments suggested specific formatting requirements for calorie declarations when there are no pre-existing signs with the name or price of the food to which the calorie declaration can be anchored. Covered establishments have the flexibility to post the calorie information in a manner that ensures that it is clear, conspicuous, and prominent.

3. Manner of Declaring Calories for Self-Service Beverages

In the proposed rule, we stated that the self-service beverage dispenser itself must have calorie declarations for each flavor or variety offered, such that the calorie declaration is clearly associated with its corresponding flavor or variety (76 FR 19192 at 19216). We received comment on calorie declarations for self-service beverages. After considering these comments, we are adding a new provision to require, for self-service beverages, that calorie declarations be accompanied by the term "fluid ounces" and, if applicable, the description of the cup size (e.g., "small," "medium").

(Comment 128) A few comments recommended that calories be posted at self-service fountain dispensers for each beverage size offered in the covered establishment. One comment asked us to permit a sign or placard placed adjacent to a fountain beverage machine to separate calorie ranges for specific subcategories, e.g., regular soda, diet soda, milk, coffees, teas, juice by cup size. A few comments recommended that calorie declarations should provide the amount of calories as a range per size.

(Response 128) We agree that calories must be posted at self-service fountain dispensers for each beverage size offered in the covered establishment. As noted previously, section 403(q)(5)(H)(iii) of the FD&C Act requires covered establishments to place adjacent to each standard menu item that is a self-service food or food on display, including self-service beverages, a sign that lists calories per displayed food item or per serving. As already discussed (see section XVII.B), § 101.11(b)(2)(iii)(A) provides several options for where and how a covered establishment could place a sign or placard.

Earlier in this document, we discussed another comment directed to the declaration of calories for self-service beverages (see Comment 126 and Response 126). A self-service standard menu item, including a self-service beverage, is subject to § 101.11(b)(2)(i) (in addition to § 101.11(b)(2)(iii)) when such food is listed on a menu or menu board (see Comment 116 and Response 116). The format requirements for variable menu items in § 101.11(b)(2)(i)(A)(4) through (b)(2)(i)(A)(7) would apply to calorie declarations on a menu or menu board. Accordingly, to the extent that self-service beverages offered for sale in different flavors or varieties are listed as single menu items on menus or menu boards (e.g., "soft drinks"), a covered establishment would be required to declare calories on such menus and menu boards for such foods using the same methods applicable to other variable menu items, including ranges, as specified in § 101.11(b)(2)(i)(A)(4) through (b)(2)(i)(A)(8). However, at the point of self-service, a self-service beverage would be subject to the requirements of section 403(q)(5)(H)(iii) of the FD&C Act and § 101.11(b)(2)(iii). For a standard menu item that is a self-service food, such as a self-service beverage, section 403(q)(5)(H)(iii) of the FD&C Act requires the covered establishment to "place adjacent to each food offered a sign that lists the calories per displayed food item or per serving." Typically, a self-service fountain beverage machine separately dispenses each flavor or variety of beverage from individual valves or dispensers that list the flavor or variety of the beverage (such as orange soda, cola, diet cola), and the consumer can see what beverage flavors and varieties are available. Otherwise, consumers would not be able to determine which flavor or variety of beverage is dispensed from a particular valve or dispenser at the self-service fountain beverage machine. Because these self-service beverages typically are presented in a manner that allows consumers to see each beverage individually, as well as the other beverages available, including other beverages offered in different flavors or varieties, the way in which these standard menu items are offered for sale is not analogous to standard menu items that come in different flavors or varieties but are listed as a single menu item on a menu or menu board. Further, because consumers can see flavor or variety of self-service beverage offered for sale, the consumer should also be able to see the number of calories contained in each flavor or variety offered for sale at the self-service machine. For these reasons, calories must be declared for each specific flavor or type of beverage available at a self-service machine rather than declared as a range.

(Comment 129) A few comments recommended that covered establishment should declare the amount of calories for self-service beverages based on the number of ounces served. A few other comments opposed declaring the number of calories per ounces served. These comments contended that it is more practical to estimate the size of a beverage with a household measure than to guess the ounces without measuring the beverage. The comments maintained that calories per ounce would be confusing. One comment stated that there is not enough space on menus for declaring the number of calories per ounce served.

(Response 129) We disagree that declaring calories based on the volume in fluid ounces for self-service beverages, as required by § 101.11(b)(2)(iii)(A)(2)(iii) of the final rule, would be overly confusing. Fluid ounces are commonly used to describe the volume of beverages in packaged food sold in the United States and, thus, consumers who purchase beverages likely would be familiar with "fluid ounces" in the context of beverages. Further, as discussed previously (see Response 125), § 101.11(b)(2)(iii)(A)(2)(iii) of the final rule specifies that, for self-service beverages, "per serving" means per total number of fluid ounces in the cup in which a self-service beverage is served and, if applicable, the description of the cup size (e.g., "140 calories per 12 fluid ounces (small)"). As an operational companion to § 101.11(b)(2)(iii)(A)(2)(iii), we also are establishing in § 101.11(b)(2)(iii)(A)(3)(iii) of the final rule specific format requirements applicable to the declaration of calories for self-service beverages. Section 101.11(b)(2)(iii)(A)(3)(iii) of the final rule requires that, for self-service beverages, calorie declarations must be accompanied by the term "fluid ounces" and, if applicable, the description of the cup size (e.g., "small," "medium"). For example, calories could be declared as "small Orange Fizz (12 fluid ounces)—150 calories." Accordingly, the calorie declaration will provide information regarding the number of fluid ounces served, and in some cases, the size of the cup, along with the number of calories. Typically, self-service beverages are offered for sale, including listed or otherwise separated by price, based on size (e.g., "small—$1.59," "12 ounces—$1.59"), and the sizes are described using general descriptors (e.g., "small," "medium," or "large,") or by fluid ounces. Therefore, in such situations, consumers will have further context regarding the number of fluid ounces served in a self-service beverage, and, in some cases, the size of the cup.

F. Applicability of Requirements for Written Nutrition Information, Succinct Statement, and Statement of Availability to Self-Service Foods and Foods on Display

In the proposed rule, we tentatively concluded that covered establishments must provide written nutrition information for self-service foods and foods on display that are standard menu items as required by section 403(q)(5)(H)(ii)(III) of the FD&C Act (76 FR 19192 at 19216).

(Comment 130) One comment argued that applying certain requirements of section 403(q)(5)(H)(ii) of the FD&C Act to self-service food and food on display is not a reasonable construction of the statute, given that calorie disclosure requirements for self-service food and food on display appear "in a wholly different subclause." The comment asserted that because the "subclause" (section 403(q)(5)(H)(iii)) of the FD&C Act) does not require additional written nutrition information or a succinct statement concerning suggested daily caloric intake and section 403(q)(5)(H)(ii) of the FD&C Act does, Congress deliberately omitted those requirements from section 403(q)(5)(H)(iii) of the FD&C Act. The comment argued that, given that every word excluded from a statute must be presumed to have been excluded intentionally, it is not permissible to interpret the statute to require covered establishments to provide additional written nutrition information and a succinct statement concerning suggested daily caloric intake for self-service food and food on display.

(Response 130) We agree in part, and disagree in part, with the comment. As we discussed in the proposed rule and Response 116, section 403(q)(5)(H)(i) of the FD&C Act states, "in the case of food that is a standard menu item . . . [the covered] establishment shall disclose the information described in subclauses (ii) and (iii)" (emphasis added). The word "and" between the references to subclauses (ii) and (iii), as opposed to a disjunctive "or," indicates that covered establishments must follow the requirements in subclause (ii) for all standard menu items, as applicable, and subclause (iii) for all standard menu items, as applicable.

We acknowledge that a principle of statutory interpretation is that "where Congress includes particular language in one section of a statute but omits it in another section of the same [statute], it is generally presumed that Congress acts intentionally and purposely in the disparate inclusion or exclusion." Russello v. U.S., 464 U.S. 16, 23 (1983) (internal citations omitted). We considered this principle when interpreting section 403(q)(5)(H) of the FD&C Act. Section 403(q)(5)(H)(ii)(III) of the FD&C Act—the section requiring additional written nutrition information—omits certain important words. Sections 403(q)(5)(H)(ii)(I), (II), and (IV) of the FD&C Act specify that certain disclosures must appear "on the menu," "on the menu board," and "on the menu or menu board," respectively. Section 403(q)(5)(H)(ii)(III) of the FD&C Act does not mention menus or menu boards at all. Because section 403(q)(5)(H)(i) of the FD&C Act states that covered establishments must disclose the information in section 403(q)(5)(H)(ii) and (iii) of the FD&C Act for standard menu items, it is reasonable to apply section 403(q)(5)(H)(ii)(III) of the FD&C Act to standard menu items, regardless of whether they appear on menus or menu boards. Therefore, the rule requires that covered establishments provide the additional written nutrition information described in section 403(q)(5)(H)(ii)(III) of the FD&C Act for all standard menu items, including self-service food and food on display regardless of whether such standard menu items appear on menus or menu boards.

We agree that the succinct statement concerning suggested daily caloric intake is required only on menus or menu boards, based on the plain language of sections 403(q)(5)(H)(ii)(I)(bb) and 403(q)(5)(H)(ii)(II)(bb) of the FD&C Act. Similarly, the statement of availability of the written nutrition information is only required on menus or menu boards, based on the plain language of section 403(q)(5)(H)(ii)(IV) of the FD&C Act.

We discuss the specific requirements related to the succinct statement and statement of availability for self-service food and food on display in the next section. We discuss the specific requirements related to the written nutrition information for self-service food and food on display in section XVII.H.

G. Succinct Statement and Statement of Availability for Self-Service Foods and Foods on Display

Proposed § 101.11(b)(2)(iii)(B) would require that for food on display identified by a menu (meaning an identifying sign) adjacent to the food itself, the statement that puts the calorie information in the context of a recommended total daily caloric intake as required by § 101.11(b)(2)(i)(B) and the statement regarding the availability of the additional written nutrition information required by § 101.11(b)(2)(i)(C) must be provided in one of two ways. Proposed § 101.11(b)(2)(iii)(B) would permit these two statements to appear either on the sign adjacent to the standard menu item or on a separate, larger sign, in close proximity to the food on display, that can be easily read as the consumer is making order selections. Proposed § 101.11(b)(2)(iii)(B) would explain that this requirement is satisfied if the two statements appear on a large menu board that can be easily read as the consumer is viewing the food on display.

In the following paragraphs, we discuss comments on this proposed provision. After considering these comments, we have revised the provision to clarify that the requirements to provide the statement that puts the calorie information in the context of a recommended total daily caloric intake (also referred to as the "succinct statement") and the statement of availability for foods on display apply to all types of food on display, including those that are self-service. Further, we are also providing further flexibility for how to satisfy those requirements.

(Comment 131) In the proposed rule, we noted that signs identifying food on display placed adjacent to such foods meet the definition of a "menu" or "menu board" within the meaning of section 403(q)(5)(H)(xi) of the FD&C Act, in that such signs are the primary writings of the establishment from which consumers make order selections (76 FR 19192 at 19217). Further, we noted that, as a result, the requirements to disclose the succinct statement and statement of availability on menus and menu boards under sections 403(q)(5)(H)(ii)(I)(bb), (II)(bb), and (IV) of the FD&C Act would apply to such small signs (76 FR 19192 at 19217). However, we noted that the requirements to post the statements on small signs seem to pose difficulties given the size of such signs, and from a consumer's perspective, it is probably unnecessary for the two statements to appear on every single individual identifying sign.

Taking these issues into consideration, along with the space on small signs that constitute menus and menu boards, as provided in section 403(q)(5)(H)(x) of the FD&C Act, we tentatively concluded that each individual sign could be considered its own menu, but that a set of signs that are in close proximity to each other, such as those that might identify items in a bakery display counter, could be viewed together as the primary writing from which consumers choose among those items to order (76 FR 19192 at 19217). As a result, we proposed in § 101.11(b)(2)(iii)(B) that covered establishments may place the succinct statement and statement of availability on individual specific signs or on a separate, larger sign, in close proximity to food on display, that can be easily read as the consumer is making his or her order selection (76 FR 19192 at 19217). In addition, we tentatively concluded that signs identifying food on display that are the primary writing from which consumers select the corresponding items to order and are in close proximity to the menu board, such that the menu board can be easily read as the consumer is viewing the food on display, could be considered part of that menu board.

One comment asserted that menu boards, tags, and other signs within an establishment are used by consumers to identify standard menu items and make order selections. The comment argued, however, that tags or other signs should not be considered menus or menu boards because a menu board lists multiple items from which a consumer can make an order selection.

One comment argued that if the succinct statement and statement of availability already appeared on a menu board, they should not have to appear again on signs adjacent or in close proximity to self-service foods or foods on display. The comment stated that the final rule should provide that posting the statement of availability and the succinct statement on the menu board of the covered establishment is sufficient to inform consumers who are selecting food on display and self-service food.

(Response 131) We agree that an individual small sign adjacent to a self-service food or food on display that contains the name (or image) and price of a standard menu item, and that can be used by a consumer to make an order selection from the establishment at the time the consumer is viewing the sign would meet the definition of a menu or menu board within the meaning of section 403(q)(5)(H)(xi) of the FD&C Act. As a result, the requirements of sections 403(q)(5)(H)(ii)(I)(bb), (II)(bb), and (IV) of the FD&C Act for a succinct statement and statement of availability apply to such signs. However, as we noted in the proposed rule, the obligation to provide the succinct statement and statement of availability on every individual small sign likely would pose difficulties given the small size of these individual signs, and it likely would not be necessary, from a consumer's perspective, for the two statements to appear on every individual sign (76 FR 19192 at 19217). Considering these factors and the limited space on these individual small signs that constitute menus or menu boards, as described by section 403(q)(5)(H)(x)(II) of the FD&C Act, we conclude that, while each individual sign could be considered its own menu, a set of signs that are in close proximity to each other could also be viewed together as the primary writing from which consumers choose among items in making order selections. Further, we conclude that a covered establishment can satisfy the requirements for posting a succinct statement and statement of availability for self-service foods and foods on display by posting such statements on the individual sign adjacent to the food itself, on a separate, larger sign, in close proximity to the food that can be easily read as the consumer is making an order selection, or on a large menu board that can be easily read as the consumer is ordering the food. Accordingly, we are retaining § 101.11(b)(2)(iii)(B) and making revisions for clarity. We have revised § 101.11(b)(2)(iii)(B) to clarify that the provision applies to food that is self-service or on display and is identified by an individual sign adjacent to the food itself where such sign meets the definition of a menu or menu board under paragraph (a) of this section. As an inadvertent error, proposed § 101.11(b)(2)(iii)(B) opened with the clause "For food on display" and did not specifically identify food that is self-service as being covered by the proposed requirements for providing the succinct statement and statement of availability on signs that are menus. As a practical matter, food that is "self-service" is "on display" and, thus, the requirements apply to "self-service food" regardless of whether "self-service food" is specified or not. Comments that addressed proposed § 101.11(b)(2)(iii)(B) from the perspective of both food on display and self-service food implicitly acknowledged that self-service foods would be subject to proposed § 101.11(b)(2)(iii)(B). Moreover, § 101.11(b)(2)(iii)(B) is a subparagraph of § 101.11(b)(2)(iii), which establishes requirements for "food that is self-service or on display." For clarity, and to ensure that covered establishments are aware that § 101.11(b)(2)(iii)(B) and the flexibility it provides applies to self-service foods identified by a menu adjacent to the food itself, we have revised the opening clause of § 101.11(b)(2)(iii)(B) to read "For food that is self-service or on display . . ." We also are making associated edits throughout the provision to remove any narrow reference only to food that is on display.

H. The Written Nutrition Information That Must Be Provided for Food That Is Self-Service or on Display

Proposed § 101.11(b)(2)(iii)(C) would require that the nutrition information in written form required by § 101.11(b)(2)(ii) be provided for food that is self-service or on display, except for packaged food that bears nutrition labeling information required by § 101.9 if the packaged food, including its label, can be examined by a consumer before purchasing the food. In the following paragraphs, we discuss comments on this proposed provision. After considering these comments, we have revised § 101.11(b)(2)(iii)(C) to clarify the regulatory requirements that apply to the nutrition labeling information on the packaged food.

(Comment 132) One comment asked us to provide more detail on what format establishments may use to provide the written nutrition information for foods on display and self-service food to ensure that the information is readily available and easily readable.

(Response 132) Section 101.11(b)(2)(ii) both requires that written nutrition information be available for standard menu items and establishes format requirements for that written nutrition information. With one exception, the format requirements of § 101.11(b)(2)(ii) apply to standard menu items that are self-service food or food on display. See § 101.11(b)(2)(ii) and the discussion of § 101.11(b)(2)(ii) in section XVI. The exception is for packaged foods, insofar as they bear nutrition labeling required by section 403(q)(5)(H)(ii)(III) of the FD&C Act and § 101.11(b)(ii)(2)(D). We discuss this exception further in Response 133.

(Comment 133) Two comments asked us to broaden the exception in § 101.11(b)(2)(iii)(C) for packaged food in compliance with § 101.9, regardless of whether the nutrition information can be examined prior to purchase. One comment pointed out that some packaged confectioneries may be placed near the cash register in a covered establishment. The comment stated that these confectioneries may be exempt from the nutrition labeling requirements of § 101.9 because they have fewer than 12 square inches of available label space or may be in gift packages. This comment stated that if a food is subject to and in compliance with § 101.9, it should not also be subject to § 101.11. The comment maintained that a food should be required to comply with one nutrition labeling regulation or the other, but not both. Another comment stated that some foods, such as food in small packages, foods with insignificant amounts of all the nutrients required on the labels of packaged food (e.g., bottled water) and foods sold in gift packages, which may provide the nutrition information inside the box or package, should be exempt from the menu labeling requirements even though their nutrient content cannot be examined by consumers prior to purchase. The comment also stated that if these foods included front of package labeling, they would lose the exemption from nutrition labeling.

(Response 133) Section 403(q)(5)(H) of the FD&C Act does not establish any new requirements regarding the labels of packaged food. Furthermore, to clarify that the requirements of § 101.11 do not affect the exemptions from nutrition labeling under § 101.9(j)(2) and (j)(3), we proposed conforming amendments to § 101.9(j)(2) and (j)(3). As discussed in the proposed rule, the NLEA amendments to the FD&C Act included an exemption, at sections 403(q)(5)(A)(i) and (ii) of the FD&C Act, for nutrition labeling for food that is "served in restaurants or other establishments in which food is served for immediate human consumption" or "sold for sale or use in such establishments" (76 FR 19192 at 19193 (citing 21 U.S.C. 343(q)(5)(A)(i)). The NLEA amendments also included an exemption for food of the type described in section 403(q)(5)(A)(i) of the FD&C Act that is primarily processed and prepared in a retail establishment, ready for human consumption, "offered for sale to consumers but not for immediate human consumption in such establishment and which is not offered for sale outside such establishment." (21 U.S.C. 343(q)(5)(A)(ii)). We issued regulations for these exemptions at § 101.9(j)(2) and (j)(3); however, these exemptions were contingent on there being no nutrient content claims or other nutrition information in any context on the labeling or in the labeling or advertising. As discussed in section IV.B, we are finalizing the conforming amendments to § 101.9(j)(2) and (j)(3). Likewise, as discussed in section IV.B, we also have made a conforming amendment to § 101.9(j)(4), which applies to foods that contain insignificant amounts of nutrients and food components required to be included in the declaration on nutrition information under § 101.9(c). As a result, a food that is exempt from the requirements of § 101.9 under § 101.9(j)(2), (j)(3), and (j)(4) would not fall out of such exemption by complying with the requirements of § 101.11. We also note that, for a standard menu item that contains insignificant amounts of all of the nutrients required in § 101.11(b)(2)(ii)(A), including, if applicable, a packaged food, a covered establishment generally would not be required to provide written nutrition information for that standard menu item (see § 101.11(b)(2)(ii)(B)).

Section 101.11 does not change the food label requirements under § 101.9(h)(3) for food products with separately packaged ingredients or foods where a package contains a variety of foods, or an assortment of foods, and is in a form intended to be used as a gift. Similarly, § 101.11 does not change the exception at § 101.9(j)(13)(i) for foods in small packages that have a total surface area of less than 12 square inches of available label space. To the extent that such foods are offered for sale in covered establishments, they generally would fall within the exceptions at § 101.9(j)(2) and (j)(3); when this is the case, the conforming amendments to § 101.9(j)(2) and (j)(3) would preserve the pre-existing exemptions under § 101.9 for such foods.

While section 403(q)(5)(H) of the FD&C Act does not establish any new requirements regarding the labels of packaged food, there may be some situations in which a covered establishment (rather than the manufacturer of a packaged food) must disclose nutrition information for a food on display or a self-service food that is a packaged food, such as a packaged food that is offered for sale at a cash register in a covered establishment. For example, if a standard menu item, such as a package of chips, is on display (e.g., a package of chips that is part of a combination meal or listed individually on a menu or menu board and is available at a cash register), the covered establishment would be required to post a calorie declaration on a sign adjacent to the package of chips and provide written nutrition information for the package of chips unless the label for the chips bears calorie and certain other nutrition information and can be examined by the consumer prior to purchase. Further, the covered establishment would be required to post a calorie declaration for the package of chips on a menu and menu board to the extent the package of chips is listed on such menu and menu board.

In the proposed rule, we tentatively concluded that a packaged food that is self-service or food on display that bears nutrition information required by section 403(q)(1) of the FD&C Act and § 101.9 satisfies the calorie disclosure requirement for self-service food or food on display in section 403(q)(5)(H)(iii) of the FD&C Act and the written nutrition information requirement of section 403(q)(5)(H)(ii)(III) of the FD&C Act (see 76 FR 19192 at 19217 and 19235). In addition, we tentatively concluded that, in such a situation, a covered establishment would still be required to post calorie declarations on menus and menu boards for packaged foods that are standard menu items and are listed on such menus and menu boards (e.g., where "chips" is listed on a menu board and refers to packaged bags of chips that are available as self-service foods or foods on display) (76 FR 19192 at 19217). We affirm these conclusions; however, we have revised the exception at § 101.11(b)(2)(iii)(C).

Under proposed § 101.11(b)(2)(iii)(C), self-service food and food on display would be subject to the written nutrition information requirement of § 101.11(b)(2)(ii), except for packaged food that bears nutrition labeling information required by § 101.9 if the packaged food can be examined by a consumer before purchasing. In response to comments regarding a food that is in compliance with § 101.9 but does not otherwise bear nutrition labeling, we have revised the exception at § 101.11(b)(2)(iii)(C) to clarify in relevant part that a covered establishment is not required to provide the written nutrition information in § 101.11(b)(2)(ii) for a packaged food, insofar as that packaged food bears the nutrition information specified in section 403(q)(5)(H)(ii)(III) of the FD&C Act and the written nutrition information requirements of § 101.11(b)(2)(ii). For example, if the package of chips described previously includes Nutrition Facts information, including the nutrition information specified in section 403(q)(5)(H)(ii)(III) of the FD&C Act and § 101.11(b)(2)(ii), a covered establishment would not be required to provide written nutrition information for the chips as required by § 101.11(b)(2)(ii), provided that the packaged food, including its label, can be examined by a consumer before purchasing the food. However, if the package of chips does not bear the nutrition information specified in section 403(q)(5)(H)(ii)(III) of the FD&C Act and § 101.11(b)(2)(ii) (e.g., because it is exempt from the nutrition label requirements of § 101.9, such as a food in a small package that has fewer than 12 square inches of available label space as provided by § 101.9(j)(13)), the covered establishment would be required to provide written nutrition information for the chips as required by § 101.11(b)(2)(ii). Moreover, if the package of chips does not bear the nutrition information specified in section 403(q)(5)(H)(ii)(III) of the FD&C Act and § 101.11(b)(2)(ii), the food would not satisfy the calorie disclosure requirement for self-service food or food on display in section 403(q)(5)(H)(iii) of the FD&C Act, and the covered establishment would be required to disclose the number of calories contained in the package of chips on a sign adjacent to the food, in accordance with § 101.11(b)(2)(iii). In either situation, the establishment would be required to post a calorie declaration for the package of chips on the menu and menu board to the extent the package of chips is listed on such menu and menu board, as required by § 101.11(b)(2)(i).

XVIII. Comments and FDA Response on Proposed § 101.11(c)(1) to (c)(5)—Determination of Nutrient Content (Final § 101.11(c)(1) to (c)(2))

Under section 403(q)(5)(H)(iv) of the FD&C Act, a covered establishment must have a reasonable basis for its nutrient content disclosures, including nutrient databases, cookbooks, laboratory analyses, and other reasonable means, as described in § 101.10. Proposed § 101.11(c)(1) would establish this reasonable basis requirement in this rule.

In addition, proposed § 101.11(c)(2), (c)(3), (c)(4), and (c)(5) would establish requirements for determining compliance with proposed § 101.11(c)(1). As discussed in the proposed rule, because the nutrition information that is required to be disclosed by covered establishments is a subset of the nutrition information required in § 101.9, we modeled proposed § 101.11(c)(2), (c)(3), (c)(4), and (c)(5) after our regulation for compliance with the nutrition labeling requirements for packaged foods in § 101.9(g) (76 FR 19192 at 19218). In brief, for purposes of compliance, proposed § 101.11(c)(2), (c)(3), (c)(4), and (c)(5) would establish the following:

- Proposed § 101.11(c)(2) would define two classes of nutrients. "Class I" nutrients would be "added" nutrients and "Class II" nutrients would be "naturally occurring" (indigenous) nutrients in standard menu items;

- Proposed § 101.11(c)(3) would establish conditions under which a standard menu item with a nutrient declaration of protein, total carbohydrate, or dietary fiber would be deemed to be misbranded under section 403(a) of the FD&C Act, including a requirement that, for Class II protein, total carbohydrate, or dietary fiber, the nutrient content of an appropriate composite of a standard menu item not be less than 80 percent of the declared value;

- Proposed § 101.11(c)(4) would establish conditions under which a standard menu item with a nutrient declaration of calories, sugars, total fat, saturated fat, trans fat, cholesterol, or sodium would be deemed to be misbranded under section 403(a) of the FD&C Act, including a requirement that the nutrient content of an appropriate composite of a standard menu item not be more than 20 percent in excess of the declared value; and

- Proposed § 101.11(c)(5) would allow for reasonable excesses of protein, total carbohydrate, dietary fiber and reasonable deficiencies of calories, sugars, total fat, saturated fat, trans fat, cholesterol, or sodium.

Comments commonly referred to the combined provisions of proposed § 101.11(c)(3) and (c)(4) as "the 80/120 rule."

In the following paragraphs, we discuss comments on proposed § 101.11(c)(1), (c)(2), (c)(3), (c)(4), and (c)(5). After considering these comments, we are:

- Finalizing § 101.11(c)(1) with several changes and making a companion change to the substantiation requirements of proposed § 101.11(c)(6) (which is being established in § 101.11(c)(3));

- Replacing proposed § 101.11(c)(2), (c)(3), (c)(4), and (c)(5) with a new § 101.11(c)(2); and

- Establishing revised certification requirements (in § 101.11(c)(3)(i)(G), (c)(3)(ii)(D), (c)(3)(iii)(E), and (c)(4)(iv)(E)) directed to reasonable steps that a covered establishment takes to ensure that the method of preparation (e.g., types and amounts of ingredients in the recipe, cooking temperatures) and amount of a standard menu item offered for sale adhere to the factors on which the nutrient values were determined.

(Comment 134) One comment asserted that the menu labeling requirements would have an impact on the manufacturers of foods sold to covered establishments, because covered establishments would look to the food manufacturers to supply them with the nutrition information that the covered establishments must provide to consumers. For the most part, food manufacturers do not currently provide restaurants and similar retail food establishments with this information. The comment maintained that some manufacturers may elect to provide the nutrition information in inserts and other forms of labeling, which will require development of guidelines on how the nutrition information should be provided to restaurant customers.

One comment asked us to consider nutritional information provided by a producer to a covered establishment to be a reasonable basis for the covered establishment's nutrition declarations. Another comment maintained that because food suppliers are not required to provide nutrition information to retailers, compliance with the rule will be challenging for covered establishments. The comment asked us to consider requiring suppliers to provide nutrition information to covered establishments.

(Response 134) The nutrition labeling provisions of this rule only apply to covered establishments as specified in § 101.11(a). Section 4205 of the ACA does not require distributors of food sold to covered establishments to provide nutrition information to those establishments. In addition, section 4205 of the ACA did not remove or amend section 403(q)(5)(G) of the FD&C Act, which provides that the nutrition labeling requirements of section 403(q)(1) through (4) of the FD&C Act do not apply to "food which is sold by a food distributor if the distributor principally sells food to restaurants and other establishments in which food is served for immediate human consumption and does not manufacture, process, or repackage the food it sells." Accordingly, this rule does not require distributors of food sold to covered establishments to provide nutrition information to covered establishments. Nevertheless, we have revised § 101.11(c)(1), in relevant part, to expressly specify that the use of Nutrition Facts on labels on packaged foods that comply with the nutrition labeling requirements of section 403(q)(1) of the FD&C Act and § 101.9 is an additional means that may be used as a reasonable basis to determine nutrient values.

We encourage cooperation between food distributors and covered establishments so that covered establishments are able to efficiently comply with the requirements of this rule. We would consider nutrition information otherwise provided by food distributors to covered establishments for food sold by such distributors to be captured within the provision that nutrient values may be determined by using "other reasonable means" provided that such nutrition information is truthful and not misleading and otherwise in compliance with the requirements of sections 403(a)(1) and (q)(5)(H) of the FD&C Act and § 101.11.

We also have revised § 101.11(c)(1) to include another example of "other reasonable means"— i.e., FDA nutrient values for raw fruits and vegetables in Appendix C of part 101 and FDA nutrient values for cooked fish in Appendix D of part 101. We developed this nutrition information to encourage retail stores that sell raw fruits, vegetables, and cooked fish to participate in the voluntary point-of-purchase nutrition program (§§ 101.42 through 101.45).

(Comment 135) Many comments agreed that a covered establishment must have a reasonable basis for its nutrient content disclosures and the means for determining them, which include nutrient databases, cookbooks, laboratory analyses, and other reasonable means, as described in § 101.10. Some comments suggested that we replace the language in proposed § 101.11(c) with the language in § 101.13(q)(5)(ii). Section 101.13(q)(5) sets forth requirements for nutrient content claims for food served in restaurants or other establishments in which food is served for immediate consumption or which is sold for sale or use in such establishments. Section 101.13(q)(5)(ii) provides that for nutrient content claims made for such food, in lieu of analytical testing, compliance may be determined using a reasonable basis for concluding that the food that bears the claim meets the definition for the claim. It continues by stating that this reasonable basis may derive from recognized databases for raw and processed foods, recipes, and other means to compute nutrient levels in the foods or meals and may be used provided reasonable steps are taken to ensure that the method of preparation adheres to the factors on which the reasonable basis was determined (e.g., types and amounts of ingredients, cooking temperatures). Furthermore, according to § 101.13(q)(5)(ii), firms making claims on foods based on this reasonable basis criterion are required to provide to appropriate regulatory officials on request the specific information on which their determination is based and reasonable assurance of operational adherence to the preparation methods or other basis for the claim.

(Response 135) We agree that some aspects of § 101.13(c)(5)(ii) that we did not include in § 101.11(c) should be added to the rule. In particular, § 101.13(c)(5)(ii) requires that reasonable steps be taken to ensure that the method of preparation adheres to the factors on which the reasonable basis was determined (e.g., types and amounts of ingredients, cooking temperatures) when the reasonable basis for a nutrient disclosure is derived using databases for raw and processed foods, recipes, or other means (e.g., means other than analytical testing). As discussed later in this document (see Comment 136), several comments opposed our proposal for using a compliance approach for determining compliance modeled after § 101.9(g) and some comments discussed the problems that can occur when the preparation of a menu item does not adhere to a recipe or deviates from the parameters used as the reasonable basis. In Response 136, we discuss the provisions of § 101.11(c)(2) that we are establishing in this rule in lieu of the provisions of proposed § 101.11(c)(2), (c)(3), (c)(4), and (c)(5) that were modeled after § 101.9(g). Those new provisions specify, in relevant part, that a covered establishment must take reasonable steps to ensure that the method of preparation (e.g., types and amounts of ingredients, cooking temperatures) and amount of a standard menu item offered for sale adhere to the factors on which its nutrient values were determined.

We also agree that § 101.11(c) should require, among other things, that a covered establishment provide to FDA on request specific information about the basis for its nutrient declarations and reasonable assurance of operational adherence to the preparation methods used as the basis for its nutrient declarations. As discussed in Response 136, we have revised the rule to establish these requirements.

We disagree that § 101.11(c) need specify that a reasonable basis may derive from recognized databases for raw and processed foods, recipes, and other means to compute nutrient levels in the foods or meals "in lieu of analytical testing." Proposed § 101.11(c)(1) already provides for the use of databases, cookbooks, and "other reasonable means" in addition to analytical testing. However, we acknowledge that this may not have been clear in part because we used the conjunction "and" in proposed § 101.11(c)(1). To make clear that any of the listed means for determining nutrient content may be used, we have revised § 101.11(c)(1) to replace the conjunction "and" with the conjunction "or" in the second sentence.

As a companion change, we have revised proposed § 101.11(c)(6)(iv)(A) (which is renumbered as § 101.11(c)(3)(iv)(A) in the final rule), which addresses the information that must be provided to FDA, within a reasonable period of time upon request, when "other reasonable means are used to provide the nutrition information." To emphasize that "other reasonable means" does not require analytical testing, § 101.11(c)(3)(iv)(A)) now requires a detailed description of the "means" (rather than the "method") used to determine the nutrition information.

We are finalizing § 101.11(c)(1) with the following additional changes:

- We are substituting the term "nutrient declarations" for the term "nutrient disclosures" for consistency in terms used throughout § 101.11. For example, § 101.11(b)(2)(i)(A) establishes requirements to "declare" calories, and § 101.11(b)(2)(i)(A)(3) refers to calorie "declarations."

- We are clarifying that nutrient databases may be used to determine nutrient values regardless of whether they use computer software programs. For example, a covered establishment may use a nutrient database that both lists nutrient values for certain food items and provides software that a covered establishment could use to calculate nutrient values for a standard menu item prepared with several of the listed foods in varying amounts. Alternatively, a covered establishment may use a nutrient database that lists nutrient values for certain food items, but does not provide such software. In such a circumstance, a covered establishment would perform and document its own calculations.

- We are substituting the term "nutrient values" for the proposed term "nutrient levels." We are making this change throughout § 101.11(c), as well as throughout the rule, to consistently use the single term "nutrient values."

- We are deleting "as described in § 101.10." Section 403(q)(5)(H)(iv) of the FD&C Act provides that a restaurant or similar retail food establishment shall have a reasonable basis for its nutrient content disclosures, including nutrient databases, cookbooks, laboratory analyses, and other reasonable means, as described in 21 CFR 101.10 (or any successor regulation) or in a related FDA guidance. Section 101.10 requires nutrition labeling for a restaurant food that bears a nutrient content or health claim, except that information on the nutrient amounts that are the basis for the claim may serve as the functional equivalent of complete nutrition information. Under § 101.10, nutrient levels may be determined by nutrient databases, cookbooks, or analyses or by other reasonable bases that provide assurance that the food or meal meets the nutrient requirements for the claim. In this rule, § 101.11(c)(1) is patterned after § 101.10, as required by section 403(q)(5)(H)(iv) of the FD&C Act, in that it provides for nutrient values to be determined by nutrient databases, cookbooks, or analyses or by other reasonable bases. However, given that we incorporated the applicable regulatory text from § 101.10 into § 101.11(c)(1), there is no need to refer to § 101.10 within § 101.11(c)(1). Indeed, including "as described in § 101.10" within § 101.11(c)(1) could mistakenly signal, to both covered establishments and investigators who would evaluate compliance with this rule, that a covered establishment must look to § 101.10 to determine how to fully comply with § 101.11(c)(1).

As finalized, § 101.11(c)(1) states that a covered establishment must have a reasonable basis for its nutrient declarations. Nutrient values may be determined by using nutrient databases (with or without computer software programs), cookbooks, laboratory analyses, or other reasonable means, including the use of Nutrition Facts on labels on packaged foods that comply with the nutrition labeling requirements of section 403(q)(1) of the FD&C Act and § 101.9, FDA nutrient values for raw fruits and vegetables in Appendix C of part 101 of the chapter, or FDA nutrient values for cooked fish in Appendix D of part 101 of the chapter.

(Comment 136) One comment agreed with our proposal for using an approach for determining compliance modeled after § 101.9(g). The comment recognized that the proposed approach is consistent with the accuracy standards for Nutrition Facts information and stated that even relatively small variances can be significant in influencing cardiovascular health.

The majority of comments opposed our proposal for using an approach for determining compliance modeled after § 101.9(g), particularly with respect to using the "80/120 rule" for compliance purposes. Some comments maintained that the proposed criteria for compliance modeled after § 101.9(g) are not consistent with § 101.10. Some comments stated that use of the "80/120 rule" for determining compliance with the menu labeling requirements of section 403(q)(5)(H) of the FD&C Act contradicts 20 years of FDA precedence regarding determining compliance for nutrient content claims made for restaurant foods. The comments referred to our statements in the final rule establishing § 101.10 regarding claims for restaurant food (58 FR 2302 at 2387, January 6, 1993) and in our 2008 guidance for restaurant food (Ref. 10). Based on these statements, the comments asserted that we understood the difficulty in determining compliance for restaurant foods making nutrient content claims or health claims and acknowledged the variations unique to restaurant foods (e.g., by recognizing that restaurant foods are generally hand assembled and, therefore, subject to individual product variation), and therefore did not require that restaurants conduct nutrient analyses for such claims. The comments asserted that reasons such as these led us to require in § 101.10 that restaurants have a reasonable basis for making a nutrient content or health claim, and that the proposed rule did not provide any factual basis or evidence that the circumstances that justified the original "reasonable basis standard" have changed.

Some comments asserted that using the "80/120 rule" for determining compliance with the menu labeling requirements of section 403(q)(5)(H) of the FD&C Act was not the intent of Congress. Some comments considered that use of the "80/120 rule" would make the reasonable basis statutory provision at section 403(q)(5)(H)(iv) of the FD&C Act irrelevant. Some comments asserted that use of the "80/120 rule" in the proposed rule contradicts the plain language of section 403(q)(5)(H)(iv) of the FD&C Act, and therefore, violates the Administrative Procedure Act (APA). One comment asserted that section 4205 of the ACA proposes a specific standard at section 403(q)(5)(H)(iv) of the FD&C Act for determining nutrient content disclosures under section 4205, and such a specific standard "does not permit an agency to impose a more rigorous standard than one required by Congress." The comment stated that under the framework articulated in Chevron, U.S.A., Inc. v. Natural Resource Defense Counsel, 467 U.S. 837 (1984), "courts ask as the threshold question of `whether Congress has directly spoken to the precise question at issue," and "[i]f the intent of Congress is clear, that is the end of the matter." The comment stated that section 4205 of the ACA is unambiguous "in adopting the pre-existing reasonable basis standard" in § 101.10 to determine compliance with the nutrition labeling requirements of section 4205, and "this reflects a clear directive to FDA which does not contemplate, nor permit, any deviation of the kind contemplated in the proposed rule."

Some comments asserted that Congress expressly directed us to consider "standardization of recipes and methods of preparation, reasonable variation in serving size and formulation of menu items ... inadvertent human error, training of food service workers, variations in ingredients, and other factors" in issuing regulations to implement section 4205 of the ACA, including those regarding reasonable basis. The comments maintained that by including this language in section 403(q)(5)(H)(x) of the FD&C Act and directing us to consider such factors, Congress demonstrated its familiarity with the challenges involved in requiring nutrition labeling for restaurant food, identifying many of the same factors that led us to implement the reasonable basis standard in § 101.10.

Some comments maintained that it is not practical to require a compliance standard for covered establishments that is the same as had been developed for packaged food manufacturers that use modern manufacturing calibrated equipment and methods for which the "80/120 rule" is appropriate. Some comments asserted that restaurant food is not standardized like packaged food. For example, some comments explained that the mere addition of five to seven extra French fries in an order of small fries would increase calories more than 20 percent and make the food product misbranded under the "80/120 rule." The comment stated, as an example, that cheese sticking together and an extra squirt of mayonnaise in a food are not negligent practices, but would make the nutrient content declaration for the food out of compliance. Another comment stated that if a lobster tail is 6 ounces rather than 5 ounces, the calories would be 20 percent higher. Some comments asserted that using the "80/120 rule" for compliance is impractical and will require frequent analysis that will add costs. Some comments contrasted manufacturers that test for nutrient variations at a single point or a handful of points of manufacture with restaurants that have thousands of points of manufacture, each of which would require separate analysis. One comment asserted that the "80/120 standard" was not practicable and is inflexible for covered establishments and would create increased and unnecessary compliance and litigation costs for covered establishments.

One comment asked us to provide flexibility for variations in portion size and recipes and allow for disparities between the amount of a food used to calculate the calories and the actual size that might be served to or taken by customers. This comment recommended that the final rule create specific guidelines for displaying caloric information for non-uniform menu items (e.g. fresh fruit or pieces of chicken).

Some comments pointed to the variability in the nutrient content of restaurant foods based on changes in ingredients and recipes, and seasonal changes in the ingredients as reasons for why complying with the "80/120 rule" would be difficult. One comment noted that moisture leaves hot foods at hot-food bars after a certain period of time and as a result nutrient values for such foods change from those values listed in recipe books. The comment asked us to expand the tolerance by 10 percent at both ends if we kept compliance requirements similar to the "80/120 rule" rather than a more flexible "reasonable basis" standard. Some comments pointed out that there is variability in menu items due to using locally grown ingredients and that the nutrient content of these ingredients can vary by region. One comment asserted that if we do not account for this variation in the final rule, it will be a disincentive to covered establishments to use local farmers and suppliers.

One comment asserted that use of the "80/120 rule" will discourage voluntary opting in by restaurants and similar retail food establishments not covered by section 403(q)(5)(H) of the FD&C Act, which would lead to less national uniformity. The comment stated that many State and local restaurant menu labeling laws measure compliance using a standard akin to "the Federal reasonable basis standard" and even where no State nutrition labeling laws apply, a restaurant making nutrient content claims would be subject to the "reasonable basis standard" under 21 U.S.C. 343(r) (i.e., § 101.10). Therefore, according to the comment, under the proposed rule, small-chain restaurants voluntarily registering with us to be subject to the Federal requirements would subject themselves to more potential liability under the "Federal 80/120 standard" and would thus be less likely to voluntarily participate in the Federal menu labeling scheme. The comment maintained that in turn, there would be less national uniformity in menu labeling, consumers would see less consistent nutrition information on menus, and State and local inspectors would have to apply a more complex patchwork of regulatory schemes.

One comment asserted that the "80/120 rule" imposes a stricter compliance standard for foods with smaller amounts of a particular nutrient that should be consumed in limited quantities (e.g., fat and cholesterol) because the "80/120 rule" measures compliance as a percentage of the declared nutrient levels. For example, a deviation of 1 gram of fat in a salad declared to have 3 grams of fat would make the covered establishment out of compliance. The comment asserted that this is a disincentive for low fat, low sodium foods and is contrary to the purpose of the rule.

One comment recommended that the amount of protein, total carbohydrates, and dietary fiber contained in an appropriate composite of a standard menu item be equal to the declared value, not at least 80 percent of the declared value.

(Response 136) Proposed § 101.11(c)(2), (c)(3), (c)(4), and (c)(5) were modeled after § 101.9(g), including use of the "80/120 rule." Based on what the comments said, we believe that some comments misinterpreted the proposed rule as requiring covered establishments to determine nutrition information through laboratory analyses only. We did not intend to suggest such a limited requirement. Laboratory analysis was merely one of several options we proposed to establish in § 101.11(c)(1) to satisfy the requirement for a reasonable basis for nutrient levels. Instead, proposed § 101.11(c)(2), (c)(3), (c)(4), and (c)(5), were provisions modeled after § 101.9(g), including use of the "80/120 rule," explaining how we would determine whether a covered establishment is in compliance with the requirement (in proposed § 101.11(c)(1)) for a covered establishment to have a reasonable basis for its nutrient disclosures. We did not intend for proposed § 101.11(c)(2), (c)(3), (c)(4), and (c)(5) to require a covered establishment to use laboratory analyses in all circumstances to determine nutrition information for standard menu items. A covered establishment would have been free to choose any reasonable basis so long as it produced accurate results.

While we do not agree with some of the comments, particularly those asserting that our proposal to use the "80/120 rule" to determine compliance would violate the APA, we agree that using the "80/120 rule" for determining compliance with the nutrition labeling requirements likely would raise practical problems such as some of those described in the comments. Given these practical problems, we have replaced proposed § 101.11(c)(2), (c)(3), (c)(4), and (c)(5) with other requirements in a new § 101.11(c)(2). First, § 101.11(c)(2) specifies that nutrient declarations for standard menu items must be accurate and consistent with the specific basis used to determine nutrient values. For example, for a nutrient declaration to be accurate, a covered establishment that relies on a nutrient database for a list of nutrient values, and then uses those nutrient values to perform its own calculation of the nutrient values in a standard menu item, must correctly add the nutrient values for all ingredients in the standard menu item taking into consideration the recipe and ingredient amounts used to prepare the standard menu item among other factors. Second, § 101.11(c)(2) also specifies that a covered establishment must take reasonable steps to ensure that the method of preparation (e.g., types and amounts of ingredients in the recipe, cooking temperatures) and amount of a standard menu item offered for sale adhere to the factors on which its nutrient values were determined. Accordingly, under § 101.11(c)(2), a covered establishment that selects a recipe from a cookbook and relies on the cookbook's nutrition information for such recipe as a basis for the establishment's nutrient declarations must take reasonable steps to ensure that employees who prepare the standard menu item do not depart from that recipe, including the recipe's instructions and ingredient amounts. For example, if a covered establishment determines nutrition information for a turkey sandwich based on a recipe along with nutrition information provided in a cookbook for the turkey sandwich, and the recipe specifies using one tablespoon of mayonnaise, the establishment must take reasonable steps to ensure that its employees use one tablespoon of mayonnaise when preparing the turkey sandwich—e.g., through appropriate instruction about the importance of the consistent application of one tablespoon of mayonnaise to satisfy the requirements of this rule.

Although we recognize inadvertent human error and variations in ingredients, covered establishments must ensure that the nutrient declarations are truthful and not misleading in part by having standard methods of preparation for standard menu items and taking reasonable steps to ensure that the methods of preparation used for a standard menu item adhere to the factors on which the nutrient levels were determined. To make clear that a covered establishment has this responsibility, we are also replacing each of the proposed requirements (in proposed § 101.11(c)(6)(i)(H), (c)(6)(ii)(D), (c)(6)(iii)(D), and (c)(6)(iv)(E)) for a certification statement regarding the recipe used to prepare the standard menu item with a requirement for a statement signed and dated by a responsible individual employed at the covered establishment certifying that the covered establishment has taken reasonable steps to ensure that the method of preparation (e.g., types and amounts of ingredients in the recipe, cooking temperatures) and amount of a standard menu item offered for sale adhere to the factors on which its nutrient values were determined. These provisions are in § 101.11(c)(3)(i)(G), (c)(3)(ii)(D), (c)(3)(iii)(E), and (c)(3)(iv)(E) of the final rule. (See the discussion of these provisions in section XIX.)

We acknowledge that the calorie content of non-uniform menu items such as whole fresh fruit and pieces of chicken vary depending on the size and, in some cases composition (e.g., chicken breast, thigh, or drumstick) of the items. A covered establishment may take such variation into consideration when determining the calorie content and calorie declaration for the menu item. For example, a covered establishment could base its nutrient declarations on the average size of a piece of fruit, or on a weighted average of nutrient values for a box of chicken that contains a fixed number of chicken breasts, thighs, or drumsticks.

In assessing compliance with § 101.11(c), we will consider the factors and criteria specified in both § 101.11(c)(1) and (c)(2), including whether the establishment took reasonable steps to ensure that the method of preparation for a standard menu item adheres to the factors on which the reasonable basis was determined. We will assess compliance on a case by case basis, taking into consideration a number of factors, including the covered establishment's nutrition labeling, the method (e.g., laboratory analysis, nutrient database, cookbook, or nutrient information provided on the labels of packaged food) used by the covered establishment to determine nutrition information, and the steps taken by the establishment to ensure that the method of preparation and amount of a standard menu item adhered to the factors on which its nutrient values were determined. Further, we may conduct our own analysis, including laboratory analysis, as needed, including if we find that nutrient declarations appear to be false or misleading or the basis upon which the covered establishment based its nutrient declaration appears to be unreasonable or is otherwise questionable.

XIX. Comments and FDA Response on Proposed § 101.11(c)(6)—Substantiation Documentation (Final § 101.11(c)(3))

Proposed § 101.11(c)(6) would require that a restaurant or similar retail food establishment provide to FDA, within a reasonable period of time upon request, information substantiating nutrient values including the method and data used to derive these nutrient levels. Proposed § 101.11(c)(6) would require that covered establishments provide the following information:

- For nutrient databases:

  o The identity of the database used.

  o The recipe or formula used as a basis for the nutrient declarations. The recipe posted on the database must be identical to that used by the restaurant or similar retail food establishment to prepare the menu item.

  o For the specified amounts of each ingredient identified in the recipe, a detailed listing (e.g., printout) of the amount of each nutrient that that ingredient contributes to the menu item.

  o If this information is not available because the nutrition information was derived from a computer program, which is designed to provide only a final list of nutrient values for the recipe, a certificate of validation attesting to the accuracy of the computer program.

  o A detailed listing (e.g., printout) of the nutrient values determined for each menu item.

  o If this information is not derived through the aid of a computer program which provides a final nutrient analysis for the menu item, worksheets used to determine the nutrient values for each of these menu items.

  o Any other information pertinent to the final nutrient levels of the menu item (e.g., information about what might cause slight variations in the nutrient profile such as moisture variations).

○ A statement signed by a responsible individual employed by the covered establishment that can certify that the information contained in the nutrient analysis is complete and accurate and that the recipe used to prepare the menu item is identical to that used for the nutrient analysis.

- For published cookbooks that contain nutritional information for recipes in the cookbook:

○ The name, author, and publisher of the cookbook used.

○ If available, information provided by the cookbook about how the nutrition information for the recipes was obtained.

○ A copy of the recipe used to prepare the menu item and a copy of the nutrition information for that menu item as provided by the cookbook.

○ A statement signed by a responsible individual employed by the covered establishment certifying that the recipe used to prepare the menu item by the restaurant or similar retail food establishment is the same recipe provided in the cookbook. (Recipes may be divided as necessary to accommodate differences in the portion size derived from the recipe and that are served as the menu item but no changes may be made to the proportion of ingredients used.).

- For analyses:

○ A copy of the recipe for the menu item used for the nutrient analysis.

○ The identity of the laboratory performing the analysis.

○ Copies of analytical worksheets used to determine and verify nutrition information.

○ A statement signed by a responsible individual employed by the covered establishment that can certify that the information contained in the nutrient analysis is complete and accurate and an additional signed statement certifying that the recipe used to prepare the menu item is identical to that used for the nutrient analysis.

- For nutrition information provided by other reasonable means:

○ A detailed description of the method used to determine the nutrition information.

○ Documentation of the validity of that method.

○ A recipe or formula used as a basis for the nutrient determination. The recipe used in determining these nutrient values must be the same recipe used by the restaurant and similar retail food establishment to prepare the item.

○ Any data derived in determining the nutrient values for the menu item; and

○ A statement signed by a responsible individual employed by the covered establishment that can certify that the information contained in the nutrient analysis is complete and accurate and that the recipe used to prepare the menu item is identical to that used for the nutrient analysis.

In the following paragraphs, we discuss comments on the proposed substantiation requirements. After considering comments, including comments (discussed in the previous section of this document) that caused us to remove proposed § 101.11(c)(2), (c)(3), (c)(4), and (c)(5), we are:

- Redesignating proposed § 101.11(c)(6) as § 101.11(c)(3);

- Clarifying the applicability of the requirements by replacing the term "restaurant or similar retail food establishment" with "covered establishment" in the introductory paragraph in § 101.11(c)(3) and in the subparagraph in § 101.11(c)(3)(ii)(D).

- Providing that the statement certifying that the information contained in the nutrient analysis is complete and accurate may be signed by a responsible individual employed by "the covered establishment or its parent entity" (proposed § 101.11(c)(6)(i)(H), (c)(6)(iii)(D), and (c)(6)(iv)(E), redesignated as § 101.11(c)(3)(i)(F), (c)(3)(iii)(D), and (c)(6)(iv)(D), respectively);

- Requiring a certification that the covered establishment has taken reasonable steps to ensure that the method of preparation (e.g., types and amounts of ingredients, cooking temperatures in the recipe) and amount of a standard menu item offered for sale adhere to the factors on which its nutrient values were determined;

- Requiring that all certification statements be dated as well as signed;

- Specifying what we mean by "the identity of the database used" in proposed § 101.11(c)(6)(i)(A) (redesignated as § 101.11(c)(3)(i)(A));

- Combining and replacing certain proposed details of the substantiation documentation when nutrient databases are used (i.e., proposed § 101.11(c)(6)(i)(C), (c)(6)(i)(D), and (c)(6)(i)(F)) with requirements (in § 101.11(c)(3)(i)(C)) to present the requirements in a simplified and streamlined format;

- Specifying what we mean by "the identity of the laboratory performing the analysis" in proposed § 101.11(c)(6)(iii)(B) (redesignated as § 101.11(c)(3)(iii)(B));

- Specifying that copies of analytical worksheets used to determine and verify nutrition information must include the analytical method in proposed § 101.11(c)(6)(iii)(C) (redesignated as § 101.11(c)(3)(iii)(C));

- Revising proposed § 101.11(c)(6)(iv)(A) (redesignated as § 101.11(c)(3)(iv)(A)) to require a detailed description of the "means" (rather than the "method") used to determine the nutrition information "by other reasonable means";

- Deleting proposed § 101.11(c)(6)(iv)(B) and redesignating proposed § 101.11(c)(6)(iv)(C), (c)(6)(iv)(D) and (c)(6)(iv)(E) as § 101.11(c)(3)(iv)(B), (c)(3)(iv)(C), and (c)(3)(iv)(D), respectively; and

- Revising proposed § 101.11(c)(6)(iv)(D) (redesignated as § 101.11(c)(3)(iv)(C)) to provide an example of any "data derived in determining the nutrient values."

In addition, as nonsubstantive editorial changes we are:

- Replacing all instances of the term "nutrient levels" with the term "nutrient values" to consistently use the same term throughout § 101.11(c);

- Replacing all instances of the term "menu item" with "standard menu item" to emphasize that the requirements for determination of nutrient content apply only to standard menu items; and

- Adding the conjunction "and" between § 101.11(c)(3)(i)(F) and § 101.11(c)(3)(i)(G), between § 101.11(c)(3)(ii)(C) and § 101.11(c)(3)(ii)(D), between § 101.11(c)(3)(iii)(D) and § 101.11(c)(3)(iii)(E), and between § 101.11(c)(3)(iv)(D) and § 101.11(c)(3)(iv)(E), to clarify that all of the items listed under § 101.11(c)(3)(i), § 101.11(c)(3)(ii), § 101.11(c)(3)(iii), and § 101.11(c)(3)(iv) are required.

(Comment 137) As discussed in more detail in section XVIII (see Comment 136), several comments opposed the nutrient determination requirements in proposed § 101.11(c)(2), (c)(3), (c)(4), and (c)(5).

(Response 137) As discussed in more detail in section XVIII (see Response 136), we are deleting those requirements from the rule. Some comments misinterpreted these provisions, e.g., by concluding that we intended to require the use of laboratory analysis as a reasonable basis in all circumstances. To reduce the potential for future misunderstanding about the substantiation provisions in the final rule, we have made the following revisions to the requirements for substantiation documentation.

First, we have revised proposed § 101.11(c)(6)(iii) (redesignated as § 101.11(c)(3)(iii) in the final rule) to clarify that the analyses governed by the provision are "laboratory analyses." Some of the specific requirements of § 101.11(c)(3)(iii)) (such as for analytical worksheets) may not apply to other means used by a covered establishment as a reasonable basis for its nutrient determinations.

Second, we are providing more specific information about the requirements for substantiation information. Specifically:

- We have revised proposed § 101.11(c)(6)(i)(A) (redesignated as § 101.11(c)(3)(i)(A) in the final rule) to specify that substantiation documentation for nutrient databases must include the name and version (including the date of the version) of the database, and, as applicable, the name of the applicable software company and any Web site address for the database. The name and version of a database would include the name and version of the computer software, if applicable. Any database suitable for use as a reasonable basis for the purposes of § 101.11 would have a name and version number; in some cases, the version number is a date. The version number is necessary to fully identify a database because databases may be updated to reflect more recent data and information, and nutrient values generated with one version of a database may be different from nutrient values generated by a different database. If, for example, a covered establishment used "version x" of a database for its nutrient determinations, and we used "version y" of that database to evaluate compliance with the nutrient determination requirements of rule, we inadvertently could conclude that the covered establishment is out of compliance with the rule if the nutrient values we obtained using "version y" do not match those obtained using "version x." Some databases may be provided by a public source (such as USDA), whereas others may be provided by a private vendor. If we have any questions about the database, we may need to contact the public source or private vendor. Some databases are available on the Internet; the Web site address would enable us to obtain any necessary followup information on an Internet-based database.

- We have revised proposed § 101.11(c)(6)(iii)(B) (redesignated as § 101.11(c)(3)(iii)(B) in the final rule) to specify that substantiation documentation for laboratory analyses must include the name and address of the laboratory. Some laboratories that conduct nutrient analyses have more than one facility, and the name of the laboratory alone would not be sufficient to identify the laboratory that conducted the analysis.

- We have revised proposed § 101.11(c)(6)(iv)(D) (redesignated as § 101.11(c)(3)(iv)(C) in the final rule) to provide "nutrition information about the ingredients used, including the source of the nutrient information" as an example of what we mean by any "data derived in determining nutrient values."

Third, we are reorganizing and combining the provisions of proposed § 101.11(c)(6)(i)(C), (c)(6)(i)(D), and (c)(6)(i)(F) (in § 101.11(c)(3)(i)(C)) to simplify the requirements and make them more clear. In particular, we reorganized the requirements to clarify that the substantiation documentation that would be provided to FDA can vary depending on characteristics of the database. For example, in some cases, the information and calculations provided by a database are transparent to a person using the database, whereas, in other cases, such information and calculations are not transparent to the user. Section § 101.11(c)(3)(i)(C) addresses these different situations in separate subparagraphs (i.e., in § 101.11(c)(3)(i)(C)(1) and (c)(3)(i)(C)(2)). Under § 101.11(c)(3)(i)(C)(1), the substantiation information for nutrient databases must include information on: (1) The amount of each nutrient that the specified amount of each ingredient identified in the recipe contributes to the menu item; and (2) How the database was used including calculations or operations (e.g., worksheets or computer printouts) to determine the nutrient values for the standard menu items. Under § 101.11(c)(3)(i)(C)(2), if the information in § 101.11(c)(3)(i)(C)(1) is not available, the substantiation documentation for nutrient databases must include certification attesting that the database will provide accurate results when used appropriately and that the database was used in accordance with its instructions.

Fourth, we have revised proposed § 101.11(c)(6)(iii)(C) (redesignated as § 101.11(c)(3)(iii)(C) in the final rule) to specify that copies of analytical worksheets used to determine and verify nutrition information must include the analytical method used to determine and verify nutrition information. An analytical worksheet cannot be evaluated for compliance purposes unless the method is identified. A key aspect of evaluating analytical results is determining whether the procedure was carried out correctly, by comparing the data in the work sheets to the procedure in the applicable analytical method.

(Comment 138) One comment recommended that covered establishments provide references for their nutrient values to consumers on request. Another comment recommended that establishments be required to maintain the reasonable basis verification only at headquarters, "and not in-store and available upon customer request or online." This comment considered that providing hard copies on site at many locations would be costly, administratively burdensome, and environmentally unsustainable.

(Response 138) We did not propose to require that the substantiation documentation be available to consumers in a covered establishment or online. The provisions for making substantiation documentation available to us were directed to our enforcement of the rule rather than to informing consumers. Hard copies of the substantiation documentation would only need to be provided to FDA "within a reasonable period of time upon request." Thus, a covered establishment need not generate any hard copies of the substantiation information until we request the information. We would request substantiation documentation from individual covered establishments during inspections. However, a covered establishment could wait to physically obtain substantiation documentation generated by its corporate headquarters or parent entity until we ask for it, provided that the covered establishment can obtain the information within a reasonable period of time.

(Comment 139) One comment stated that it was unclear whether each independently operated unit, including a franchisee, will have to substantiate the accuracy of the nutrient information. Some comments disagreed that the responsible person of the covered establishment needs to sign a statement certifying that the nutrient analysis is complete and accurate and that recipes used to prepare menu items are identical to those used for the nutrient analysis. The comments asserted that this information is mostly gathered at corporate headquarters and there is no comparable requirement for packaged food.

(Response 139) We agree, in part, and disagree, in part, with these comments. We agree that the responsible individual certifying that the nutrient analysis is complete and accurate need not be employed at the covered establishment; instead, the individual could be employed at the establishment's corporate headquarters or parent entity. Whether such individual is employed at the covered establishment or the establishment's corporate headquarters or parent entity, it is critical that the individual who signs the certification has a factual basis for certifying that the nutrient analysis is complete and correct.

We disagree that a responsible individual employed at the covered establishment's corporate headquarters or parent entity, rather than a responsible individual employed at the covered establishment, could sign a certification regarding the use of a recipe within a covered establishment. A responsible individual employed at the establishment's corporate headquarters or parent entity likely would not have a factual basis for certifying the actions of a specific covered establishment because the individual would not be present in the establishment where the standard items are prepared, and, thus, likely could not certify the actions the establishment takes to comply with the rule.

After considering these comments, we have revised the requirements for certification statements (i.e., proposed § 101.11(c)(6)(i)(H), (c)(6)(ii)(D), (c)(6)(iii)(D), and (c)(6)(iv)(E), which we have renumbered in the final rule as described in the following sentences) to distinguish certifications that must be signed and dated by a responsible individual employed at the covered establishment from certifications that may be signed and dated by a responsible individual employed at either the covered establishment or at its corporate headquarters or parent entity. First, § 101.11(c)(3)(i)(F), (c)(3)(iii)(D), and (c)(6)(iv)(D) of the final rule require a statement signed and dated by a responsible individual, employed at the covered establishment or its corporate headquarters or parent entity, who can certify that the information contained in the nutrient analysis is complete and accurate. We are using the term "parent entity" in addition to "corporate headquarters" because some business entities may not be "corporations."

Second, § 101.11(c)(3)(i)(G), (c)(3)(ii)(D), (c)(3)(iii)(E), and (c)(6)(iv)(E) of the final rule require a statement signed and dated by a responsible individual employed at the covered establishment certifying that the covered establishment has taken reasonable steps to ensure that the method of preparation (e.g., types and amounts of ingredients in the recipe, cooking temperatures) and amount of a standard menu item offered for sale adhere to the factors on which its nutrient values were determined.

We are requiring that all certification statements be dated as well as signed. A date is standard practice on such documents and would be necessary, for example, to establish whether a certification signed in advance by a responsible individual at the parent entity can address nutrient analyses conducted over time.

(Comment 140) One comment opposed the proposed requirement that a covered establishment turn over its recipes to a governmental agency, because a covered establishment cannot be assured that its proprietary information will be protected and will not make it into the hands of competitors or unscrupulous governmental employees looking to sell or pass on trade secrets.

(Response 140) While we understand that some establishments may have concerns about the confidentiality of information inspected by FDA under § 101.11, we emphasize that we protect confidential information from disclosure, consistent with applicable statutes and regulations. Our disclosure of information is subject to the Freedom of Information Act (FOIA) (5 U.S.C. 552), the Trade Secrets Act (18 U.S.C. 1905), the FD&C Act, and our implementing disclosure regulations under part 20 (21 CFR part 20), which include protection for confidential commercial or financial information and trade secrets. To the extent that the comment is asserting that we have no procedures in place to protect the confidentiality of proprietary information, we disagree. We receive trade secret or confidential information on a regular and recurring basis. As noted previously, trade secrets and commercial or financial information that are privileged or confidential are protected from disclosure under the FOIA, the Trade Secrets Act, the FD&C Act, and our implementing disclosure regulations (see, e.g., 21 U.S.C. 331(j), 18 U.S.C. 1905; 21 CFR 20.61(c)). Our disclosure regulations set forth specific procedures for assuring such protection (see part 20). A covered establishment that provides substantiation documentation to us may identify any information in such documentation that the establishment considers to be trade secret or confidential commercial or financial information (21 CFR 20.61(d)). Information so marked will not be disclosed to the extent such information is protected under the FOIA and our disclosure regulations (part 20).

(Comment 141) A few comments asserted that the proposed requirement that a responsible individual of the covered establishment certify that the recipe used for the standard menu item is identical to that used for the nutrient analysis is unreasonable and beyond the scope of the law. The comments considered that Congress directed us (in section 403(q)(5)(H)(x)(II)(aa) of the FD&C Act) to consider standardization of recipes, reasonable variation in serving size and formulation of menu items, inadvertent human error, training of food service workers, variations in ingredients, and other factors. One comment noted that this certification is not required by statute, and considered that it is not clear what regulatory purpose it would serve. The comments asserted that it is unreasonable to expect a covered establishment to prepare a standard menu item in a manner that is identical to the recipe on each given day. A few comments opposed asking employees to attest that they have followed recipes exactly and considered such a requirement to be unfair to employees because there are several factors that affect the recipe such as seasonal variations, market availability of certain ingredients, and modifying recipes to accommodate regional taste preferences. One comment suggested deleting the following proposed requirements in § 101.11(c)(6):

- For nutrient databases

○ The recipe posted on the database must be identical to that used by the restaurant or similar retail food establishment to prepare the menu item.

○ For the specified amounts of each ingredient identified in the recipe, a detailed listing (e.g., printout) of the amount of each nutrient that that ingredient contributes to the menu item.

○ If this information is not available because the nutrition information was derived from a computer program, which is designed to provide only a final list of nutrient values for the recipe, a certificate of validation attesting to the accuracy of the computer program.

○ A statement signed by a responsible individual employed by the covered establishment that can certify that the information contained in the nutrient analysis is complete and accurate and that the recipe used to prepare the menu item is identical to that used for the nutrient analysis.

- For published cookbooks that contain nutritional information for recipes in the cookbook:

○ A copy of the recipe used to prepare the menu item and a copy of the nutrition information for that menu item as provided by the cookbook.

○ A statement signed by a responsible individual employed by the covered establishment certifying that the recipe used to prepare the menu item by the restaurant or similar retail food establishment is the same recipe provided in the cookbook. (Recipes may be divided as necessary to accommodate differences in the portion size derived from the recipe and that are served as the menu item but no changes may be made to the proportion of ingredients used.)

- For analyses:

○ A statement signed by a responsible individual employed by the covered establishment that can certify that the information contained in the nutrient analysis is complete and accurate and an additional signed statement certifying that the recipe used to prepare the menu item is identical to that used for the nutrient analysis.

- For nutrition information provided by other reasonable means:

○ The word "detailed" from the provision in § 101.11(c)(6)(iv)(A).

○ Documentation of the validity of that method.

○ A statement signed by a responsible individual employed by the covered establishment that can certify that the information contained in the nutrient analysis is complete and accurate and that the recipe used to prepare the menu item is identical to that used for the nutrient analysis.

(Response 141) As discussed in Response 136, we are replacing each requirement (in proposed §§ 101.11(c)(6)(i)(H), (c)(6)(ii)(D), (c)(6)(iii)(D), and (c)(6)(iv)(E)) that a responsible individual of the covered establishment certify that the recipe used for the standard menu item is identical to that used for the nutrient analysis used to prepare the standard menu item with a requirement for a statement signed and dated by a responsible individual employed at the covered establishment certifying that the establishment has taken reasonable steps to ensure that the method of preparation (e.g., types and amounts of ingredients in the recipe, cooking temperatures) and amount of a standard menu item offered for sale adhere to the factors on which its nutrient values were determined. Therefore, § 101.11(c) will not require a responsible individual of the covered establishment to certify that the recipe used for the standard menu item is identical to that used for the nutrient analysis used to prepare the standard menu item; nor will it require that a covered establishment prepare a standard menu item using a recipe that is identical to that used in a database (as proposed in § 101.11(c)(6)(i)(B)). Nevertheless, a covered establishment must ensure that its nutrition labeling is truthful and not misleading and that it has a reasonable basis for its nutrient content disclosures, as further discussed in Response 136.

As requested in Comment 136 and discussed in Response 136, we have revised the rule to require (in § 101.11(c)(2)) that the covered establishment take reasonable steps to ensure that the method of preparation (e.g., types and amounts of ingredients in the recipe, cooking temperatures) and amount of a standard menu item offered for sale adhere to the factors on which its nutrient values were determined. As discussed in Response 135, we have revised proposed § 101.11(c)(6)(iv)(A) (which is renumbered as § 101.11(c)(3)(iv)(A) in the final rule), which addresses the information that must be provided to FDA, within a reasonable period of time upon request, when "other reasonable means are used to provide the nutrition information." To emphasize that "other reasonable means" does not require analytical testing, § 101.11(c)(3)(iv)(A)) requires a detailed description of the "means" (rather than the "method") used to determine the nutrition information.

We also have removed proposed § 101.11(c)(6)(iv)(B), which would have required documentation of the validity of the method for "nutrition information provided by other reasonable means." As evidenced by the examples we now provide of "other reasonable means" in § 101.11(c)(1), "documentation of validity of that method" generally would not apply to "other reasonable means" that are reasonably foreseeable.

Other than by removing proposed § 101.11(c)(6)(iv)(B) and the proposed provisions requiring that the recipe used to prepare a standard menu item be identical to the recipe used to determine the nutrition information for the standard menu item described previously, we are not deleting the remaining specific proposed provisions that one comment recommended deleting. The comment provided no explanation or basis for deleting those specific provisions. Further, these provisions establish requirements for substantiating determination of nutrient content for standard menu items provided by covered establishments. As we discussed in the proposed rule (76 FR 19192 at 19219), to determine whether a covered establishment has a reasonable basis for its nutrient content disclosures, as required by section 403(q)(5)(H) of the FD&C Act, and whether a standard menu item is otherwise misbranded under section 403(a)(1) of the FD&C Act, we must have access to the information substantiating the covered establishment's determination of nutrient content. Without these requirements, which provide access to substantiation documentation, we would not be able to efficiently determine whether a covered establishment's nutrition labeling is truthful and not misleading. Further, without access to substantiation documentation of the basis of a covered establishment's nutrient content disclosures, including recipe and ingredient information, we would not be able to determine whether an establishment has a reasonable basis for its nutrition content disclosures, as required by section 403(q)(5)(H)(iv) of the FD&C Act. Accordingly, such requirements are necessary for the efficient enforcement of the FD&C Act.

XX. Comments and FDA Response on Proposed Section 101.11(d)—Voluntary Registration To Elect To Be Subject to the Rule

Proposed § 101.11(d)(1) would provide that a restaurant or similar retail food establishment that is not part of a chain with 20 or more locations doing business under the same name and offering for sale substantially the same menu items could voluntarily register to provide the nutrition information required by § 101.11(b), and that in doing so they would no longer be subject to non-identical State or local nutrition labeling requirements. Proposed § 101.11(d)(2) would provide that the authorized official of a restaurant or similar retail food establishment as defined, may register with FDA. Proposed § 101.11(d)(3) would list the types of information (in brief, the contact information of each restaurant or similar retail food establishment, as well as contact information of an official onsite, trade names the restaurant or similar retail food establishment uses, preferred mailing address, and certification) that a restaurant or similar retail food establishment would need to provide to us in order to register voluntarily. Proposed § 101.11(d)(3) and (d)(4) would also describe the mechanism for submission by email, fax, mail, or online form. Finally, proposed § 101.11(d)(5) would require re-registration every other year within 60 days prior to the expiration of the current registration with FDA, and would provide that registration will automatically expire if not renewed.

In the following paragraphs, we discuss comments on these proposed provisions. We are finalizing them with the following changes for clarity.

- We are amending the titles of § 101.11(d)(4) and (d)(5) by replacing the question mark in each title with a period because these titles are not questions.

- We are deleting the revision date of Form FDA 3757 (i.e., 7/10) from § 101.11(d)(3). The FDA form number is sufficient to identify the form. Moreover, the revision date may change as a result of the renewal of the form every 3 years under the Paperwork Reduction Act.

- We are moving proposed § 101.11(d)(3)(vi) and (d)(3)(vii) to be subparagraphs of § 101.11(d)(4) rather than § 101.11(d)(3) and redesignating them as § 101.11(d)(4)(i) and (d)(4)(ii), respectively. These provisions are directed to "How to register" rather than to "What information is required?"

- For clarity, we are adding the form number (i.e., Form FDA 3757) to the second sentence of § 101.11(d)(4).

- For completeness, we have added ".gov" to the end of the email address provided for voluntary registration under § 101.11(d)(4)(i). The complete email address now reads "menulawregistration@fda.hhs.gov."

- We have revised the format of the cross-reference, within § 101.11(d)(4) to § 101.11(d)(3) to read "paragraph (d)(3) of this section" rather than "§ 101.11(d)(3)." We note that the proposed rule had identified the cross-reference as "§ 101.11(c)(3)." We revised this to "§ 101.11(d)(3)" in the correction document, but did not revise the format at that time.

(Comment 142) One comment supported the proposed registration requirements. One comment recommended that retail food establishments not covered by section 403(q)(5)(H) of the FD&C Act, regardless of whether they have fewer than 20 locations or if the sale of food is not the primary business activity, be allowed to elect to become subject to the requirements of section 403(q)(5)(H) of the FD&C Act by registering biannually with us. One comment referred to our discussions in the proposed rule that establishments such as cafeterias in schools and hospitals would not be covered by the rule under the proposed definition of "restaurant or similar retail food establishment" (see Footnote 1 at 76 FR 19192 at 19197 and discussion at 19230). This comment asked us to clarify whether there are some establishments (e.g., hospitals or school cafeterias) that are not restaurants or similar retail food establishments and therefore cannot voluntarily register to be subject to the Federal menu labeling requirements. The comment also asked us to clarify whether certain food service contractor facilities can voluntarily register even if other facilities in the overall set of operations do not. The comment recommended that we allow a restaurant or similar retail food establishment to voluntarily register on an establishment-by-establishment basis and not require the chain or company to make a single corporate-wide determination. The comment asked us to allow a food service contract business to register some of their establishments in order to make well-informed decisions on whether to register the other establishments and modify their establishments and contracts accordingly ("rolling adoption"). The comment also asked if there were requirements for opting out of the Federal requirements after voluntarily registering. The comment asked whether a restaurant or similar retail food establishment is required to be covered by the menu labeling requirements for a specific length of time, once it has voluntarily registered.

(Response 142) The final rule defines "restaurant or similar retail food establishment" to mean a retail establishment that offers for sale restaurant-type food, except if it is a school as defined in 7 CFR 210.2 or 220.2. Under § 101.11(d), a restaurant or similar retail food establishment, as defined in § 101.11(a), that is not part of a chain with 20 or more locations doing business under the same name and offering for sale substantially the same menu items (and, thus, is not subject to the requirements of section 403(q)(5)(H) of the FD&C Act) may voluntarily register to be subject to the requirements established in this rule. It does not matter whether the sale of food is the establishment's primary business activity, because the definition of restaurant or similar retail food establishment in this rule does not include a primary business test. Many establishments that would not have been a "restaurant or similar retail food establishment" under the definition we proposed (including establishments in hospitals) would be a restaurant or similar retail food establishment under the definition established in this rule (see the discussion of the definition of restaurant or similar retail food establishment in section VI.B). Whether any such establishment is automatically covered by the rule generally would depend on whether the establishment satisfies all other criteria in the definition of "covered establishment" (i.e., part of a chain with 20 or more locations doing business under the same name (regardless of the type of ownership, e.g., individual franchises) and offering for sale substantially the same menu items).

Section 403(q)(5)(H)(ix) of the FD&C Act provides that an authorized official of any restaurant or similar retail food establishment not subject to the requirements of section 403(q)(5)(H) may elect to become subject to the requirements by registering with FDA. Accordingly, any establishment that meets the definition for a restaurant or similar retail food establishment, as provided in § 101.11(a), that is not already subject to the requirements of section 403(q)(5)(H) of the FD&C Act can voluntarily register to become subject to the requirements under § 101.11(d). Establishments that do not meet the definition of "restaurant or similar retail food establishment" (e.g., drug stores that do not offer for sale any restaurant-type food) cannot voluntarily register.

Under § 101.11(d), an authorized official is permitted to register an individual restaurant or similar retail food establishment on an establishment-by-establishment basis, in that the authorized official may register a single restaurant or similar retail food establishment or multiple restaurants or similar retail food establishments within a chain on a single registration form, provided that the individual is authorized to do so for all of the restaurants or similar retail food establishments included on the form (Form FDA 3757) submitted. Whether a decision to register is made on an establishment-by-establishment basis or is a corporate-wide decision applying to many or all establishments within a chain is a matter for the restaurant or similar retail establishments and any corporate management to determine. This is as true for restaurants or similar retail food establishments operated by contractors as it is for other restaurants or similar retail food establishments.

The rule does not establish a date by which a restaurant or similar retail food establishment must register in order to "opt in" as a covered establishment and, thus, establishments within a chain could approach the voluntary registration using the "rolling adoption" requested by one comment.

A restaurant or similar retail food establishment that has voluntarily registered under § 101.11 must comply with the requirements of sections 403(a)(1), 403(f), and 403(q)(5)(H) of the FD&C Act and § 101.11 for 2 years after the date of registration and may not "opt out" until the 2 years has passed. If the restaurant or similar retail food establishment wants to "opt out," the mechanism to do so would be to let the registration lapse (i.e., not re-register) after the 2 years have passed.

XXI. Comments and FDA Response on Proposed § 101.11(e)—Signatures

Proposed § 101.11(e) would provide that signatures obtained under the voluntary registration provisions that meet the definition of electronic signatures in § 11.3(b)(7) would be exempt from the requirements of part 11 of the CFR (requirements for electronic records and signatures).

We received no comments on this proposed provision and are finalizing it without change.

XXII. Comments and FDA Response on Proposed § 101.11(f)—Misbranding

Proposed § 101.11(f) would provide that "a standard menu item offered for sale in a covered establishment" would be "deemed misbranded under sections 201(n), 403(a), and/or 403(q) of the Federal Food, Drug, and Cosmetic Act if its label or labeling is not in conformity" with the requirements for nutrition labeling and determination of nutrient content at § 101.11(b) and (c).

While we received no comments on this proposed provision, we are finalizing this provision with one change. We are including a reference to section 403(f) of the FD&C Act to clarify that failure to comply with the requirements of § 101.11(b) could cause a food to be misbranded under section 403(f) of the FD&C Act. Section 403(f) of the FD&C Act provides that a food shall be deemed misbranded "if any word, statement, or other information required by or under authority of this Act to appear on the label or labeling is not prominently placed thereon with such conspicuousness (as compared with other words, statements, designs, or devices, in the labeling) and in such terms as to render it likely to be read and understood by the ordinary individual under customary conditions of purchase and use." For example, as discussed in Response 127, if a calorie declaration for a standard menu item that is a self-service food or food on display is not declared in a manner that complies with § 101.11(b)(2)(iii)(A)(3)(ii), in that the declaration is not clear and conspicuous, the standard menu item would be misbranded under section 403(f) of the FD&C Act in addition to section 403(q) of the FD&C Act.

XXIII. Comments and FDA Response on Effective Date

A. Proposed Effective Date and Request for Comment

The proposed rule specified that the final rule would become effective 6 months from the date of its publication in the Federal Register (76 FR 19192 at 19219). We noted that compliance is expected to yield significant public health benefits because consumers will have calorie and other nutrition information when they make menu choices. Because of this benefit, we stated that it is reasonable to make the requirements effective as soon as practicable. We recognized, however, the potential difficulties of implementing the rule in this timeframe, and requested comment on whether the effective date should be extended for a greater period of time after the publication of the final rule. In particular, we requested comment on whether a 9-month or 1-year implementation timeframe would be more appropriate.

We also requested comment, supported by data, concerning how much time is needed for covered establishments to come into compliance with the rule, including, if possible, data on whether specific provisions of the rule can be more quickly implemented than others. We also requested comment on whether we should provide for staggered implementation based on the size of a chain or of a specific franchisee and again requested that suggestions be supported by data.

B. Comments on Proposed Effective Date

(Comment 143) Many comments supported our proposed 6-month effective date. Some comments noted that State and local jurisdictions with menu labeling requirements implemented and enforced the requirements in 6 or 7 months. One comment stated that many large chains have already conducted nutrient analyses for their menu items. In contrast, another comment reported the implementation time frames for 12 State and local requirements. This comment noted that restaurants subject to State or local menu labeling requirements have had no less than 6 months to comply with such requirements. This comment reported that one city (Philadelphia) provided more than 1 year for compliance and one State (Oregon) provided 6 months for implementation of Phase 1 of its requirements, and an additional year for compliance with Phase 2 of its requirements. This comment urged us to allow establishments at least 1 year to come into compliance with the Federal requirements.

Several comments opposed the 6-month effective date and requested an effective date of at least 1 year. Some comment noted that an effective date of at least 1 year would be necessary for covered establishments to develop and install redesigned menus. In particular, one comment from national associations representing a number of restaurants estimated that there are 250,000 to 275,000 covered restaurants in the United States, not including similar retail food establishments that would be covered under the rule. This comment recommended that we adopt an implementation period of not less than 1 year after the publication of the final rule and noted that extending the time period to 1 year would allow most restaurants to incorporate adding calorie declarations to menus and associated menu redesigns with regular menu replacement cycles, thereby reducing costs. This comment identified several specific steps necessary for covered establishments to comply with the rule, including:

- "Digest the final rule," including determining what are menus and menu boards, what are standard menu items, what are custom orders, and what are temporary menu items or otherwise excluded foods;

- Determine nutrient content levels and ensure that their bases for determining such nutrient information are sound;

- Prepare and print written nutrition information;

- Redesign menus and menu boards to include calories;

- Roll out new menus and menu boards simultaneously to chain restaurants nationwide;

- Update food preparation procedures to ensure consistency and ensure that reasonable steps are in place to ensure standard menu items are prepared consistently;

- Create processes where information related to standard menu items, e.g., ingredients supplier data, is periodically updated; and

- Develop and conduct training.

This comment also presented the following estimated time frames to conduct some of these steps:

- Four weeks to digest the requirements of the rule;

- Twenty-four weeks to design new layouts, obtain reviews and approvals, and for production and kitting; and

- Eight weeks for shipping.

Other comments that supported a 1-year effective date presented similar reasons, noting that a 1 year effective date would allow restaurants to properly review the final rule, analyze covered food items, and incorporate nutrition labeling into their truck stop and travel plaza restaurants. Some comments expressed concern that demand for menu item nutrient analysis and redesigning menu boards will skyrocket upon publication of the final rule, thereby overwhelming testing laboratories and companies that design menus and menu boards.

(Response 143) We agree that covered establishments will need more than 6 months to come into compliance with the rule, including making changes to menus and menus boards. While some establishments already are subject to State or local nutrition labeling requirements for foods sold in such establishments, others are not. Moreover, even those establishments that already are subject to State or local requirements nutrition labeling requirements may not be required to disclose such nutrition information in the format and manner specified in section 403(q)(5)(H) of the FD&C Act and this rule. We carefully considered the activities and associated time frames identified by the comments, including the comment from national organizations representing restaurants, and we agree that the rule should provide for an effective date of 1 year to comply with the Federal requirements. Most comments, even the comment noting that one State and one local government provided more than 1 year for full implementation, requested an effective date of "at least 1 year."

We also agree that a time frame that enables establishments to make changes to menus and menu boards during a time period that coincides with their regular menu replacement cycles would save time and resources. In addition, we acknowledge that companies that design and produce menu boards will receive many orders to update menu boards to comply with the rule. We note that a covered establishment that experiences difficulty obtaining new menus or menu boards as a result of increased demand as the effective date draws near will have other ways to comply with the rule without replacing the menus or menu boards. For example, we would not object if a covered establishment declares calorie information by applying stickers or pieces of paper to menus or menu boards. For packaged foods, we have taken the position for some time that the Nutrition Facts label may be printed on a sticker and affixed to a package, as long as the sticker adheres to the product under the intended storage conditions (Ref. 38; see L16). We also have long taken the position that stickers may be used to make changes in labeling such as correcting label mistakes provided that the final label is correct and complies with all regulations at the time of retail sale, the stickers do not cover other mandatory labeling, and the stickers adhere tightly (Ref. 38, see L55).

Likewise, we acknowledge that there could be some increased demand for nutrient analysis by testing laboratories as the effective date draws near. Importantly, the rule does not require analytical testing of standard menu items; analytical testing is merely one option available to a covered establishment to determine nutrient values. Other options include use of nutrient databases, cookbooks, or other reasonable means, including the use of Nutrition Facts on labels on packaged foods that comply with the nutrition labeling requirements of section 403(q)(1) of the FD&C Act and § 101.9, FDA nutrient values for raw fruits and vegetables in Appendix C of part 101, or FDA nutrient values for cooked fish in Appendix D (see § 101.11(c)(1)). In addition, as noted by the comments, many establishments that are part of large chains have already determined nutrient values for their menu items. As discussed in Response 138 and Response 139, this rule provides that corporate headquarters or a parent entity, rather than each individual covered establishment, may determine and certify nutrient values, as requested by comments. Thus, to the extent establishments' corporate headquarters or parent entity have determined nutrient values for standard menu items offered for sale in such establishments, individual covered establishments can come into compliance with this rule without significantly overwhelming testing laboratories, even if such establishments choose analytical testing as the means to determine nutrient values.

For all of these reasons, and as discussed in more detail in section XXIII.C, we have established an effective date for this rule that is 1 year from the date of publication of this document. Thus, the final rule is effective on December 1, 2015.

(Comment 144) One comment that recommended a minimum of 12 to 18 months for establishments to comply with the rule provided information about its experience from a 2010 rollout of new menu boards for all its domestic stores. This comment identified the following steps and corresponding time frames for this 2010 rollout:

- 2 months to develop new menu board templates for the seven types of menu boards for its various types of store locations (mall stores, mall kiosks, mall carts, stadium stores, stadium carts, etc.);

- 8 months to develop, program, and test an ordering site to accommodate more than 850 individual store menus;

- 2 months to receive the orders and lay out all custom menu boards; and

- 2 months to produce and ship new menu boards to its stores.

(Response 144) We appreciate that this comment provided its specific experience from a company-wide rollout of new menu boards. The steps identified by this comment are similar to the steps identified by the comment from national associations representing restaurants, although with longer timeframes. However, as discussed in Comment 143 these national associations also noted that extending the time period to 1 year would allow most restaurants to incorporate adding calorie declarations to menus and associated menu redesigns with regular menu replacement cycles. We therefore disagree that the time frames experienced by one entity during a company-initiated rollout of new menu boards should determine the time frame for compliance by all covered establishments.

(Comment 145) Some comments requested an effective date of more than 12 months. One comment requested an 18-month effective date because it considered that many requirements are still unclear. Another comment requested an 18-month to 2-year effective date for similar retail food establishments, even if there is a shorter time for restaurants. According to this comment, establishments need time to comply properly with the requirements and rushing through compliance could result in mistakes that may be confusing to consumers and would require additional industry resources to correct.

A few comments requested a 2-year effective date. One comment asserted that there will be a steep learning curve and time is needed to train employees and develop and print display materials. A few comments maintained that a 2-year compliance period is appropriate because, according to one comment, we used a 2-year uniform compliance period when implementing the NLEA. According to another comment, a 2-year timeframe is reasonable as long as nutrition information is available in brochures and online.

(Response 145) We disagree that an effective date over 1 year (such as 18 months or 2 years, as suggested by the comments) is necessary. Many comments seeking a longer effective date focused on the need to train employees. Such training does not need to wait until all implementation activities are complete—e.g., such training can begin while an establishment is waiting for delivery of its revised menus and menu boards.

We also disagree with the comment asserting that similar retail food establishments need more time than restaurants to comply with the rule. The comment provided no basis for why similar retail food establishments should be treated differently from restaurants or why such establishments would need more time for compliance than restaurants.

We discuss the applicability of the uniform compliance date in section XXIII.C.

(Comment 146) One comment asserted that there will be an unfair competitive advantage for larger companies because of the ability of larger companies to leverage their market position with the menu board producers. One comment requested a grace period to come into compliance if a covered establishment has adopted and followed a reasonable program to monitor changing nutrient values and update menus and menu boards at reasonable intervals coinciding with typical cycles.

(Response 146) In the proposed rule, we specifically requested that comments about whether we should provide for staggered implementation based on the size of a chain or of a specific franchisee be supported by data. The comment asserting that there will be an unfair competitive advantage for larger companies (because of their ability to leverage their market position with the menu board producers) provided no data for its assertion; therefore we have no information that could assist us in considering whether or how much additional time might be appropriate. Further, as discussed in Response 143, covered establishments can use a number of ways to comply with this rule without replacing menus or menu boards; for example, they can apply stickers or pieces of paper to menus or menu boards. For these reasons, we do not believe there is a sufficient basis to establish a staggered implementation period based on the size of the chain or of a specific franchise.

Nevertheless, we can work with establishments that are not in compliance by the effective date of this rule on a case-by-case basis, taking into consideration a number of factors, including specific steps an establishment has taken towards compliance.

(Comment 147) One comment requested that we allow 1 year for implementation, rather than 6 months, to provide covered establishments with adequate time to come into compliance given contractual requirements. For example, the comment said that it maintains a database with over 35,000 recipes which, in turn, may be modified or adapted by the specific restaurant or similar retail food establishment for local needs and tastes, limitations of the establishment, contractual specifications, and other restrictions (e.g., an establishment's determinations as to types of offerings). In addition, the comment stated that contractors rely on suppliers to provide nutritional information and, therefore, we should allow adequate time to retrieve data from these sources.

(Response 147) As discussed in section XXIII.C, we are establishing an effective date of 1 year from the date of publication of this rule. We note that the comment refers to recipes that may be modified or adapted by a specific restaurant or similar retail food establishment. In section VI.F, we discuss how such modifications can affect whether an establishment is offering for sale substantially the same menu items (and, thus, satisfies this criterion in the definition of covered establishment).

C. Effective Date and Compliance Date for This Rule

We are establishing the effective date to be 1 year from the date of publication of this document, i.e., the final rule is effective on December 1, 2015, (see DATES). We believe that extending the effective date from 6 months to 1 year provides sufficient time for covered establishments to come into compliance with the requirements without a significant negative impact on public health.

We expect covered establishments to come into compliance with the requirements of this rule by

December 1, 2015, i.e., the same date as the effective date of this rule. Although we are issuing this final rule after January 1, 2013, there is sufficient justification for establishing a compliance date of December 1, 2015, to enforce the provisions of this final rule, rather than January 1, 2016, which FDA has established as the next uniform compliance date for other food labeling changes required by food labeling regulations that are issued between January 1, 2013, and December 31, 2014 (77 FR 70885; November 28, 2012). Typically, our uniform compliance dates for food labeling regulations focus on changes made to the requirements for labels of packaged foods and seek to minimize the economic impact of such label changes, in relevant part, by allowing manufacturers to come into compliance with such regulations by one particular compliance date rather than several different dates (e.g., 77 FR 70885; 75 FR 78155 (December 15, 2010)). By providing one uniform compliance date, we enable manufacturers to avoid multiple short-term label revisions that would otherwise occur if not for the uniform compliance date. However, this rule does not establish requirements for the labels of packaged foods, and therefore would not cause food label revisions comparable to other food labeling regulations typically addressed by our uniform compliance dates. In addition, standard menu items offered for sale in covered establishments were not subject to Federal nutrition labeling requirements before the enactment of section 4205 of the ACA. As a result, unlike packaged foods, standard menu items currently are not subject to several different Federal food labeling regulations that may provide for different compliance dates. Further, a comment from national associations representing restaurants reported that extending the time period from the 6 months that we proposed, to 1 year, would allow most restaurants to comply with the rule as part of regular menu replacement cycles, thereby lessening costs. For these reasons, along with the reasons discussed previously, we believe that 1 year is sufficient time for covered establishments to come into compliance with the requirements of this rule. Waiting until FDA's next uniform compliance date of January 1, 2016, would create unnecessary delay in the enforcement of this rule and could minimize public health benefits.

XXIV. Comments and FDA Response on Compliance

In the proposed rule, we noted that some provisions of section 4205 of the ACA became requirements immediately upon enactment of the law and that we intended to exercise enforcement discretion until after we had completed notice and comment rulemaking. We encouraged our State and local partners to proceed in a similar way. We requested comment on how we should implement the rule, including whether specific provisions of the rule can be more quickly implemented than others (76 FR 19192 at 19220).

(Comment 148) One comment asked us to develop a protocol for checking the accuracy of the nutritional information provided by covered establishments. One comment recommended that we undertake random testing as resources allow. Another comment recommended that testing be done annually and kept on a public file to ensure that the portions continue to be within 5 percent tolerance of the original nutritional information. The comment suggested that if deviations are found, the company would either retest in 30 days or pay a penalty fee that would be passed to a childhood obesity campaign.

(Response 148) The rule provides several options for how covered establishments can determine nutrition information. While analytical testing of standard menu items may be appropriate in some cases (e.g., when the reasonable basis that a covered establishment uses to determine nutrient values is analytical testing), we expect our routine approach to evaluating the accuracy of the nutrition information to be based on the particular facts at issue, including the reasonable basis used by the covered establishment, which may be means other than analytical testing. Consistent with our approach to inspection of food processing facilities, we do not expect to establish a public file with the results of any testing we conduct. Under the Freedom of Information Act and our regulations in part 20, a person who wishes to see the results of our inspections may submit a request to do so.

Regarding the comment suggesting that we develop a protocol for checking the accuracy of the nutritional information provided by covered establishments, we decline to include such a protocol for checking the accuracy of the nutritional information in the rule at this time. Section 101.11(c) includes requirements for determining nutrient content and section XVII further discusses such requirements, including the requirement that nutrient declarations be accurate and consistent with the specific basis used to determine nutrient values. After we have had experience in evaluating compliance with the rule, we will consider whether to develop such a protocol.

(Comment 149) A few comments asked us to clarify our enforcement strategy and quickly establish an enforcement protocol. One comment stated that the proposed rule is virtually silent on how the menu labeling requirements will be enforced and encouraged us to permit the industry to comment on our enforcement strategy before it is included in the rule. One comment recommended that we issue guidance documents to the industry to better clarify matters of uncertainty that will persist following issuance of the rule.

One comment asked us to provide details on the penalties for noncompliance. Another comment recommended that we issue warning letters prior to instituting civil penalties against a covered establishment, particularly if the proposed rule's ambiguities are not clarified in the final rule. The comment maintained that a covered establishment may have made a good faith effort to comply and that warning letters will encourage compliance and inform establishments how they have fallen short of compliance. The comment recommended that we use a tiered penalty structure, whereby minor violations (e.g., inadequate font size of nutrition information) are treated less harshly than more serious violations (e.g., a clear lack of effort to place calorie information on printed menus). The comment also encouraged us to have a progressive penalty system for violations, whereby first violations are treated less harshly (e.g., a warning letter) than repeated violations. The comment maintained that this is especially crucial in the first few years the rules are being implemented as covered establishments familiarize themselves with the new requirements.

(Response 149) We are establishing these regulations under sections 201(n), 403(a)(1), 403(f), and 403(q)(5)(H) of the FD&C Act, as well as under section 701(a) of the FD&C Act. As discussed in the proposed rule and in section XXII, failure to comply with the rule will render the food misbranded under section(s) 201(n), 403(a), 403(f), or 403(q) of the FD&C Act (76 FR 19192 at 19219). Penalties are already set forth in the FD&C Act, and violations of § 101.11 may result in enforcement action consistent with those penalties. For example, introducing, delivering for introduction, or receiving a misbranded food in interstate commerce, or misbranding a food while it is in interstate commerce or being held for sale after shipment in interstate commerce, are prohibited acts under section 301 of the FD&C Act (21 U.S.C. 331), carrying criminal penalties under section 303 of the FD&C Act (21 U.S.C. 333). In addition, under section 302 of the FD&C Act (21 U.S.C. 332), the United States can bring a civil action in Federal court to enjoin a person who commits a prohibited action. Under section 304(a)(1) of the FD&C Act (21 U.S.C. 334(a)(1)), a food that is misbranded when introduced into or while in interstate commerce or while held for sale after shipment in interstate commerce may be seized by order of a Federal court. We expect to issue guidance to help covered establishments with compliance.

The tiered enforcement approach described by the comment is similar to the approach we currently take for other misbranded food, and we generally expect our enforcement approach to misbranding violations of this rule to be similar to that for other misbranded food. Nevertheless, enforcement will be considered on a case-by-case basis depending on the specific facts and circumstances.

(Comment 150) One comment asked us to focus our enforcement actions on helping with compliance, rather than seeking monetary penalties, at least until establishments have an opportunity to fully adopt the requirements. This comment maintained that flexibility is needed in the initial phases of implementation for facilities that operate under Federal Government contracts so that they can continue to comply with requirements mandated by specific Government Agencies. As a result, the comment recommended that we provide flexibility for contract food providers that provide services to Government facilities under a specified program.

(Response 150) We recognize that covered establishments will need time to comply with the nutrition labeling requirements of this rule during the initial phase of implementation. To provide more time to do so, this rule is not becoming effective until 1 year after the date of publication of this document (see the discussion in section XXIII.C of this document).

A covered establishment has responsibility to comply with all requirements of the rule. We acknowledge that a covered establishment may need to update its business and contractual relationships with its suppliers in order to do so.

(Comment 151) One comment asked us to permit stores to register points of contact to which we will address enforcement because experience shows that involving "corporate parents" of individual franchises or the owner of multi-store chains is the most effective way to manage enforcement issues. The comment recommended that we notify these contacts in the event of an enforcement action. Similarly, the comment recommended that we designate specific contacts for informal guidance and advice and develop a menu labeling hotline telephone number or email address to which store operators can ask specific questions. The comment considered that doing so would increase compliance and ease the administrative burden on its members.

(Response 151) Each individual restaurant or similar retail food establishment is responsible for disclosing the required nutrition information for its standard menu items and otherwise complying with the requirements of sections 403(q)(5)(H), 403(a)(1), and 403(f) of the FD&C Act and § 101.11. Persons exercising authority and supervisory responsibility over such establishments may also be held liable for violations of the FD&C Act. See Response 3. Our decisions regarding enforcement actions will be determined on a case by case basis. In general, we intend to notify a "corporate parent" as appropriate (see e.g., Refs. 39 and 40). Although § 101.11(d) provides for voluntary registration for restaurants and similar retail food establishments that are not subject to the nutrition labeling requirements of section 403(q)(5)(H) of the FD&C Act, and requires contact information, these requirements only apply to such establishments that would not be subject to the rule without registering.

We already maintain a telephone hotline where industry may contact us for questions about compliance with our regulations (1-888-SAFEFOOD (1-888-723-3366)). Staff who are assigned to the hotline will have or obtain the information to answer questions about this rule. In addition, a covered establishment may direct questions to the contact person identified in this document (see FOR FURTHER INFORMATION CONTACT), to the contact telephone number provided in any subsequent guidance, and to a general email mailbox for industry questions (industry@fda.gov). A covered establishment also may send written inquiries to Center for Food Safety and Applied Nutrition (HFS-009), Food and Drug Administration, 5100 Paint Branch Pkwy., College Park, MD 20740.

(Comment 152) A few comments recommended that we preapprove menus and menu boards. One of these comments recommended that we do so even if a fee was required. The comment maintained that an approval process would alleviate covered establishments from having to pay the costs to replace menus that they thought met the menu labeling requirements.

(Response 152) We decline the request of these comments. Section 403(q)(5)(H) of the FD&C Act does not require that we preapprove menus and menu boards, nor do we have the resources to do so at this time. Section 403(q)(5)(H) of the FD&C Act and this rule set forth and specify the requirements for menus and menu boards such that a covered establishment should be able to determine whether its menu or menu board meets the applicable requirements. Further, a covered establishment may contact us with questions about compliance, as discussed previously in Response 151.

(Comment 153) One comment asked us to clarify that compliance is the responsibility of each establishment and that if someone fails to comply, only that standard menu item in the particular establishment is misbranded. The comment expressed concern that without clarity on this point, States and localities may cite franchisors for violations by franchisees, and plaintiffs' attorneys may sue franchisors for violations by franchisees under consumer protection laws.

(Response 153) With regard to what food is misbranded if there is a failure to comply with the regulations, this would be determined based on the particular facts of the situation (see also Response 3).

(Comment 154) Some comments asked us to allow flexibility for when a covered establishment must update menus to reflect changes in nutrient content. One of these comments asked us to clarify that any temporary inconsistencies resulting from periodic updating will not result in a violation of the law. The comment expressed concern that nutrient values may change because of ingredient changes, use of different suppliers, suppliers updating nutritional analysis with no changes in formulation, and reformulation of menu items based on consumer feedback. The comment asked us to state that values found not current will not raise a compliance issue if the covered establishment can demonstrate that it has adopted a reasonable program to monitor changing values and that it updates materials at reasonable intervals based on the manner and frequency in which it changes menus and other labeling. The comment also recommended that covered establishments be able to update their menus and menu boards at reasonable intervals coinciding with typical cycles to change menus and, at a maximum, values that require updating be updated at least once a year. One comment asked that the final rule clearly state that covered establishments are responsible for maintaining the accuracy of their nutrient declarations, including keeping this information up-to-date as their menus change.

(Response 154) Nutrition labeling for a standard menu item must be truthful and not misleading, consistent with the specific basis used to determine nutrient values, and otherwise in compliance with the requirements of sections 403(a)(1), 403(f), and 403(q)(5)(H) of the FD&C Act and § 101.11. We recognize that changes in nutrition information for standard menu items could cause a covered establishment to change a menu or menu board even if the list of menu items has not changed. In general, revised nutrition must be posted before serving the food. Compliance will be determined on a case-by-case basis depending on the specific facts and circumstances. We recommend that a covered establishment coordinate changes in menu items that are significant enough to affect nutrient content with the introduction of new items that also require updating a menu or menu board to help minimize costs. As discussed in Response 143, covered establishment may also use measures such as stickers to update nutrient content on menus or menu boards.

(Comment 155) Several comments requested clarification on who would enforce the rule. One comment asked that delegation of inspection authority to the States be explicit, and asserted that the provision in 21 U.S.C. 337 authorizing States to enforce Federal law has rarely been used. This comment stated that we could use 21 U.S.C 372(a)(1)(A) to provide technical assistance and funding to States and locals for enforcement. The comment suggested that we set up a simple process for local health inspectors to report violations to us, e.g., a postcard to be filled in and sent to us with a tear off receipt to be left with the restaurant manager. The comment also suggested that we develop a system to collect and store reports of violations in a database. A few comments recommended that the final rule specify that enforcement procedures of States are not affected by section 4205 of the ACA.

One comment recommended that we work with headquarters of chain restaurants and similar retail food establishments to ensure compliance and then have our District Offices assess compliance in the States.

One comment stated that States and locals cannot be expected to enforce the Federal menu labeling requirements without significant funding. The comment stated that the enforcement process in its State is already overburdened and, therefore, the Federal Government should enforce the requirements. Other comments recommended that we rely on States and localities and provide training and funding. A few comments stated that historically restaurant inspections are done by the States and localities, and one comment recommended that we use the contractual regime of food safety inspections used with the enforcement of the NLEA. One comment stated that local restaurant inspectors can add the enforcement of menu labeling to their current inspections. One comment recommended that we enforce fines and penalties for noncompliance and direct any resulting funds to inspection programs enforcing the menu labeling requirements.

One comment stated that it is not always practical for States and locals to enforce section 4205 of the ACA as delegates of FDA; rather we should encourage and support enactment of identical requirements that fit into local and State food codes.

One comment suggested that the rule include specific provisions that would be binding on State and local jurisdictions relative to enforcing the rule. The comment stated that the right to a notice of a violation, the opportunity to cure a violation, and the opportunity to have a re-inspection before an adverse decision by the enforcing agent, e.g. a citation, vary enormously from jurisdiction to jurisdiction, at the State and at the local level. The comment suggested that we include specifics such as:

- The enforcement agency at initial inspection provides written notice of violations;

- The enforcement agency gives the establishment a period of time to cure the violations (e.g., 15-30 days);

- The enforcement agency would re-inspect after cure period; and

- If violations are not cured, the enforcement agency would issue adverse decision applying fine or other action that would apply under the enforcement agency's regulations or applicable State or local laws.

The comment stated that these actions would only apply to calorie labeling and not to other violations related to safety.

(Response 155) Collectively, these comments address three mechanisms by which States (and, in some cases, local jurisdictions) could have a role in enforcing the provisions of section 403(q)(5)(H) of the FD&C Act and this rule:

- In general, a State or political subdivision of a State may establish food nutrition labeling requirements that are identical to applicable Federal requirements, including the requirements of this rule. In this case, the State or local jurisdiction would act on its own behalf to enforce its own requirements, albeit requirements that are identical to the Federal requirements.

- Under 702(a)(1)(A) of the FD&C Act (21 U.S.C. 372(a)(1)(A)), FDA is authorized to conduct examinations and investigations for the purposes of the FD&C Act through any health, food, or drug officer or employee of any State, Territory, or political subdivision thereof (such as a locality), duly commissioned to act on behalf of FDA. In this case, the State or local representative would act on our behalf to enforce the Federal requirements.

- In general, under section 310(b) of the FD&C Act (21 U.S.C. 337(b)), a State may bring in its own name and within its jurisdiction proceedings for the civil enforcement, or to restrain violations, of section 403(q) of the FD&C Act, including the nutrition labeling requirements for standard menu items under section 403(q)(5)(H) of the FD&C Act, if the food that is the subject of the proceedings is located in the State provided that other requirements and conditions are met. In this case, the State acts on its own behalf to enforce the Federal requirements.

We have successfully partnered with States to conduct examinations and inspections in other contexts, including inspections of food processing facilities on our behalf (Ref. 41). We expect to continue to cooperatively leverage the resources of Federal, State, and local Government Agencies as we strive to obtain industry-wide compliance with this rule.

XXV. Final Regulatory Impact Analysis

FDA has examined the impacts of this final rule under Executive Order 12866, Executive Order 13563, the Regulatory Flexibility Act (5 U.S.C. 601-612), and the Unfunded Mandates Reform Act of 1995 (Pub. L. 104-4). Executive Orders 12866 and 13563 direct Agencies to assess all costs and benefits of available regulatory alternatives and, when regulation is necessary, to select regulatory approaches that maximize net benefits (including potential economic, environmental, public health and safety, and other advantages; distributive impacts; and equity). We have developed a detailed Regulatory Impact Analysis (RIA) that presents the benefits and costs of this final rule (Ref. 42) which is available at http://www.regulations.gov (enter Docket No. FDA-2011-F-0172). The full economic impact analyses of FDA regulations are no longer (as of April 2012) published in the Federal Register but are submitted to the docket and are available at http://www.regulations.gov. We also post the full economic impact analyses of FDA regulations at the following Web site:
http://www.fda.gov/AboutFDA/ReportsManualsForms/Reports/EconomicAnalyses/default.htm.

This rule is designated an "economically" significant rule, under section 3(f)(1) of Executive Order 12866. Accordingly, the rule was reviewed by OMB. In particular, Executive Order 12866 directs each Agency engaged in rulemaking to "identify the problem that it intends to address"—that is, the essential purpose of the rule. As a separate step in its rulemaking, Executive Order 12866 directs the Agency to "assess both the costs and the benefits of the intendedregulation . . . , recognizing that some costs and benefits are difficult to quantify."

Executive Order 13563 confirms that "each agency is directed to use the best available techniques to quantify anticipated present and future benefits and costs as accurately as possible. Where appropriate and permitted by law, each Agency may consider (and discuss qualitatively) values that are difficult or impossible to quantify." Here, the essential purpose of the rule is to make nutrition information for certain foods available to consumers in a direct, accessible, and consistent manner to enable consumers to make informed and healthful dietary choices. The full analysis—contained in the RIA—of anticipated and quantifiable costs and benefits from the promulgation of the rule does not alter this fundamental purpose. Nor does it fully capture the unquantifiable benefits of greater consumer understanding regarding dietary choices and their impact on health.

The Regulatory Flexibility Act requires Agencies to analyze regulatory options that would minimize any significant impact of a rule on small entities. According to our analysis, we believe that the final rule will have a significant economic impact on a substantial number of small entities, and we have accordingly analyzed regulatory options that would minimize the economic impact of the rule on small entities consistent with statutory objectives. We have crafted the final rule to provide flexibility for compliance.

Section 202(a) of the Unfunded Mandates Reform Act of 1995 requires that Agencies prepare a written statement, which includes an assessment of anticipated costs and benefits, before proposing "any rule that includes any Federal mandate that may result in the expenditure by State, local, and tribal governments, in the aggregate, or by the private sector, of $100,000,000 or more (adjusted annually for inflation) in any one year." The current threshold after adjustment for inflation is $141 million, using the most current (2013) Implicit Price Deflator for the Gross Domestic Product. FDA has determined that this final rule has met the threshold under the Unfunded Mandates Reform Act.

The analyses that we have performed to examine the impacts of this final rule under Executive Order 12866, Executive Order 13563, the Regulatory Flexibility Act, and the Unfunded Mandates Reform Act of 1995 are included in the RIA (Ref. 42).

We had prepared a "Preliminary Regulatory Impact Analysis" (Ref. 43) in connection with the proposed rule. We also included sections titled "Summary of Preliminary Regulatory Impact Analysis" and "Initial Regulatory Flexibility Analysis" in the preamble to the proposed rule (76 FR 19192 at 19220 through 19225). We received comments on our analysis of the impacts presented in those sections, and the RIA (Ref. 42) contains our responses to those comments.

XXVI. Paperwork Reduction Act of 1995

This final rule contains information collection provisions that are subject to review by OMB under the Paperwork Reduction Act of 1995 (the PRA) (44 U.S.C. 3501-3520). A description of these provisions is given in this section of the document with estimates of the annual reporting, recordkeeping, and third-party disclosure burden. Included in each burden estimate is the time for reviewing instructions, searching existing data sources, gathering and maintaining the data needed, and completing and reviewing each collection of information.

We had included a section titled "Paperwork Reduction Act of 1995" in the preamble to the proposed rule (76 FR 19192 at 19225 through 19229). We received one comment on our analysis of the burdens presented in that section.

(Comment 156) One comment stated that the recordkeeping burdens of the proposed rule would impose millions of dollars in cost per year. The comment stated that these burdens are needless.

(Response 156) We disagree that the burdens are needless. Providing accurate, clear, and consistent nutrition information, including the calorie content of foods, in restaurants and similar retail food establishments will make such nutrition information available to consumers in a direct and accessible manner to enable consumers to make informed and healthful dietary choices.

We invite comments on these topics: (1) Whether the proposed collection of information is necessary for the proper performance of FDA's functions, including whether the information will have practical utility; (2) the accuracy of FDA's estimate of the burden of the proposed collection of information, including the validity of the methodology and assumptions used; (3) ways to enhance the quality, utility, and clarity of the information to be collected; and (4) ways to minimize the burden of the collection of information on respondents, including through the use of automated collection techniques, when appropriate, and other forms of information technology.

Title: Information Collection Provisions of the Final Rule on Food Labeling: Nutrition Labeling of Standard Menu Items in Restaurants and Similar Retail Food Establishments

A. Reporting Requirements

Description of Respondents: The likely respondents to this information collection are restaurants and similar retail food establishments that voluntarily elect to be subject to the Federal requirements of this rule by registering with FDA. These establishments include chain retail food establishments and eating and drinking places such as full- and limited-service restaurants, snack bars (including, for example, ice cream, donut, and bagel shops and similar establishments), cafeterias and drinking places, managed food service facilities, grocery stores, supermarkets, convenience stores, general merchandise stores, lodging facilities, recreational venues, sports venues, performing arts venues, and movie theaters.

Description: Restaurants and similar retail food establishments not subject to the ACA's requirements may voluntarily elect to be subject to the Federal requirements by registering with FDA. Authorized officials for restaurants and similar retail food establishments must provide FDA with the following information on Form FDA 3757: Their contact information including name, address, phone number, and email address for their authorized official; the contact information including name, address, phone number, and email address for each restaurant or similar retail food establishment being registered, as well as the name and contact information for an official onsite, such as the owner or manager, for each specific restaurant or similar retail food establishment; all trade names the restaurant or similar retail food establishment uses; preferred mailing address, if different from location address for each establishment; and certification that the information submitted is true and accurate, that the person submitting it is authorized to do so, and that each registered restaurant or similar retail food establishment will be subject to the requirements of section 403(q)(5)(H) of the FD&C Act and § 101.11 of the final rule.

To keep the establishment's registration active, the authorized official of the restaurant or similar retail food establishment must register every other year within 60 days prior to the expiration of the establishment's current registration with FDA. Registration will automatically expire if not renewed.

Table 1—Estimated Reporting Burden 1

21 CFR part 101	Number of respondents	Number of responses per respondent per year	Total annual responses	Average burden per response (in hours)	Total hours
Initial Burden (annualized over 3 years):					
§ 101.11(d) Initial Registration	3,559	1	3,559	2	7,118
Annual Burden:					

| § 101.11(d) Registration Renewal | 5,340 | 1 | 5,340 | 0.5 (30 minutes) | 2,670 |
| Total Burden Hours | | | | | 9,788 |

We lack data on the number of restaurants and similar retail food establishments that might voluntarily register to comply with this final rule. We do not expect the net benefit for voluntary registration for many non-covered establishments to be positive and in the RIA (Ref. 42) we indicate that as of the conducting of this analysis, no establishments have voluntarily registered with FDA. Therefore we did not estimate a significant burden in the RIA. However, in the event that a few register anyway, or find positive incentive to do so, for the purposes of this PRA analysis, we estimate the burden such establishments will face. We believe that implementation of the final rule, and the resulting attention to the nutrition content of standard menu items, may give non-covered establishments an incentive to voluntarily disclose calorie and other nutrition information. We believe that the only types of establishments that would likely face a positive incentive to voluntarily register are some restaurants and some grocery, convenience, and general merchandise stores that do not already provide this information in some form or another at the point of purchase. We estimate that 5 percent of these establishments may register, or 10,678 [(5% volunteer × 47% no nutrition info × 348,200 non-covered restaurants) + (5% volunteer × 49,900 non-covered grocery, convenience, and general merchandise stores)] (Refs. 44 and 45). We estimate it will require approximately 2 hours per initial registration. Given 10,678 establishments and one initial registration per establishment at 2 hours per registration, we estimate the initial hourly burden for these establishments is 21,356 hours (10,678 establishments × 1 initial registration per establishment × 2 hours per registration). Annualizing this value over 3 years yields 7,118 hours per year (10,678 establishments/3 years × 1 initial registration per establishment × 2 hours per registration). (10,678 establishments/3 years = 3,559 establishments per year.)

We expect that renewal registrations will require substantially less time because establishments are expected to be able to affirm or update the existing information in an online account in a way similar to other FDA firm registration systems. We estimate that re-registration will take 30 minutes (0.5 hours) for each registrant. This would indicate that biennial registration would impose a burden of 5,340 hours (10,678 establishments × 0.5 hours) every 2 years, or 2,670 hours every year (10,678 establishments/2 years × 0.5 hours).

B. Recordkeeping Requirements

The preamble to the proposed rule provided an estimate of the recordkeeping burden, which consisted of the burden associated with nutrition analysis and the burden associated with generating, providing, or maintaining records. Upon further consideration, we have omitted the burden estimate associated with generating or maintaining records previously estimated in the proposed rule because the rule does not require restaurants and similar retail food establishments to generate or maintain records. This section now includes only the burden estimate associated with providing information substantiating nutrient values of standard menu items to FDA as required by the final rule. Further, as discussed in section C of this analysis, we have included a burden estimate for nutrition analysis as part of the third party disclosure burden, since the total time, effort, or financial resources expended by covered establishments to declare nutrition information likely includes time, effort, or financial resources to determine the nutrition content of covered menu items.

Description of Respondents

The likely respondents to this information collection are restaurants and similar retail food establishments that are subject to the Federal requirements of this rule or that volunteer to be subject to the rule. These establishments include chain retail food establishments and eating and drinking places such as full- and limited-service restaurants, snack bars (including, for example, ice cream, donut, and bagel shops and similar establishments), cafeterias and drinking places, and managed food service facilities. Chain retail food establishments would also include some grocery stores, supermarkets, convenience stores, general merchandise stores, lodging facilities, recreational venues, sports venues, performing arts venues, and movie theaters (Ref. 46).

Description

The paperwork burden for the recordkeeping requirements of the final rule is to provide substantiation of the nutrient values of standard menu items to FDA. The likely respondents for the nutrition analysis are restaurants and similar retail food establishments that are subject to the Federal requirements of this rule or that volunteer to be subject to the rule. These establishments must produce records with information substantiating nutrient values for their standard menu items.

The likely respondents are the universe of retail food establishments and retail chains that are covered by the final rule. Our estimate includes eating and drinking places such as full- and limited-service restaurants, snack bars including, for example, ice cream, donut, and bagel shops and similar establishments, cafeterias and drinking places, and managed food service facilities. Covered establishments also include some grocery stores, supermarkets, convenience stores, general merchandise stores, lodging facilities, recreational venues, sports venues, performing arts venues, and movie theaters.

Table 2—Estimated Recordkeeping Burden 1

21 CFR part 101	Number recordkeepers	Annual frequency per recordkeeper	Total annual records	Hours per record	Total hours
Initial Burden (Annualized over 3 years)					
§ 101.8(c)(2)(i)(A) Initial Nutrition Analysis Records	69,017	1	69,017	0.25 (15 minutes)	17,254
Annual Burden					
§ 101.8(c)(2)(i)(A) Recurring Nutrition Analysis Records	30,059	1	30,059	0.25 (15 minutes)	7,515
Total Burden Hours					24,769

Initial Nutrition Analysis

We estimate the annual number of the largest restaurant chains that will need to produce substantiation of their standard menu items to be 541 (503 covered restaurant chains + 38 voluntary restaurant chains) with an average of 117 unique menu items that will require an initial nutrition analysis. This leads to 63,297 (541 chains × 117 items) individual chains-specific restaurant records. In addition to chain-level nutrition analysis, each individual restaurant establishment will likely have a small variety of standard menu items that are unique to the individual establishment. We estimate there are 11,684 restaurants establishments (10,866 covered + 818 voluntary) with establishment-specific items. Each of these restaurant establishments has an average of five establishment-specific menu items. This leads to 58,420 (11,684 establishments × 5 items) individual establishment-specific restaurant records.

In addition to restaurants, other similar retail food establishments have both chain-specific and establishment-specific menu items. Other covered retail food establishments include: Grocery stores, supermarkets, convenience stores, general merchandise stores, lodging facilities, recreational venues, sports venues, performing arts venues, and movie theaters. We estimate there are 691 grocery, convenience, and general merchandise (GCGM) store chains (660 covered + 31 voluntary) with an average of 40 menu items each (= 27,640 records); 5,309 GCGM establishments (5,060 covered + 249 voluntary) with an average of 5 establishment-specific menu items each (= 26,545 records); 50 managed food service (MFS) chains with an average of 80 menu items (= 4,000 records); 450 MFS establishments with an average of 5 establishment-specific menu items (= 2,250 records); 100 lodging chains with an average of 40 menu items (= 4,000 records); 620 lodging establishments with an average of 5 establishment-specific menu items (= 3,100 records); 250 sports, recreation and entertainment (SRE) chains with an average of 59 menu items (= 14,750 records); and 610 SRE establishments with an average of 5 establishment-specific menu times (= 3,050 records). In total, we estimate there are 207,052 records (63,297 restaurant chain-level + 58,420 restaurant establishment-level + 27,640 GCGM chain-level + 26,545 GCGM establishment-level + 4,000 MFS chain-level + 2,250 MFS establishment-level + 4,000 lodging chain-level + 3,100 lodging establishment-level + 14,750 SRE chain-level + 3,050 SRE establishment-level). Annualized over 3 years, this value yields 69,017 (= 207,052 records/3 years) per year. We estimate that each nutrition analysis will require a burden of 15 minutes to produce each record. We estimate the total recordkeeping burden for the initial nutrition analysis to be 17,254.25 hours (= 69,017 records × 0.25 hours per record).

Recurring Nutrition Analysis

From Mintel Menu Insights data, we estimate that restaurant chains introduced, on average, 24 new menu items in 2009 (Ref. 47). Because the final requirements do not apply to temporary menu items, daily specials, and foods that are part of a customary market test, only a fraction of these items will need nutrition analysis. We estimate that existing restaurant chains or individual establishments would need new nutrition analysis for 25 percent of new standard menu items, or six new standard menu items per year. If in addition to these new standard menu items, chains need nutrition analysis on 6 reformulated standard menu items, there would be a total of 12 nutrition analyses per chain needed on an annual basis. Thus we estimate there will be 26,904 annual records associated with new or reformulated items of covered chains [= (1,151 restaurant chains + 691 GCGM chains + 50 MFS chains + 100 lodging chains + 250 SRE chains) × 12 menus items].

In addition we estimate that each year there will be the number of covered chains to increase in each category as companies expand. As discussed in the final RIA, each year there will be some existing non-covered chains that, through expansion of their business, will become subject to the rule's requirements (for example, a chain expanding from 19 to 20 locations). We estimate there will be 20 new restaurant chains, each with an average of 117 menu items; 5 new GCGM chains each with an average of 40 menu items; 3 new MFS chains each with an average of 80 menu items; 2 new lodging chains each with an average of 40 menu items; 5 new SRE chains each with an average of 59 menu items. Thus we estimate there will be 3,155 annual records [= (20 restaurants × 117 items) + (5 GCGM × 40 items) + (3 MFS × 80 items) + (2 lodging × 40 items) + (5 SRE × 59 items] associated with nutrition analysis for new covered chains.

Based on data from FDA's Recordkeeping Cost Model, we estimate that it will take approximately

15 minutes per standard menu item for providing the information of nutrition analysis to FDA (Ref. 48). We estimate the total recurring recordkeeping burden for the nutrition analysis to be 7,515 hours [(26,899 records for new/reformulated standard menu items under existing chains + 3,155 records for items under new chains) × 0.25 hours per record)].

C. Third-Party Disclosure Requirements

Description of Respondents: Restaurants and similar retail food establishments that are subject to statutory menu labeling requirements or that voluntarily elect to be subject to the Federal requirements by registering with FDA.

Description: There will be five types of third-party disclosure burdens under the rule related to: Initial nutrition analysis, initial menu replacement, chain-level written nutrition information, establishment-level nutrition information, recurring nutrition analysis, and recurring menu replacement.

Table 3—Estimated Third Party Disclosure Burden

21 CFR Part 101	Number of respondents	Number of disclosures per respondent	Total annual disclosures	Average burden per disclosure	Total hours	Total operating and maintenance costs
Initial Burden (Annualized over 3 years)						
§ 101.8(c)(2)(i)(A) Initial Nutrition Analysis	69,017	1	69,017	4	276,068	
§ 101.8(c)(2)(i)(A) Initial Menu Replacement	106,168	1	106,168	0.5 (30 minutes)	53,084	$248,767,000
§ 101.8(c)(2)(i)(A) Written Nutrition Information Chain-level	1,632	1	1,632	3	4,896	
§ 101.8(c)(2)(i)(A) Written Nutrition Information Establishment-level	18,673	1	18,673	0.5 (30 minutes)	9,337	
Annual Burden						
§ 101.8(c)(2)(i)(A) Recurring Nutrition Analysis	30,054	1	30,054	4	120,216	
§ 101.8(c)(2)(i)(A) Recurring Menu Replacement	700	1	700	0.5 (30 minutes)	350	$529,000
Total					463,951	$249,296,000

Initial Nutrition Analysis

The first burden is the time and effort expended by restaurants and other retail food establishments to determine the nutrition content of their covered menu items, which we refer to as "Nutrition Analysis." A nutrition analysis entails the burden of determining nutrition content for covered and voluntary establishment menus by analyzing the food product and summarizing the nutritional information results. Note that the recordkeeping portion of this burden was estimated in the previous subsection.

Our estimate for the annual number of the restaurant and similar retail food chains and individual establishments that will be burdened with initial nutrition analysis is identical to our estimate for the chains and establishments under the recordkeeping subsection. The total number of respondents estimated for the third-party disclosure burden of initial nutrition analysis is 207,052. Annualized over 3 years, this value becomes 69,017. We estimate that each nutrition analysis will require a burden of 4 hours (this estimate of 4 hours was used in the final RIA (Ref. 42)), thus total burden for the initial nutrition analysis is 276,068 hours (207,052 records/3 years × 4 hours per record).

Recurring Nutrition Analysis

The second burden is the time and effort expended by restaurants and other retail food establishments in recurring nutrition analysis. As discussed in the recordkeeping subsection of this PRA, recurring nutrition analysis will be required for new and reformulated standard menu items. Our estimate for the annual number of the restaurant and similar retail food chains and individual establishments that will be burdened with recurring nutrition analysis is identical to our estimate for the chains and establishments under the recordkeeping subsection. The total number of respondents estimated for the third-party disclosure burden of recurring nutrition analysis is 30,054. We estimate that each nutrition analysis will require a burden of 4 hours (this estimate of 4 hours was used in the final RIA (Ref. 42)), thus total third party disclosure burden recurring nutrition analysis is 120,216 hours (30,054 records × 4 hours per record).

Initial Menu Replacement

The third burden is for the time expended by restaurants and similar retail food establishments to physically produce and install the menus, menu boards that include the new calorie declarations, which we refer to as "Calorie Declaration Signs." As described in the final RIA (Ref. 42), chain retail food establishments will need to redesign and replace their existing menus and menu boards in order to comply with the final requirements. For full service restaurants and drinking places with only personal menus and no menu boards, this burden will be relatively low. Most menus are replaced frequently anyway as they wear out, are lost, or as prices and menu items change. For many of these establishments, the burden of updating menus to comply with the final requirements would be limited to design and associated administrative hours.

The longer lifespan of menu boards in limited-service eating places would likely require the redesign of menu/menu boards and the replacement of one or more menu boards. In addition, some chains would need to update self-serve and display signs. The number of menus that an establishment will keep on hand is highly variable. A full-service restaurant, where each order is placed using a menu, will need more than a quick-service establishment that uses menus just for takeout orders. The number of menus is also tied to the seating capacity of the restaurant, and whether the menu is laminated or paper. Because paper menus are more fragile and cheaper to print in bulk, an establishment may keep a large reserve in stock, whereas establishments using more durable and expensive laminated menus may only keep a few extra on hand. Estimates for the burden of updating menu boards, other major displays that serve as menus, such as electronic displays, or major materials needed to disclose calories for self-serve or displayed foods to comply with the final requirements, will vary widely across chains and establishments because of different menu board and display types.

As described in the RIA, we estimate that the average full-service restaurant establishment must discard and reprint one menu for each seat, plus 10 extra, for a total of 91 menus per restaurant each year. We estimate that GCGM stores have an average of two menu boards per establishment based on public comments that we received. We estimate that MFS and SRE establishments will each have an average of one menu board. Lodging establishments generally have menus instead of menu boards, and we estimate the menu replacement burden for establishments in the lodging sector to be 87 menu replacements per establishment. Since each covered and voluntarily registered establishment will need to replace menus and/or menu boards, we estimate this total value to be 318,505 (= 248,610 restaurants + 53,095 GCGM + 4,500 MFS + 6,200 lodging + 6,100 SRE). (In the previous calculation, 248,610 restaurants = 231,200 covered restaurants + 17,410 voluntary; and 53,095 GCGM = 50,600 covered + 2,495 voluntary.) Annualized over 3 years, this value becomes 106,168 (= 318,505/3 years). We estimate the labor burden for ordering new menus and menu boards to be 30 minutes (0.5 hours) per establishment. Thus the total burden for initial menu replacement is 53,084 hours per year. At an average wage (which includes an extra 50 percent to account for overhead costs and employee benefits) of $30 per hour for managers across the covered industries, the labor burden comes to $1,593,000 (= 53,084 hours × $30 per hour). In the final RIA (Ref. 42), we estimated the total average costs associated with initial menu replacement to be $250.36 million. This value takes into consideration costs of menu/menu board design, printing, and installation. Subtracting the labor costs of ordering new menus, $1,593,000, from the total costs for initial menu replacement, $250,360,000, yields total initial operating and maintenance costs of $248,767,000.

Recurring Menu Replacement for New Chains

The fourth burden is for the time expended by new restaurants and similar retail food establishments to physically replace menus and menu boards that include the new calorie declarations. All restaurants and similar retail food chains that become covered as the number of their associated establishments grows beyond the coverage threshold of 20 will need to replace their menus and menu boards. We estimated in the final RIA (Ref. 42) that the annual number of new covered restaurants and similar retail food establishments is 700. Again, we estimate the labor burden for ordering new menus and menu boards to be 30 minutes (0.5 hours) per establishment. Thus the total annual burden for recurring menu replacement is 350 hours per year. At an average wage (which includes an extra 50 percent in overhead costs and employee benefits) of $30 per hour for managers across the covered industries, the recurring labor burden comes to $11,000 (= 350 hours × $30 per hour). In the final RIA, we estimated the total average annual operating and maintenance costs associated with recurring menu replacement to be $540,000. This value takes into consideration costs of menu/menu board design, printing, and installation. Subtracting the recurring labor costs of ordering new menus, $11,000, from the total costs for recurring menu replacement of $540,000, yields total recurring operating and maintenance costs of $529,000.

Written Nutrition Information

The fifth burden is for the time expended by restaurants and similar retail food establishments to make written nutrition information available to customers upon request. The number of chains (and associated establishments) that do not already provide this information was estimated in the recordkeeping subsection under initial nutrition analysis, or 1,632 chains (503 covered restaurant + 38 voluntary restaurant + 660 covered GCGM + 31 voluntary GCGM + 50 covered MFS + 100 covered lodging + 250 covered SRE) and 18,673 establishments with establishment specific-menu items (10,866 covered restaurant + 818 voluntary restaurant + 5,060 covered GCGM + 249 voluntary GCGM + 450 covered MFS + 620 covered lodging + 610 covered SRE). We estimate the time it takes to provide written nutrition information at the chain level to be 3 hours per respondent. Since the average number of establishment-specific menu items is only five per establishment, we estimate the time it takes to provide written nutrition information at the establishment level (for those menu items that are specific only to the establishment) to be 30 minutes per respondent. Thus the total burden hours for chain-level and establishment level written nutrition information disclosure are 4,896 and 9,336.5 hours, respectively. Therefore the total third party disclosure burden for the rule is 463,950.5 hours with total operating and maintenance costs of $249,296,000.

To ensure that comments on information collection are received, OMB recommends that written comments be faxed to the Office of Information and Regulatory Affairs, OMB, Attn: FDA Desk Officer, FAX: 202-395-7285, or emailed to oira_submission@omb.eop.gov. All comments should be identified with the OMB Control Number 0910-NEW, and title "Information Collection Provisions of the Final Rule on Food Labeling: Nutrition Labeling of Standard Menu Items in Restaurants and Similar Retail Food Establishments." Also include the FDA docket number found in brackets in the heading of this document.

In compliance with the Paperwork Reduction Act of 1995 (44 U.S.C. 3507(d)), we have resubmitted the information collection provisions of this final rule to OMB for review, because the final rule provides additional modifications to § 101.11. These requirements will not be effective until we obtain OMB approval. Interested persons are requested to submit comments regarding information collection to OMB (see DATES and ADDRESSES).

Prior to the effective and compliance date of this final rule, we will publish a notice in the Federal Register announcing OMB's decision to approve, modify, or disapprove the information collection provisions in this final rule. An Agency may not conduct or sponsor, and a person is not required to respond to, a collection of information unless it displays a currently valid OMB control number.

XXVII. Federalism

We have analyzed this final rule in accordance with the principles set forth in Executive Order 13132. Section 4(a) of the Executive order requires Agencies to "construe . . . a Federal statute to preempt State law only where the statute contains an express preemption provision or there is some other clear evidence that the Congress intended preemption of State law, or where the exercise of State authority conflicts with the exercise of Federal authority under the Federal statute." Federal law includes an express preemption provision that preempts "any requirement for nutrition labeling of food that is not identical to the requirement of section 403(q) [of the FD&C Act] [21 U.S.C. 343(q)]", except that this provision does not apply "to food that is offered for sale in a restaurant or similar retail food establishment that is not part of a chain with 20 or more locations doing business under the same name (regardless of the type of ownership of the locations) and offering for sale substantially the same menu items unless such restaurant or similar retail food establishment complies with the voluntary provision of nutrition information requirements under section 403(q)(5)(H)(ix) [of the FD&C Act]." In the proposed rule, we provided an interpretation of the preemptive provisions of section 4205 of the ACA, as well as an alternative interpretation (76 FR 19192 at 19203). (21 U.S.C. 343-1(a)(4)). The final rule creates requirements for nutrition labeling of food under section 403(q) of the FD&C Act that would preempt certain non-identical State and local nutrition labeling requirements.

Section 4205 of the ACA also includes a Rule of Construction providing that "Nothing in the amendments made by [section 4205] shall be construed—(1) to preempt any provision of State or local law, unless such provision establishes or continues into effect nutrient content disclosures of the type required under section 403(q)(5)(H) of the Federal Food, Drug, and Cosmetic Act [21 U.S.C. 343(q)(5)(H)] (as added by subsection(b)) and is expressly preempted under subsection (a)(4) of such section; (2) to apply to any State or local requirement respecting a statement in the labeling of food that provides for a warning concerning the safety of the food or component of the food; or (3) except as provided in section 403(q)(5)(H)(ix) of the Federal Food, Drug, and Cosmetic Act [21 U.S.C. 343(q)(5)(H)(ix)] (as added by subsection (b)), to apply to any restaurant or similar retail food establishment other than a restaurant or similar retail food establishment described in section 403(q)(5)(H)(i) of such Act." (See Pub. L. 111-148, Sec. 4205(d), 124 Stat. 119, 576 (2010).)

We interpret the provisions of section 4205 of the ACA related to preemption to mean that States and local governments may not impose nutrition labeling requirements for food sold in a covered establishment, as defined in § 101.11(a), unless the State or local requirements are identical to the Federal requirements. In other words, States and localities cannot have additional or different nutrition labeling requirements for food sold either in (1) chain retail food establishments or (2) restaurants and similar retail food establishments not subject to the requirements of section 403(q)(5)(H) of the FD&C Act that voluntarily elect to be subject to the requirements by registering biannually under section 403(q)(5)(H)(ix).

Otherwise, for certain food that is not subject to the nutrition labeling requirements of section 403(q)(5)(H) of the FD&C Act, States and localities may establish or continue to impose nutrition labeling requirements. First, States and localities can have nutrition labeling requirements for food sold in restaurants or similar retail food establishments that are not part of a chain with 20 or more locations doing business under the same name and offering for sale substantially the same menu items that have not voluntarily registered under section 403(q)(5)(H)(ix) of the FD&C Act.

Second, States and localities can have nutrition labeling requirements for foods offered for sale in other establishments described in sections 403(q)(5)(A)(i) or (ii) of the FD&C Act that are exempt from the nutrition labeling requirements of sections 403(q)(1) to (q)(4) of the FD&C Act under section 403(q)(5)(A)(i) or (ii) of the FD&C Act, provided that such food is not required to have nutrition labeling under section 403(q)(5)(H) of the FD&C Act. For example, certain foods sold in schools and transportation carriers would not be required to have nutrition labeling under sections 403(q)(1) to (q)(4) of the FD&C Act (see section 403(q)(5)(A)(i) and (ii) of the FD&C Act and § 101.9(j)(2) and (j)(3)), or under section 403(q)(5)(H) of the FD&C Act because these establishments are not covered establishments within the meaning of § 101.11(a). Under our interpretation of the Rule of Construction in section 4205(d)(1) of the ACA, nutrition labeling for food sold from such establishments would not be "nutrient content disclosures of the type required under section 403(q)(5)(H)(viii) [of the FD&C Act]" and, therefore, would not be preempted. As a result, States and localities would be able to continue to require nutrition labeling for foods sold from establishments that are exempt from the nutrition labeling requirements of section 403(q)(1) to (q)(4) of the FD&C Act and not subject to nutrition labeling requirements of section 403(q)(5)(H) of the FD&C Act.

In addition, the express preemption provisions of section 403(A)(a)(4) of the FD&C Act do not preempt any State or local requirement respecting a statement in the labeling of food that provides for a warning concerning the safety of the food or component of the food.

The preamble to the proposed rule (76 FR 19192 at 19229 to 19230) described an alternative interpretation of the preemption provisions of section 4205 of the ACA that could leave less room for States and localities to require nutrition labeling for food sold in restaurants or similar retail food establishments. Under this alternative interpretation, State or local nutrition labeling requirements for food sold in establishments that are not "restaurants or similar retail food establishments," would be ineligible for the exception to the preemption in section 403(A)(a)(4) of the FD&C Act, because that exception by its literal terms only covers nutrition labeling requirements for food offered for sale in certain restaurants or similar retail food establishments, specifically those not subject to the nutrition labeling requirements of section 403(q)(5)(H) of the FD&C Act. Under this alternative interpretation, States and localities could not have nutrition labeling requirements for certain foods offered for sale in non-restaurants and similar retail food establishments unless they successfully petitioned us. Federal law provides that, upon petition, FDA may exempt State or local requirements from the express preemption provisions of section

403A(a)(4) of the FD&C Act under certain conditions. (See 21 U.S.C. 343-1(b).) We have issued regulations at § 100.1 (21 CFR 100.1) describing the petition process that is available to State and local governments to request such exemptions from preemption.

In addition, under this alternative interpretation, there would be foods in certain establishments for which the Federal Government has not required nutrition labeling and for which States and localities would also be precluded from establishing such labeling requirements unless they successfully petitioned us and a rulemaking was completed. This approach would risk creating a regulatory gap that would be inconsistent with the purposes of section 4205 of the ACA. It would also impose a restriction and burden on the States and localities that is inconsistent with the Federalism principles expressed in Executive Order 13132, as well as a substantial administrative burden on FDA in the event States petition for exemption.

We requested comment on our interpretation of section 4025 of the ACA related to preemption, as well as the alternative interpretation. We also requested comment on the use of the petition process in this context and on other potential interpretations that interested persons could identify as appropriate given both the preemption-related language of section 4205 of the ACA and the statutory goals.

(Comment 157) Several comments agreed with our interpretation of the preemption provisions of section 4205 of the ACA. A few of these comments recommended that the final rule include an explicit statement that the scope of the law's preemptive effect is coextensive with the law's nutrition labeling requirements; that is, the only State and local provisions that are preempted are those that explicitly require the type of menu labeling set forth in section 4205 of the ACA at a covered establishment. For example, the comments stated that if we decide not to cover movie theaters, hospitals, and other establishments or decide to exempt alcohol beverages from menu labeling in the final rule, then States and localities can enact laws to cover them. Another comment stated that an express statement about preemption will encourage States and localities to pass laws that fill in the gaps and to pass identical laws.

One comment disagreed with our proposed interpretation of the preemption provisions and its outcome. The comment stated that narrowing the exception for preemption is consistent with Congress' purpose to preempt the growing patchwork of State and local menu labeling laws. In addition, the comment stated that, while the alternative interpretation would result in a "regulatory gap" with some establishments not covered by Federal, State, and local menu labeling laws, Congress could amend the FD&C Act, if it chose to do so.

(Response 157) We agree with the comments asserting that the preemptive effect of the Federal menu labeling requirements of section 4205 of the ACA is limited to State and local requirements that impose additional or different nutrition labeling requirements for food that is covered by the Federal requirements of section 403(q)(5)(H) of the FD&C Act and § 101.11. We also agree that the alternative interpretation described in the proposed rule (76 FR 19192 at 19230) would restrict State and local authorities and create a regulatory gap that would be inconsistent with the purposes and language of section 4205 of the ACA and the Federalism principles expressed in Executive Order 13132.

We disagree with the comment that suggested that the alternative interpretation is more consistent with congressional intent to preempt the "patchwork" of State and local laws on menu labeling and that the solution for the "regulatory gap" under that interpretation would be for Congress to amend the FD&C Act again. Congress did create a uniform national menu labeling scheme for certain foods in certain facilities described in section 4205 of the ACA. However, nothing in the legislative history suggests that Congress intended to create a category of foods in establishments for which neither the Federal Government nor State or local governments could require menu labeling. We think it is more consistent with the purposes of section 4205 of the ACA, which provides valuable nutrition information to consumers, to allow State and local governments to require menu labeling for food not covered by Federal law. The language of section 4205(c) of the ACA amending section 403A of the FD&C Act is consistent with our final interpretation. This amendment includes an exception from preemption for food sold in restaurants or similar retail food establishments that are not restaurants or establishments subject to the requirements of 403(q)(5)(H) of the FD&C Act.

For these reasons, we interpret the provisions of section 4205 of the ACA related to preemption to mean that State and local governments may not establish or continue in effect nutrition labeling requirements for food covered by the Federal requirements of section 403(q)(5)(H) of the FD&C Act and § 101.11, unless the State or local requirements are identical to the Federal requirements of section 403(q)(5)(H) of the FD&C Act and § 101.11. In other words, States and localities cannot have additional or different nutrition labeling requirements for food sold either from: (1) Chain retail food establishments; or (2) restaurants and similar retail food establishments not otherwise subject to the requirements of section 403(q)(5)(H) and § 101.11 who voluntarily elect to be subject to those requirements by registering biannually with FDA in accordance with section 403(q)(5)(H)(ix) of the FD&C Act and § 101.11(d). For food sold in restaurants and similar retail establishments not subject to the nutrition labeling requirements of section 403(q)(5)(H) of the FD&C Act, States and localities may impose nutrition labeling requirements.

(Comment 158) Several comments agreed with our interpretation of the Rule of Construction. One comment agreed that warning statements are not preempted but asked us to clarify that this does not mean just microbiological hazards.

A few comments recommended that we codify the Rule of Construction. The comments asserted that the absence of codified provisions in the rule regarding the Rule of Construction could lead to confusion in properly interpreting the statute. The comments maintained that the lack of codified provisions in the rule for a similar Rule of Construction in the NLEA (see 21 U.S.C. 343-1 note) has led to confusion and to court decisions that have not taken that rule into account. The comments maintained that ensuring that the Rule of Construction is explicitly set out in Title 21 of the Code of Federal Regulations could help to avoid similar problems with the menu labeling law.

(Response 158) With respect to our interpretation of the Rule of Construction in section 4205(d) of the ACA, we reiterate that State or local requirements for statements in food labeling providing for warnings concerning food safety are not preempted. We agree with the comment that food safety in this context is not limited to microbiological hazards. We are not persuaded by the comments suggesting that we add a codified statement to § 101.11 restating the Rule of Construction at section 4205(d) of the ACA. We have highlighted the existence of the Rule of Construction and have explained our interpretation of section 4205(d) of the ACA both in the preamble to the proposed rule and in the preamble to this final rule. We do not think that codifying the Rule of Construction in section 4205(d) in our regulations is needed either to prevent confusion in interpreting the statute or to assure that courts consider section 4205(d) when appropriate.

(Comment 159) Some comments asked us to address the meaning of "identical" in section 403A(a)(4) of the FD&C Act, which excludes from preemption State and local requirements that are identical to Federal requirements under section 403(q) of the FD&C Act. The comments recommended that the final rule explicitly state that "identical" refers to the effect of the law and does not mean that a State or local requirement must be identical in wording of the law.

(Response 159) In response to the comments asserting that we revise the rule to clarify the meaning of "identical" within the context of section 403A(a)(4) of the FD&C Act, we note that we have already issued a regulation at § 100.1 that explains the meaning of "not identical to" in the context of section 403A of the FD&C Act in describing the petition process available to State and local governments to request an exemption from the express preemption provisions of section 403A of the FD&C Act under section 403A(b). Section 100.1(c)(4) provides in relevant part that, within the context of section 403A of FD&C Act, "not identical to" does not refer to the specific words in the State or local requirement but instead means that the State or local requirement directly or indirectly imposes obligations or contains provisions concerning the labeling of food that: (1) Are not imposed by or contained in the applicable provision (including any implementing regulation) of section 403 of the FD&C Act; or (2) differ from those specifically imposed by or contained in the applicable provision (including any implementing regulation) of section 403 of the FD&C Act.

Accordingly, a State or local nutrition labeling requirement for food covered by the requirements of section 403(q)(5)(H) of the FD&C Act and § 101.11 that directly or indirectly imposes obligations or contains labeling provisions that: (1) Are not imposed by or contained in section 403(q) of the FD&C Act and § 101.11; or (2) differ from those specifically imposed by or contained in section 403(q) of the FD&C Act and § 101.11 would be "not identical to" the Federal requirements and therefore would be preempted under section 403A(a)(4) of the FD&C Act. Because the meaning of the phrase "not identical to," within the context of section 403A of the FD&C Act, is already described in § 100.1 and is further explained here, we decline to revise the rule to clarify the meaning of "identical" as suggested by the comments.

(Comment 160) A few comments recommended that we support development of State and local laws that are identical. The comments recommended that we help the States and localities by making staff available to help assess the proposed language of State or local law for potential conflicts with Federal law and providing model legislation, which should be made part of the Model Food Code.

(Response 160) As discussed in section XXIV, a State or local jurisdiction may establish requirements, identical to those established in this rule, in its own food codes and then enforce its own food codes. Whether we can help States and localities assess the proposed language of State or local law for potential conflicts with Federal law will depend on resources available at the time of any requests for such assistance. However, at this time, we do not expect to have resources to provide model legislation for use by States and localities. We recommend that States and localities who wish to establish requirements, in their own food codes, identical to those established in this rule adapt § 101.11 for their own use.

(Comment 161) One comment asked us to describe the basis on which establishments that opt into the program can be assured that preemption applies. The comment asserted that if a facility complies with the Federal requirements under its food service contract as agreed to by the Federal Government, that establishment must be fully protected from State and local menu labeling action. The comment also stated that a facility's compliance with the terms of a Federal Government contract must suffice as certification that the facility is in compliance with all FDA menu labeling provisions and the facility should be permitted to opt into our program without any additional requirements.

(Response 161) As provided in 403(q)(5)(H)(ix) of the FD&C Act, authorized officials of restaurants and similar retail establishments that are not subject to the requirements of section 403(q)(5)(H) may elect to be subject to those requirements by registering biannually with FDA, as specified in § 101.11(d). Under section 403A(a)(4) of the FD&C Act, an establishment that "complies with the voluntary provision of nutrition information requirements of 403(q)(5)(H)(ix)" brings itself within the scope of Federal preemption of State and local laws. The comment appears essentially to be seeking FDA's assurances that a facility's compliance with the terms of a Federal contract to provide food services would (1) suffice for "opting in" to the voluntary program and (2) guarantee that State and local menu labeling action against the facility is prohibited. We decline to provide such assurances. The requirements for voluntarily "opting in" to be subject to the Federal menu labeling requirements are set forth in § 101.11(d). Preemption of certain State and local requirements follows from voluntarily becoming subject to the requirements of § 101.11. The effects of following the terms of Federal contracts to procure food services are outside the scope of this rulemaking.

XXVIII. Environmental Impact

We have determined under 21 CFR 25.30(k) that this action is of a type that does not individually or cumulatively have a significant effect on the human environment. Therefore, neither an environmental assessment nor an environmental impact statement is required.

XXIX. References

The following references have been placed on display in the Division of Dockets Management (HFA-305), Food and Drug Administration, 5630 Fishers Lane, Rm. 1061, Rockville, MD 20852, and may be seen by interested persons between 9 a.m. and 4 p.m., Monday through Friday, and are available electronically at http://www.regulations.gov. (FDA has verified all the Web site addresses in this reference section, but FDA is not responsible for any subsequent changes to the Web sites after this document publishes in the Federal Register).

1. Flegal, K.M., M.D. Carroll, C.L. Ogden, et al., "Prevalence and Trends in Obesity Among U.S. Adults 1999-2008," Journal of the American Medical Association, 303:235-241, 2010.

2. Ogden, C.L., M.D. Carroll, L.R. Curtin, et al., "Prevalence of High Body Mass Index in U.S. Children and Adolescents, 2007-2008," Journal of the American Medical Association, 303:242-249, 2010.

3. U.S. Department of Health and Human Services (DHHS) and USDA, "2010 Dietary Guidelines for Americans," 7th ed., Washington DC: U.S. Government Printing Office, 2010. Available at http://www.cnpp.usda.gov/DGAs2010-PolicyDocument.htm. Accessed on November 3, 2014.

4. Lin, B.H., J. Guthrie, and E. Frazão. "Nutrient Contribution of Food Away From Home," America's Eating Habits: Changes and Consequences, chapter 12, Elizabeth Frazão (ed.), USDA Agriculture Information Bulletin No. (AIB-750), pp. 213-242, May 1999.

5. FDA Reports & Research Internet Web page: "Backgrounder—Keystone Forum on Away-From-Home Foods: Opportunities for Preventing Weight Gain and Obesity Report," Keystone Center, June 2006.

6. USDA, Economic Research Service, "Table 10: Food Away From Home as a Share of Food Expenditures," Food CPI and Expenditures: Food Expenditure Tables. Available at http://www.ers.usda.gov/data-products/food-expenditures.aspx. Accessed on November 3, 2014.

7. Burton, S., E.H. Creyer, J. Kees, et al., "Attacking the Obesity Epidemic: The Potential Health

Benefits of Providing Nutrition Information in Restaurants," American Journal of Public Health, 96(9):1669-1675, September 2006.

8. FDA, "Draft Guidance for Industry: Questions and Answers Regarding Implementation of the Menu Labeling Provisions of Section 4205 of the Patient Protection and Affordable Care Act of 2010," 2010.

9. 112th Congress, House of Representatives, H. Rept. 112-101, "Agriculture, Rural Development, Food and Drug Administration, and Related Agencies Appropriations Bill, 2012," June 3, 2011.

10. FDA, "Guidance for Industry: A Labeling Guide for Restaurants and Other Retail Establishments Selling Away-From-Home Foods," April 2008.

11. Food Marketing Trends. "U.S. Grocery Shopper Trends", 2010.

12. Sutherland Statutes 21.4, 7th ed., 2009.

13. 155 Cong. Rec. S5522 (May 14, 2009) (statement of Senator Harkin).

14. Commissioner, New York State Department of Agriculture and Markets and Commissioner, New York State Department of Health. "Memorandum of Understanding Between the New York State Department of Health and the New York State Department of Agriculture and Markets Concerning the Inspection of Food Service Establishments and Food Processing Establishments", 2010.

15. Webster's Third New International Dictionary, p. 369, 2002.

16. The American Heritage Online Dictionary. Available at http://ahdictionary.com/word/search.html?q=chain. Accessed on November 3, 2014.

17. Merriam-Webster Dictionary. Available at http://www.merriam-webster.com/dictionary/chain. Accessed on November 3, 2014.

18. Webster's Third New International Dictionary, pp. 1327-1328, 2002.

19. The American Heritage Online Dictionary. Available at http://ahdictionary.com/word/search.html?q=location. Accessed on November 3, 2014.

20. The American Heritage Online Dictionary. Available at http://ahdictionary.com/word/search.html?q=writing. Accessed on November 3, 2014.

21. Merriam-Webster Dictionary. Available at http://www.merriam-webster.com/dictionary/writing. Accessed on November 3, 2014.

22. Webster's Third New International Dictionary, p. 2641, 2002.

23. Merriam-Webster Dictionary. Available at http://www.merriam-webster.com/dictionary/primary. Accessed on November 3, 2014.

24. The American Heritage Online Dictionary. Available at http://ahdictionary.com/word/search.html?q=primary. Accessed on November 3, 2014.

25. Webster's Third New International Dictionary, p. 1800, 2002.

26. 2A Sutherland Statutory Construction 137, 7th ed., 2009.

27. McDonald's and North America Consumer and Business Insights, "Drive-Thru Caloric Information Online Customer Satisfaction Survey", 2011.

28. FDA Memorandum, Chung-Tung Jordan Lin, to the File, "Review of Comment Submitted by McDonald's USA to Docket No. FDA-2011-F-0172, on the Use of Stanchions at Drive-Through Windows to Disclose Calories in Standard Menu Items in Restaurants and Similar Retail Food Establishments," January 27, 2012.

29. Harkin, DeLauro Respond to Proposed Menu Labeling Rules. April 1, 2011. Available at http://www.harkin.senate.gov/press/release.cfm?i=332329. Accessed on November 3, 2014.

30. U.S. Department of the Treasury, Alcohol and Tobacco Tax and Trade Bureau. TTB Ruling Number: 2013-2, May 28, 2013.

31. Cunningham, S.K., The Bartender's Black Book, 10th ed., 2011.

32. Comment from Hyman, Phelps, and McNamara on behalf of Dominoes, Appendix 3, 2011.

33. FDA Memorandum, Chung-Tung Jordan Lin, to the File, "Review of Comment Submitted by Culver Franchising Systems, Inc,. to Docket No. FDA-2011-F-0172, on the Calorie Declaration Option of Not Using Caloric Ranges for Combination Meals and Variable Menu Items," February 29, 2012.

34. California Health and Safety Code, Section 114377.

35. New York City Health Code, Section 81.08.

36. Baltimore City Health Code Section 6-507.

37. County Council for Montgomery County Maryland, Resolution No. 16-134, 2007.

38. FDA, "Guidance for Industry: A Food Labeling Guide," 2008.

39. FDA, "Regulatory Procedures Manual," chapter 4.

40 FDA, "Regulatory Procedures Manual," chapter 6, section 5.

41. FDA, "State Contracts," available at http://www.fda.gov/ForFederalStateandLocalOfficials/PartnershipsContracts/StateContracts/default.htm, 2012.

42. FDA, "Food Labeling: Nutrition Labeling of Standard Menu Items in Restaurants and Similar Retail Food Establishments. Final Regulatory Impact Analysis," Docket No. FDA-2011-F-0172, 2014.

43. "Food Labeling: Nutrition Labeling of Standard Menu Items in Restaurants and Similar Retail Food Establishments. Notice of Proposed Rulemaking," Docket No. FDA-2011-F-0172, Preliminary Regulatory Impact Analysis, 2011.

44. U.S. Census Bureau. County Business Patterns, United States NAICS 2000-2008. October 18,

2010.

45. Wootan, M.G., M. Osborn. "Availability of Nutrition Information From Chain Restaurants in the United States. American Journal of Preventive Medicine, 30(3):266-268, 2006.

46. U.S. Census Bureau. North American Industry Classification System. 2007. October 18, 2010.

47. Mintel Menu Insights. New Menu Items at Restaurants. 2010.

48. Eastern Research Group I. Evaluation of Recordkeeping Costs for Food Manufacturers, Final Report. Sertkaya, A, A. Berlind, S. Erdem, editors. Contract No. 223-01-2461, Task Order Number 5. 2007.

LIST OF SUBJECTS

Administrative practice and procedure, Computer technology, Reporting and recordkeeping requirements.

Food labeling, Nutrition, Reporting and recordkeeping requirements.

Therefore, under the Federal Food, Drug, and Cosmetic Act and under authority delegated to the Commissioner of Food and Drugs, 21 CFR parts 11 and 101 are amended as follows:

REGULATORY TEXT

PART 11 ELECTRONIC RECORDS ELECTRONIC SIGNATURES

1. The authority citation for 21 CFR part 11 continues to read as follows:

Authority:

21 U.S.C. 321-393; 42 U.S.C. 262.

2. Section 11.1 is amended by adding paragraph (g) to read as follows:

§ 11.1 Scope.

* * * * *

(g) This part does not apply to electronic signatures obtained under § 101.11(d) of this chapter.

PART 101 FOOD LABELING

3. The authority citation for 21 CFR part 101 continues to read as follows:

Authority:

15 U.S.C. 1453, 1454, 1455; 21 U.S.C. 321, 331, 342, 343, 348, 371; 42 U.S.C. 243, 264, 271.

4. Section 101.9 is amended by revising paragraph (j)(1)(i), the introductory text of paragraphs (j)(2) and (3), and the first sentence of paragraph (j)(4) to read as follows:

§ 101.9 Nutrition labeling of food.

* * * * *

(j) * * *

(1)(i) Food offered for sale by a person who makes direct sales to consumers (e.g., a retailer) who has annual gross sales made or business done in sales to consumers that is not more than $500,000 or has annual gross sales made or business done in sales of food to consumers of not more than $50,000, Provided, That the food bears no nutrition claims or other nutrition information in any context on the label or in labeling or advertising. Claims or other nutrition information subject the food to the provisions of this section, § 101.10, or § 101.11, as applicable.

* * * * *

(2) Except as provided in § 101.11, food products that are:

* * * * *

(3) Except as provided in § 101.11, food products that are:

* * * * *

(4) Except as provided in § 101.11, foods that contain insignificant amounts of all of the nutrients and food components required to be included in the declaration of nutrition information under paragraph (c) of this section, Provided, That the food bears no nutrition claims or other nutrition information in any context on the label or in labeling or advertising. * * *

* * * * *

5. Section 101.10 is revised to read as follows:

§ 101.10 Nutrition labeling of restaurant foods whose labels or labeling bear nutrient content claims or health claims.

Nutrition labeling in accordance with § 101.9 shall be provided upon request for any restaurant food or meal for which a nutrient content claim (as defined in § 101.13 or in subpart D of this part) or a health claim (as defined in § 101.14 and permitted by a regulation in subpart E of this part) is made, except that information on the nutrient amounts that are the basis for the claim (e.g., "low fat, this meal provides less than 10 grams of fat") may serve as the functional equivalent of complete nutrition information as described in § 101.9. For the purposes of this section, restaurant food includes two categories of food. It includes food which is served in restaurants or other establishments in which food is served for immediate human consumption or which is sold for sale or use in such establishments. It also includes food which is processed and prepared primarily in a retail establishment, which is ready for human consumption, which is of the type described in the previous sentence, and which is offered for sale to consumers but not for immediate human consumption in such establishment and which is not offered for sale outside such establishment. For standard menu items that are offered for sale in covered establishments (as defined in § 101.11(a)), the information in the written nutrition information required by § 101.11(b)(2)(ii)(A) will serve to meet the requirements of this section. Nutrient levels may be determined by nutrient databases, cookbooks, or analyses or by other reasonable bases that provide assurance that the food or meal meets the nutrient requirements for the claim. Presentation of nutrition labeling may be in various forms, including those provided in § 101.45 and other reasonable means.

6. Section 101.11 is added to subpart A to read as follows:

§ 101.11 Nutrition labeling of standard menu items in covered establishments.

(a) Definitions. The definitions of terms in section 201 of the Federal Food, Drug, and Cosmetic Act apply to such terms when used in this section. In addition, for purposes of this section:

Authorized official of a restaurant or similar retail food establishment means the owner, operator, agent in charge, or other person authorized by the owner, operator, or agent in charge to register the restaurant or similar retail food establishment, which is not otherwise subject to section 403(q)(5)(H) of the Federal Food, Drug, and Cosmetic Act, with FDA for the purposes of paragraph (d) of this section.

Combination meal means a standard menu item that consists of more than one food item, for example a meal that includes a sandwich, a side dish, and a drink. A combination meal may be represented on the menu or menu board in narrative form, numerically, or pictorially. Some combination meals may include a variable menu item or be a variable menu item as defined in this paragraph where the components may vary. For example, the side dish may vary among several options (e.g., fries, salad, or onion rings) or the drinks may vary (e.g., soft drinks, milk, or juice) and the customer selects which of these items will be included in the meal.

Covered establishment means a restaurant or similar retail food establishment that is a part of a chain with 20 or more locations doing business under the same name (regardless of the type of ownership, e.g., individual franchises) and offering for sale substantially the same menu items, as well as a restaurant or similar retail food establishment that is registered to be covered under paragraph (d) of this section.

Custom order means a food order that is prepared in a specific manner based on an individual customer's request, which requires the covered establishment to deviate from its usual preparation of a standard menu item, e.g., a club sandwich without the bacon if the establishment usually includes bacon in its club sandwich.

Daily special means a menu item that is prepared and offered for sale on a particular day, that is not routinely listed on a menu or menu board or offered by the covered establishment, and that is promoted by the covered establishment as a special menu item for that particular day.

Doing business under the same name means sharing the same name. The term "name" refers to either:

(i) The name of the establishment presented to the public; or

(ii) If there is no name of the establishment presented to the public (e.g., an establishment with the generic descriptor "concession stand"), the name of the parent entity of the establishment. When the term "name" refers to the name of the establishment presented to the public under paragraph (i) of this definition, the term "same" includes names that are slight variations of each other, for example, due to the region, location, or size (e.g., "New York Ave. Burgers" and "Pennsylvania Ave. Burgers" or "ABC" and "ABC Express").

Food on display means restaurant-type food that is visible to the customer before the customer makes a selection, so long as there is not an ordinary expectation of further preparation by the consumer before consumption.

Food that is part of a customary market test means food that appears on a menu or menu board for less than 90 consecutive days in order to test consumer acceptance of the product.

Location means a fixed position or site.

Menu or menu board means the primary writing of the covered establishment from which a customer makes an order selection, including, but not limited to, breakfast, lunch, and dinner menus; dessert menus; beverage menus; children's menus; other specialty menus; electronic menus; and menus on the Internet. Determining whether a writing is or is part of the primary writing of the covered establishment from which a customer makes an order selection depends on a number of factors, including whether the writing lists the name of a standard menu item (or an image depicting the standard menu item) and the price of the standard menu item, and whether the writing can be used by a customer to make an order selection at the time the customer is viewing the writing. The menus may be in different forms, e.g., booklets, pamphlets, or single sheets of paper. Menu boards include those inside a covered establishment as well as drive-through menu boards at covered establishments.

Offering for sale substantially the same menu items means offering for sale a significant proportion of menu items that use the same general recipe and are prepared in substantially the same way with substantially the same food components, even if the name of the menu item varies, (e.g. "Bay View Crab Cake" and "Ocean View Crab Cake"). "Menu items" in this definition refers to food items that are listed on a menu or menu board or that are offered as self-service food or food on display. Restaurants and similar retail food establishments that are part of a chain can still be offering for sale substantially the same menu items if the availability of some menu items varies within the chain. Having the same name may indicate, but does not necessarily guarantee, that menu items are substantially the same.

Restaurant or similar retail food establishment means a retail establishment that offers for sale restaurant-type food, except if it is a school as defined by 7 CFR 210.2 or 220.2.

Restaurant-type food means food that is:

(i) Usually eaten on the premises, while walking away, or soon after arriving at another location; and

(ii) Either:

(A) Served in restaurants or other establishments in which food is served for immediate human consumption or which is sold for sale or use in such establishments; or

(B) Processed and prepared primarily in a retail establishment, ready for human consumption, of the type described in paragraph (ii)(A) of this definition, and offered for sale to consumers but not for immediate human consumption in such establishment and which is not offered for sale outside such establishment.

Self-service food means restaurant-type food that is available at a salad bar, buffet line, cafeteria line, or similar self-service facility and that is served by the customers themselves. Self-service food also includes self-service beverages.

Standard menu item means a restaurant-type food that is routinely included on a menu or menu board or routinely offered as a self-service food or food on display.

Temporary menu item means a food that appears on a menu or menu board for less than a total of 60 days per calendar year. The 60 days includes the total of consecutive and non-consecutive days the item appears on the menu.

Variable menu item means a standard menu item that comes in different flavors, varieties, or combinations, and is listed as a single menu item.

(b) Requirements for nutrition labeling for food sold in covered establishments—(1) Applicability. (i) The labeling requirements in this paragraph (b) apply to standard menu items offered for sale in covered establishments.

(ii)(A) The labeling requirements in this paragraph (b) do not apply to foods that are not standard menu items, including:

(1) Items such as condiments that are for general use, including those placed on the table or on or behind the counter; daily specials; temporary menu items; custom orders; food that is part of a customary market test; and

(2) Self-service food and food on display that is offered for sale for less than a total of 60 days per calendar year or fewer than 90 consecutive days in order to test consumer acceptance.

(B) The labeling requirements of paragraph (b)(2)(iii) of this section do not apply to alcoholic beverages that are foods on display and are not self-service foods.

(2) Nutrition information. (i) Except as provided by paragraph (b)(2)(i)(A)(8) of this section, the following must be provided on menus and menu boards:

(A) The number of calories contained in each standard menu item listed on the menu or menu board, as usually prepared and offered for sale. In the case of multiple-serving standard menu items, this means the calories declared must be for the whole menu item listed on the menu or menu board as usually prepared and offered for sale (e.g., "pizza pie: 1600 cal"); or per discrete serving unit as long as the discrete serving unit (e.g., pizza slice) and total number of discrete serving units contained in the menu item are declared on the menu or menu board, and the menu item is usually prepared and offered for sale divided in discrete serving units (e.g., "pizza pie: 200 cal/slice, 8 slices"). The calories must be declared in the following manner:

(1) The number of calories must be listed adjacent to the name or the price of the associated standard menu item, in a type size no smaller than the type size of the name or the price of the associated standard menu item, whichever is smaller, in the same color, or a color at least as conspicuous as that used for the name of the associated standard menu item, and with the same contrasting background or a background at least as contrasting as that used for the name of the associated standard menu item.

(2) To the nearest 5-calorie increment up to and including 50 calories and to the nearest 10-calorie increment above 50 calories, except that amounts less than 5 calories may be expressed as zero.

(3) The term "Calories" or "Cal" must appear as a heading above a column listing the number of calories for each standard menu item or adjacent to the number of calories for each standard menu item. If the term "Calories" or "Cal" appears as a heading above a column of calorie declarations, the term must be in a type size no smaller than the smallest type size of the name or price of any menu item on that menu or menu board in the same color or a color at least as conspicuous as that used for that name or price and in the same contrasting background or a background at least as contrasting as that used for that name or price. If the term "Calories" or "Cal" appears adjacent to the number of calories for the standard menu item, the term "Calories" or "Cal" must appear in the same type size and in the same color and contrasting background as the number of calories.

(4) Additional requirements that apply to each individual variable menu item:

(i) When the menu or menu board lists flavors or varieties of an entire individual variable menu item (such as soft drinks, ice cream, doughnuts, dips, and chicken that can be grilled or fried), the calories must be declared separately for each listed flavor or variety. Where flavors or varieties have the same calorie amounts (after rounding in accordance with paragraph (b)(2)(i)(A)(2) of this section), the calorie declaration for such flavors or varieties can be listed as a single calorie declaration adjacent to the flavors or varieties, provided that the calorie declaration specifies that the calorie amount listed represents the calorie amounts for each individual flavor or variety.

(ii) When the menu or menu board does not list flavors or varieties for an entire individual variable menu item, and only includes a general description of the variable menu item (e.g. "soft drinks"), the calories must be declared for each option with a slash between the two calorie declarations where only two options are available (e.g., "150/250 calories") or as a range in accordance with the requirements of paragraph (b)(2)(i)(A)(7) of this section where more than two options are available (e.g., "100-250 calories").

(iii) When the menu or menu board describes flavors or varieties for only part of an individual variable menu item (such as different types of cheese offered in a grilled cheese sandwich (e.g., "Grilled Cheese (Cheddar or Swiss)"), the calories must be declared for each option with a slash between the two calorie declarations where only two options are available (e.g., "450/500 calories") or as a range in accordance with the requirements of paragraph (b)(2)(i)(A)(7) of this section where more than two options are available (e.g., "450-550 calories").

(5) Additional requirements that apply to a variable menu item that is offered for sale with the option of adding toppings listed on the menu or menu board. When the menu or menu board lists toppings that can be added to a menu item (such as pizza or ice cream):

(i) The calories must be declared for the basic preparation of the menu item as listed (e.g., "small pizza pie," "single scoop ice cream").

(ii) The calories must be separately declared for each topping listed on the menu or menu board (e.g., pepperoni, sausage, green peppers, onions on pizza; fudge, almonds, sprinkles on ice cream), specifying that the calories are added to the calories contained in the basic preparation of the menu item. Where toppings have the same calorie amounts (after rounding in accordance with paragraph (b)(2)(i)(A)(2) of this section), the calorie declaration for such toppings can be listed as a single calorie declaration adjacent to the toppings, provided that the calorie declaration specifies that the calorie amount listed represents the calorie amount for each individual topping.

(iii) The calories for the basic preparation of the menu item must be declared for each size of the menu item. The calories for each topping listed on the menu or menu board must be declared for each size of the menu item, or declared using a slash between the two calorie declarations for each topping where only two sizes of the menu item are available (e.g., "adds 150/250 cal") or as a range for each topping in accordance with the requirements of paragraph (b)(2)(i)(A)(7) of this section where more than two sizes of the menu item are available (e.g., "adds 100-250 cal"). If a slash between two calorie declarations or a range of calorie declarations is used, the menu or menu board must indicate that the variation in calories for each topping arises from the size of the menu item to which the toppings are added.

(iv) If the amount of the topping included on the basic preparation of the menu item decreases based on the total number of toppings ordered for the menu item (such as is sometimes the case with pizza toppings), the calories for each topping must be declared as single values representing the calories for each topping when added to a one-topping menu item, specifying that the calorie declaration is for the topping when added to a one-topping menu item.

(6) Additional requirements that apply to a combination meal. Except as provided in paragraph (b)(2)(i)(A)(6)(iv) of this section:

(i) When the menu or menu board lists two options for menu items in a combination meal (e.g., a sandwich with a side salad or chips), the calories must be declared for each option with a slash between the two calorie declarations (e.g., "350/450 calories").

(ii) When the menu or menu board lists three or more options for menu items in a combination meal (e.g., a sandwich with chips, a side salad, or fruit), the calories must be declared as a range in accordance with the requirements of paragraph (b)(2)(i)(A)(7) of this section (e.g., "350-500 calories").

(iii) When the menu or menu board includes a choice to increase or decrease the size of a combination meal, the calorie difference must be declared for the increased or decreased size with a slash between two calorie declarations (e.g., "Adds 100/150 calories," "Subtracts 100/150 calories") if the menu or menu board lists two options for menu items in the combination meal, or as a range in accordance with the requirements of paragraph (b)(2)(i)(A)(7) of this section (e.g., "Adds 100-250 calories," "Subtracts 100-250 calories") if the menu or menu board lists three or more options for menu items in the combination meal.

(iv) Where the menu or menu board describes an opportunity for a consumer to combine standard menu items for a special price (e.g., "Combine Any Sandwich with Any Soup or Any Salad for $8.99"), and the calories for each standard menu item, including each size option as described in paragraph (b)(2)(i)(A)(6)(iii) of this section if applicable, available for the consumer to combine are declared elsewhere on the menu or menu board, the requirements of paragraphs (b)(2)(i)(A)(6)(i), (ii), and (iii) of this section do not apply.

(7) Additional format requirements for declaring calories for an individual variable menu item, a combination meal, and toppings as a range, if applicable. Calories declared as a range must be in the format "xx-yy," where "xx" is the caloric content of the lowest calorie variety, flavor, or combination, and "yy" is the caloric content of the highest calorie variety, flavor, or combination.

(8) Exception for a variable menu item that has no clearly identifiable upper bound to the range of calories: If the variable menu item appears on the menu or menu board and is a self-service food or food on display, and there is no clearly identifiable upper bound to the range, e.g., all-you-can-eat buffet, then the menu or menu board must include a statement, adjacent to the name or price of the item, referring customers to the self-service facility for calorie information, e.g., "See buffet for calorie declarations." This statement must appear in a type size no smaller than the type size of the name or price of the variable menu item, whichever is smaller, and in the same color or a color at least as conspicuous as that used for that name or price, with the same contrasting background or a background at least as contrasting as that used for that name or price.

(9) Additional requirements that apply to beverages that are not self-service. For beverages that are not self-service, calories must be declared based on the full volume of the cup served without ice, unless the covered establishment ordinarily dispenses and offers for sale a standard beverage fill (i.e., a fixed amount that is less than the full volume of the cup per cup size) or dispenses a standard ice fill (i.e., a fixed amount of ice per cup size). If the covered establishment ordinarily dispenses and offers for sale a standard beverage fill or dispenses a standard ice fill, the covered establishment must declare calories based on such standard beverage fill or standard ice fill.

(B) The following statement designed to enable consumers to understand, in the context of a total daily diet, the significance of the calorie information provided on menus and menu boards: "2,000 calories a day is used for general nutrition advice, but calorie needs vary." For menus and menu boards targeted to children, the following options may be used as a substitute for or in addition to the succinct statement: "1,200 to 1,400 calories a day is used for general nutrition advice for children ages 4 to 8 years, but calorie needs vary."; or "1,200 to 1,400 calories a day is used for general nutrition advice for children ages 4 to 8 years and 1,400 to 2,000 calories a day for children ages 9 to 13 years, but calorie needs vary."

(1) This statement must be posted prominently and in a clear and conspicuous manner in a type size no smaller than the smallest type size of any calorie declaration appearing on the same menu or menu board and in the same color or in a color at least as conspicuous as that used for the calorie declarations and with the same contrasting background or a background at least as contrasting as that used for the calorie declarations.

(2) For menus, this statement must appear on the bottom of each page of the menu. On menu pages that also bear the statement required by paragraph (b)(2)(i)(C) of this section, this statement must appear immediately above, below, or beside the statement required by paragraph (b)(2)(i)(C) of this section.

(3) For menu boards, this statement must appear on the bottom of the menu board, immediately above, below, or beside the statement required by paragraph (b)(2)(i)(C) of this section.

(C) The following statement regarding the availability of the additional written nutrition information required in paragraph (b)(2)(ii) of this section must be on all forms of the menu or menu board: "Additional nutrition information available upon request."

(1) This statement must be posted prominently and in a clear and conspicuous manner in a type size no smaller than the smallest type size of any calorie declaration appearing on the same menu or menu board and in the same color or in a color at least as conspicuous as that used for the caloric declarations, and with the same contrasting background or a background at least as contrasting as that used for the caloric declarations.

(2) For menus, the statement must appear on the bottom of the first page with menu items immediately above, below, or beside the succinct statement required by paragraph (b)(2)(i)(B) of this section.

(3) For menu boards, the statement must appear on the bottom of the menu board immediately above, below, or beside the succinct statement required by paragraph (b)(2)(i)(B) of this section.

(ii) The following nutrition information for a standard menu item must be available in written form on the premises of the covered establishment and provided to the customer upon request. This nutrition information must be presented in the order listed and using the measurements listed, except as provided in paragraph (b)(2)(ii)(B) of this section. Rounding of these nutrients must be in compliance with § 101.9(c). The information must be presented in a clear and conspicuous manner, including using a color, type size, and contrasting background that render the information likely to be read and understood by the ordinary individual under customary conditions of purchase and use. Covered establishments may use the abbreviations allowed for Nutrition Facts for certain packaged foods in § 101.9(j)(13)(ii)(B):

(A)(1) Total calories (cal);

(2) Calories from fat (fat cal);

(3) Total fat (g);

(4) Saturated fat (g);

(5) Trans fat (g);

(6) Cholesterol (mg);

(7) Sodium (mg);

(8) Total carbohydrate (g);

(9) Dietary fiber (g);

(10) Sugars (g); and

(11) Protein (g).

(B) If a standard menu item contains insignificant amounts of all the nutrients required to be disclosed in paragraph (b)(2)(ii)(A) of this section, the establishment is not required to include nutrition information regarding the standard menu item in the written form. However, if the covered establishment makes a nutrient content claim or health claim, the establishment is required to provide nutrition information on the nutrient that is the subject of the claim in accordance with § 101.10. For standard menu items that contain insignificant amounts of six or more of the required nutrients, the declaration of nutrition information required by paragraph (b)(2)(ii)(A) of this section may be presented in a simplified format.

(1) An insignificant amount is defined as that amount that allows a declaration of zero in nutrition labeling, except that for total carbohydrates, dietary fiber, and protein, it must be an amount that allows a declaration of "less than one gram."

(2) The simplified format must include information, in a column, list, or table, on the following nutrients:

(i) Total calories, total fat, total carbohydrates, protein, and sodium; and

(ii) Calories from fat, and any other nutrients identified in paragraph (b)(2)(ii)(A) of this section that are present in more than insignificant amounts.

(3) If the simplified format is used, the statement "Not a significant sourceof ___ " (with the blank filled in with the names of the nutrients required to be declared in the written nutrient information and calories from fat that are present in insignificant amounts) must be included at the bottom of the list of nutrients.

(C) For variable menu items, the nutrition information listed in paragraph (b)(2)(ii)(A) of this section must be declared as follows for each size offered for sale:

(1) The nutrition information required in paragraph (b)(2)(ii)(A) of this section must be declared for the basic preparation of the item and, separately, for each topping, flavor, or variable component.

(2) Additional format requirements for toppings if the amount of the topping included on the basic preparation of the menu item decreases based on the total number of toppings ordered for the menu item (such as is sometimes the case with pizza toppings). The nutrients for such topping must be declared as single values representing the nutrients for each topping when added to a one-topping menu item, specifying that the nutrient declaration is for the topping when added to a one-topping menu item.

(3) If the calories and other nutrients are the same for different flavors, varieties, and variable components of the combination meal, each variety, flavor, and variable component of the combination meal is not required to be listed separately. All items that have the same nutrient values could be listed together with the nutrient values listed only once.

(D) The written nutrition information required in paragraph (b)(2)(ii)(A) of this section may be provided on a counter card, sign, poster, handout, booklet, loose leaf binder, or electronic device such as a computer, or in a menu, or in any other form that similarly permits the written declaration of the required nutrient content information for all standard menu items. If the written nutrition information is not in a form that can be given to the customer upon request, it must be readily available in a manner and location on the premises that allows the customer/consumer to review the written nutrition information upon request.

(iii) The following must be provided for a standard menu item that is self-service or on display.

(A) Calories per displayed food item (e.g., a bagel, a slice of pizza, or a muffin), or if the food is not offered for sale in a discrete unit, calories per serving (e.g., scoop, cup), and the serving or discrete unit used to determine the calorie content (e.g., "per scoop" or "per muffin") on either: A sign adjacent to and clearly associated with the corresponding food; (e.g., "150 calories per scoop"); a sign attached to a sneeze guard with the calorie declaration and the serving or unit used to determine the calorie content above each specific food so that the consumer can clearly associate the calorie declaration with the food, except that if it is not clear to which food the calorie declaration and serving or unit refers, then the sign must also include the name of the food, e.g., "Broccoli and cheese casserole—200 calories per scoop"; or a single sign or placard listing the calorie declaration for several food items along with the names of the food items, so long as the sign or placard is located where a consumer can view the name, calorie declaration, and serving or unit of a particular item while selecting that item.

(1) For purposes of paragraph (b)(2)(iii)(A) of this section, "per displayed food item" means per each discrete unit offered for sale, for example, a bagel, a slice of pizza, or a muffin.

(2) For purposes of paragraph (b)(2)(iii)(A) of this section, "per serving" means, for each food:

(i) Per serving instrument used to dispense the food offered for sale, provided that the serving instrument dispenses a uniform amount of the food (e.g., a scoop or ladle);

(ii) If a serving instrument that dispenses a uniform amount of food is not used to dispense the food, per each common household measure (e.g., cup or tablespoon) offered for sale or per unit of weight offered for sale, e.g., per quarter pound or per 4 ounces; or

(iii) Per total number of fluid ounces in the cup in which a self-service beverage is served and, if applicable, the description of the cup size (e.g., "140 calories per 12 fluid ounces (small)").

(3) The calories must be declared in the following manner:

(i) To the nearest 5-calorie increment up to and including 50 calories and to the nearest 10-calorie increment above 50 calories except that amounts less than 5 calories may be expressed as zero.

(ii) If the calorie declaration is provided on a sign with the food's name, price, or both, the calorie declaration, accompanied by the term "Calories" or "Cal" and the amount of the serving or displayed food item on which the calories declaration is based must be in a type size no smaller than the type size of the name or price of the menu item whichever is smaller, in the same color, or a color that is at least as conspicuous as that used for that name or price, using the same contrasting background or a background at least as contrasting as that used for that name or price. If the calorie declaration is provided on a sign that does not include the food's name, price, or both, the calorie declaration, accompanied by the term "Calories" or "Cal" and the amount of the serving or displayed food item on which the calorie declaration is based must be clear and conspicuous.

(iii) For self-service beverages, calorie declarations must be accompanied by the term "fluid ounces" and, if applicable, the description of the cup size (e.g., "small," "medium").

(B) For food that is self-service or on display and is identified by an individual sign adjacent to the food itself where such sign meets the definition of a menu or menu board under paragraph (a) of this section, the statement required by paragraph (b)(2)(i)(B) of this section and the statement required by paragraph (b)(2)(i)(C) of this section. These two statements may appear on the sign adjacent to the food itself; on a separate, larger sign, in close proximity to the food that can be easily read as the consumer is making order selections; or on a large menu board that can be easily read as the consumer is viewing the food.

(C) The nutrition information in written form required by paragraph (b)(2)(ii) of this section, except for packaged food insofar as it bears nutrition labeling information required by and in accordance with paragraph (b)(2)(ii) of this section and the packaged food, including its label, can be examined by a consumer before purchasing the food.

(c) Determination of nutrient content. (1) A covered establishment must have a reasonable basis for its nutrient declarations. Nutrient values may be determined by using nutrient databases (with or without computer software programs), cookbooks, laboratory analyses, or other reasonable means, including the use of Nutrition Facts on labels on packaged foods that comply with the nutrition labeling requirements of section 403(q)(1) of the Federal Food, Drug, and Cosmetic Act and § 101.9, FDA nutrient values for raw fruits and vegetables in Appendix C of this part, or FDA nutrient values for cooked fish in Appendix D of this part.

(2) Nutrient declarations for standard menu items must be accurate and consistent with the specific basis used to determine nutrient values. A covered establishment must take reasonable steps to ensure that the method of preparation (e.g., types and amounts of ingredients, cooking temperatures) and amount of a standard menu item offered for sale adhere to the factors on which its nutrient values were determined.

(3) A covered establishment must provide to FDA, within a reasonable period of time upon request, information substantiating nutrient values including the method and data used to derive these nutrient values. This information must include the following:

(i) For nutrient databases:

(A) The name and version (including the date of the version) of the database, and, as applicable, the name of the applicable software company and any Web site address for the database. The name and version of a database would include the name and version of the computer software, if applicable;

(B) The recipe or formula used as a basis for the nutrient declarations;

(C)(1) Information on:

(i) The amount of each nutrient that the specified amount of each ingredient identified in the recipe contributes to the menu item; and

(ii) How the database was used including calculations or operations (e.g., worksheets or computer printouts) to determine the nutrient values for the standard menu items;

(2) If the information in paragraph (c)(3)(i)(C)(1) of this section is not available, certification attesting that the database will provide accurate results when used appropriately and that the database was used in accordance with its instructions;

(D) A detailed listing (e.g., printout) of the nutrient values determined for each standard menu item.

(E) Any other information pertinent to the final nutrient values of the standard menu item (e.g., information about what might cause slight variations in the nutrient profile such as moisture variations);

(F) A statement signed and dated by a responsible individual, employed at the covered establishment or its corporate headquarters or parent entity, who can certify that the information contained in the nutrient analysis is complete and accurate; and

(G) A statement signed and dated by a responsible individual employed at the covered establishment certifying that the covered establishment has taken reasonable steps to ensure that the method of preparation (e.g., types and amounts of ingredients in the recipe, cooking temperatures) and amount of a standard menu item offered for sale adhere to the factors on which its nutrient values were determined.

(ii) For published cookbooks that contain nutritional information for recipes in the cookbook:

(A) The name, author, and publisher of the cookbook used;

(B) If available, information provided by the cookbook or from the author or publisher about how the nutrition information for the recipes was obtained;

(C) A copy of the recipe used to prepare the standard menu item and a copy of the nutrition information for that standard menu item as provided by the cookbook; and

(D) A statement signed and dated by a responsible individual employed at the covered establishment certifying that that the covered establishment has taken reasonable steps to ensure that the method of preparation (e.g., types and amounts of ingredients in the recipe, cooking temperatures) and amount of a standard menu item offered for sale adhere to the factors on which its nutrient values were determined. (Recipes may be divided as necessary to accommodate differences in the portion size derived from the recipe and that are served as the standard menu item but no changes may be made to the proportion of ingredients used.)

(iii) For laboratory analyses:

(A) A copy of the recipe for the standard menu item used for the nutrient analysis;

(B) The name and address of the laboratory performing the analysis;

(C) Copies of analytical worksheets, including the analytical method, used to determine and verify nutrition information;

(D) A statement signed and dated by a responsible individual, employed at the covered establishment or its corporate headquarters or parent entity, who can certify that the information contained in the nutrient analysis is complete and accurate; and

(E) A statement signed and dated by a responsible individual employed at the covered establishment certifying that the covered establishment has taken reasonable steps to ensure that the method of preparation (e.g., types and amounts of ingredients in the recipe, cooking temperatures) and amount of a standard menu item offered for sale adhere to the factors on which its nutrient values were determined.

(iv) For nutrition information provided by other reasonable means:

(A) A detailed description of the means used to determine the nutrition information;

(B) A recipe or formula used as a basis for the nutrient determination;

(C) Any data derived in determining the nutrient values for the standard menu item, e.g., nutrition information about the ingredients used with the source of the nutrient information;

(D) A statement signed and dated by a responsible individual, employed at the covered establishment or its corporate headquarters or parent entity, who can certify that the information contained in the nutrient analysis is complete and accurate; and

(E) A statement signed and dated by a responsible individual employed at the covered establishment certifying that the covered establishment has taken reasonable steps to ensure that the method of preparation (e.g., types and amounts of ingredients in the recipe, cooking temperatures) and amount of a standard menu item offered for sale adhere to the factors on which its nutrient values were determined.

(d) Voluntary registration to be subject to the menu labeling requirements—(1) Applicability. A restaurant or similar retail food establishment that is not part of a chain with 20 or more locations doing business under the same name and offering for sale substantially the same menu items may voluntarily register to be subject to the requirements established in this section. Restaurants and similar retail food establishments that voluntarily register will no longer be subject to non-identical State or local nutrition labeling requirements.

(2) Who may register? The authorized official of a restaurant or similar retail food establishment as defined in paragraph (a) of this section, which is not otherwise subject to paragraph (b) of this section, may register with FDA.

(3) What information is required? Authorized officials for restaurants and similar retail food establishments must provide FDA with the following information on Form FDA 3757:

(i) The contact information (including name, address, phone number, and email address) for the authorized official;

(ii) The contact information (including name, address, phone number, and email address) of each restaurant or similar retail food establishment being registered, as well as the name and contact information for an official onsite, such as the owner or manager, for each specific restaurant or similar retail food establishment;

(iii) All trade names the restaurant or similar retail food establishment uses;

(iv) Preferred mailing address (if different from location address for each establishment) for purposes of receiving correspondence; and

(v) Certification that the information submitted is true and accurate, that the person submitting it is authorized to do so, and that each registered restaurant or similar retail food establishment will be subject to the requirements of section 403(q)(5)(H) of the Federal Food, Drug, and Cosmetic Act and this section.

(4) How to register. Authorized officials of restaurants and similar retail food establishments who elect to be subject to requirements in section 403(q)(5)(H) of the Federal Food, Drug, and Cosmetic Act can register by visiting http://www.fda.gov/food/ingredientspackaginglabeling/labelingnutrition/ucm217762.htm. FDA has created a form (Form 3757) that contains fields requesting the information in paragraph (d)(3) of this section and made the form available at this Web site. Registrants must use this form to ensure that complete information is submitted.

(i) Information should be submitted by email by typing complete information into the form (PDF), saving it on the registrant's computer, and sending it by email to menulawregistration@fda.hhs.gov.

(ii) If email is not available, the registrant can either fill in the form (PDF) and print it out (or print out the blank PDF and fill in the information by hand or typewriter), and either fax the completed form to 301-436-2804 or mail it to FDA, CFSAN Menu and Vending Machine Registration, White Oak Building 22, Rm. 0209, 10903 New Hampshire Ave., Silver Spring, MD 20993.

(5) When to renew the registration. To keep the establishment's registration active, the authorized official of the restaurant or similar retail food establishment must register every other year within 60 days prior to the expiration of the establishment's current registration with FDA. Registration will automatically expire if not renewed.

(e) Signatures. Signatures obtained under paragraph (d) of this section that meet the definition of electronic signatures in § 11.3(b)(7) of this chapter are exempt from the requirements of part 11 of this chapter.

(f) Misbranding. A standard menu item offered for sale in a covered establishment shall be deemed misbranded under sections 201(n), 403(a), 403(f) and/or 403(q) of the Federal Food, Drug, and Cosmetic Act if its label or labeling is not in conformity with paragraph (b) or (c) of this section.

Dated: November 19, 2014.
Leslie Kux,
Associate Commissioner for Policy.
[FR Doc. 2014-27833 Filed 11-25-14; 8:45 am]
BILLING CODE 4164-01-P

Made in the USA
Columbia, SC
10 January 2020